Social Research and Educational Studies Series

Series Editor
Robert G. Burgess,
Professor of Sociology,
University of Warwick

Social Research and Educational Studies Series: 8

The Ethics of Educational Research

Edited by

Robert G. Burgess

RoutledgeFalmer
Taylor & Francis Group

LONDON AND NEW YORK

First published 1989
By RoutledgeFalmer, 11 New
Fetter Lane, London EC4P 4EE

Transferred to Digital Printing 2004

British Library Cataloguing in Publication Data
The ethics of educational research. — (Social research and educational studies series; 8)
  1. Education. Research. Ethical aspects
  I. Burgess, Robert G. II. Series 174'.937
ISBN 1-85000-297-5
ISBN 1-85000-298-3 Pbk

Library of Congress Cataloging-in-Publication Data
The ethics of educational research/edited by Robert G. Burgess.
  p. cm. — (Social research and educational studies series: 8)
Bibliography: p.
Includes index.
ISBN 1-85000-297-5
ISBN 1-85000-298-3 (pbk.)
  1. Education–Research. 2. Research ethics.
  I. Burgess, Robert G. II. Series.
LB1028.E73 1989
370'.78–dc20   89-32352 CIP

Jacket design by Caroline Archer

Typeset in 11/13 point Bembo by
Alresford Typesetting & Design, New Farm Road, Alresford, Hants.

Contents

Series Editor's Preface

The purpose of the *Social Research and Educational Studies* series is to provide authoritative guides to key issues in educational research. The series includes overviews of fields, guidance on good practice and discussions of the practical implications of social and educational research. In particular, the series deals with a variety of approaches to conducting social and educational research. Contributors to this series review recent work, raise critical concerns that are particular to the field of education, and reflect on the implications of research for educational policy and practice.

Each volume in the series draws on material that will be relevant for an international audience. The contributors to this series all have wide experience of teaching, conducting and using educational research. The volumes are written so that they will appeal to a wide audience of students, teachers and researchers. Altogether, the volumes in the *Social Research and Educational Studies* series provide a comprehensive guide for anyone concerned with contemporary educational research.

The series will include individually-authored books and edited volumes on a range of themes in education including: qualitative research, survey research, the interpretation of data, self-evaluation, research and social policy, analyzing data, action research, the politics and ethics of research.

This volume examines a range of ethical issues that arise in different styles and stages of educational research. It also provides a discussion of ethical issues that are involved in conducting empirical studies in education. All the contributors provide examples of ethical dilemmas that they have confronted in their own research. In this sense, the chapters give access to a discussion of actual problems that confront educational researchers and the ways in which they attempt to handle them. This collection of papers is intended for researchers, lecturers and students who are interested in examining the ethical dilemmas involved in the conduct of social and educational research.

Robert Burgess

University of Warwick

Preface

Much of the literature on social and educational research is concerned with the design, collection and analysis of research data. While many of the discussions focus on technical procedures, they avoid ethical questions about the conduct of social investigation. It is this gap in the literature that this book is intended to fill.

The chapters collected together in this volume are intended to provide a contribution to discussions on the ethics of social and educational research in general. Accordingly, part one provides accounts of the ethical issues involved in a range of research methods used by social and educational researchers, while part two provides examples of the ethical issues that researchers encounter in particular projects or fields of study devoted to education. All the accounts provided in this volume discuss ethical principles and ethical issues in relation to examples drawn from specific studies. In this respect, the chapters locate discussions of ethical principles in research experience.

All the chapters included in this volume were specially commissioned. The chapters by John Bibby, Ivor Bundell and David Raffe, Alison Kelly, David Bridges and myself were originally presented at a symposium on 'research ethics' that I organized at an annual conference of the British Educational Research Association. These chapters, in common with others in the volume, have been redrafted so that they can be used by undergraduate and postgraduate students and teachers studying for higher degrees as well as researchers. It is to be hoped that these chapters assist readers in handling ethical issues in their own research as well as considering ethical problems that surround social and educational investigations that they might design, evaluate and on occasion participate in.

I would like to thank friends and colleagues who have engaged in debates and discussions about research ethics in formal and informal sessions which have contributed to my interest and understanding in this field. Secondly, I am indebted to Malcolm Clarkson of the Falmer Press who has patiently waited for this book to take shape. His encouragement has been a great help. Finally, I am again indebted to Pat Langhorn for providing first class secretarial support in the final stages of the preparation of these papers for publication.

Robert Burgess

Ethics and Educational Research: An Introduction

Robert G. Burgess

Ethical questions are the subject of interdisciplinary discussions and debates. Philosophers have examined abstract concepts, while sociologists and psychologists have focused on extreme cases and research 'scandals' in the course of locating ethical issues in their research experience. In these circumstances, we might expect philosophers, sociologists and psychologists involved in the study of education to bring together their expertise to focus on ethical questions in educational research. Yet a brief glance at the research literature and research studies reveals that this topic is absent from debate. Apart from a collection of essays edited by Adelman (1984) there are few examples of educational researchers discussing the ethical questions associated with their research experience. While it might be argued there are few scandals in educational research (or scandals that become public) it is difficult for researchers to deny that ethical, moral and political questions do not surround their day to day experience of education and educational research.

The Oxford English Dictionary (1976) defines ethics as:

> Relating to morals, treating of moral questions; morally correct, honourable . . . Set of principles of morals . . . Science of morals, moral principles, rules of conduct, whole field of moral science (p. 355).

Such a definition focuses on moral principles that Cassell and Jacobs (1987) consider may 'seem to have little relation to our daily activities as researchers, teachers, students and practitioners' (p. 1). In addition, they point out how the concept of 'ethics' is used to reprove behaviour of others. However they argue:

> We do not wish to make this seem merely a matter of isolated choices in crucial situations. Much of our lives proceeds undramatically, and often our decisions are almost imperceptible, so that only with hindsight are we aware that our course of action

had consequences that we had not foreseen and now regret (*ibid*, p. 1).

Accordingly, they go on to argue:

> To improve ethical adequacy . . . we must consider not only exceptional cases but everyday decisions, and reflect not only upon the conduct of others but also upon our own actions (*ibid*, p. 1).

While Cassell and Jacobs were writing in the context of anthropological study their comments have relevance for social and educational research.

Much of the literature on ethical issues in sociology has focused on research 'scandals' that have provided an opportunity to discuss research sponsorship, secrecy and deception and questions concerning the publication of data. Among these extreme examples there are few reported studies in education apart from Punch's (1986) account of researching Dartington Hall, an independent progressive school in south-west England. Fifteen years elapsed between Maurice Punch starting research in Dartington Hall and publishing an account of his research experience. Much of this delay resulted from the way in which the research process took on political, moral and personal dimensions. Punch engaged in a struggle with his research sponsors (the Trustees of Dartington Hall) as he had signed a document agreeing not to publish any material from the study without the written consent of the chairman of the Trust. In the event, attempts were made to prevent publication — a situation that raised issues concerning research sponsorship, confidentiality, identification, freedom to publish and the nature of professional standards (Punch, 1986, pp. 70–84). However, Burgess (1984, 1985) has shown that similar issues not only arise in dramatic circumstances in educational research but also in the day-to-day experience of conducting research in a comprehensive school. Among the questions that he raises in his reflection on some of the ethical problems in his research are: what should individuals be told about the conduct of social research? Is secret research justifiable? Is secret research desirable? What data can be collected 'openly'? How should data be disseminated? What protection can be given to those individuals who participate in social and educational research? Some of these questions are also raised in the educational projects that are discussed in this volume and to which we now turn.

Ethics and Educational Research Methods

In the first part of this volume the chapters focus on different research strategies and research techniques where authors highlight particular ethical problems associated with their use in educational inquiry. The first chapter by David Raffe, Ivor Bundell and John Bibby discusses ethical problems associated with the use of a survey research design. Here, they focus on their experience of working on the Scottish Young People's Survey. Within their chapter they discuss the problems of informed consent, the problems of using data-sets and the legal and professional codes that have been established to protect those involved in survey research. Similar themes are also raised by Pamela Sammons on issues that occur in investigations that use statistical methods in education. Her chapter highlights the way in which recent legislation has made it a requirement for schools to provide statistical evidence on examination results. However, as Sammons points out there is no legislation about how to interpret or use the results. She also provides some discussion of the technical expertise required if researchers are to uphold the codes of ethics provided for statisticians. However, as she illustrates from her own research, it is not possible to straightforwardly apply principles involved in moral codes. For example, in considering the principle of informed consent, circumstances can occur when it would be inappropriate to convey the purpose of an investigation.

It is this discussion of the way in which principles are put into practice that is the focus of Robert Burgess' account of conducting ethnographic research in the course of restudying a comprehensive school. Burgess illustrates the ethical implications involved in relationships between the researcher and the researched when gaining access, and handling field relations. Here principles of informed consent, and questions concerning harm, deception, confidentiality and anonymity are raised in discussion.

Some of these themes were also of importance to Sheila Riddell when conducting feminist research in two rural comprehensive schools. Riddell's research also illustrates how feminist investigations raise questions about honesty, power relations and the responsibility of the researcher to the researched. Here, Riddell uses evidence from her study to question the circumstances under which covert research is appropriate, and the extent to which it is more appropriate for women to interview women rather than men. Finally, she questions whether collaboration is the answer to ethical issues surrounding hierarchical relationships between researcher and researched given that questions could be asked about the relationship between a feminist researcher collaborating with men and boys in analyzing data.

Some of these issues are also raised for action researchers as Alison Kelly demonstrates in some reflections on her project 'Girls Into Science and Technology'. This project involved a range of ethical issues: the values of the researcher, the power of the researcher, the problem of informed consent and the manner in which research data are presented to the participants in the project.

In a final chapter in the first section of the book Helen Simons examines the ethical issues associated with case study research and evaluation. In common with researchers working within other traditions of social research Simons highlights the key concerns as confidentiality, informed consent, anonymity and the right to privacy and to knowledge. Among the fascinating questions she raises is whether guidelines can be produced for educational researchers and evaluators and the circumstances in which they require revision. Certainly, this is an issue to which we return in the second part of the volume.

Ethical Issues in Empirical Research

The chapters in part two include researchers' discussions of the ethical issues involved in some projects and areas of study in education. We begin with a chapter from David Bridges which provides an illustration of case study research in action. Bridges was looking at police training from the perspective of an educational researcher as his case studies were to be used in police training. Central to the whole discussion is the question of control of publication by the commissioning body as the researchers were required to sign the Official Secrets Act. While this is an unusual requirement for educational researchers it does provide an example of the ways in which a researcher can handle research sponsors.

Similar themes are also highlighted in Jon Nixon's account of conducting a Technical and Vocational Educational Initiative (TVEI) evaluation. Here, Nixon demonstrates how researchers engaged in evaluation also need to consider questions of confidentiality and the negotiation of procedures to release a report on the project findings. His study highlights the political as well as the ethical tensions involved in educational research. It is this issue that is also raised by Harry Torrance in his discussion of research on assessment. He also demonstrates how researchers need to consider relationships with the researched and the way in which research reports may relate to policy and practice.

Pauline Foster's chapter examines questions of policy and practice and the ways in which policy issues modified her research design. Again, she demonstrates how the political context involves the researcher in negotiations and compromises during the course of the research. Her chapter also raises the question whose side are we on? — an issue that is the central focus of the chapter by Barry Troyna and Bruce Carrington working in the field of race and education. They demonstrate how ethical issues are involved in all aspects of the research from the initial research design and formulation of the research problem through to the point of publication. They end by pointing us towards a collaborative model of research-based investigation which in common with many 'solutions' to ethical issues is the subject of considerable debate in the research community and among the contributors to this book who have highlighted the ethical dilemmas involved in educational research.

Some Ethical Dilemmas in Educational Research

The accounts that are provided in this volume should allow the reader to construct an agenda of topics for consideration in research practice. They include:

(a) *Research sponsorship.* Questions of sponsorship have been widely debated in the literature; especially as far as the intervention of sponsors in research activities is concerned (Barnes, 1979; Bulmer, 1982). Here, we need to consider the extent to which research funders influence research activity. Is it a case of those who pay for research projects also 'call the tune'? (See the chapters by Simons, Nixon, Troyna and Carrington). However, sponsorship does not only apply to a gatekeeping role as far as funding is concerned but also in establishing field relations. Here, questions need to be asked about power relations and the way these assist or impede research (see the chapters by Riddell, Kelly and Foster).

(b) *Research relations.* Much of the ethnographic literature considers relationships between the researcher and the researched. Yet this has quickly been translated into a debate about the merits and demerits of overt and covert research as it applies to participant observation (Erikson, 1967, 1968; Denzin, 1968; Bulmer, 1980, 1982; Homan, 1980). However, this is a very narrow interpretation of this issue. The chapters by Bibby *et al*, Burgess, Riddell, Kelly, Simons, Torrance and Foster all illustrate how ethical issues concerning research relations are not confined to the use of participant observation nor for that matter to questions of 'open' as opposed to 'closed' research. Instead questions of access, power, harm, deception, secrecy and confidentiality are all issues that the researcher has to consider and resolve often in the research context.

(c) *Informed consent* has a central place in the ethics literature and refers to the voluntary consent of the individual to participate in research. In turn, it is argued that individuals involved in research shall not in any way be harmed (*cf.* Diener and Crandall, 1978; Reiser *et al*, 1977). Again the chapters in this collection demonstrate that informed consent is not a principle that merely applies to field relations in ethnographic research. Instead, it applies to survey work (see the chapter by Raffe *et al*), to statistical investigations (see the chapter by Sammons), and to action research (see the chapter by Kelly) as well as to ethnographic studies (see the chapter by Burgess). Furthermore, these chapters also demonstrate that informed consent is not a universal principle that is unproblematic to use in research investigations.

(d) *Data dissemination* is another key area where ethical considerations are involved (*cf.* Barnes, 1979; Bulmer, 1982). Key issues concern confidentiality (see the chapters by Burgess, Simons, Bridges, Torrance and Nixon), the extent to which data can be reported back (see the chapters by Sammons, Burgess, Kelly, Simons and Bridges) and the extent to which research reports can be used by policy makers (see the chapters by Sammons, Torrance and Nixon) and in educational practice (see the chapters by Bridges and Nixon).

Resolving the Dilemmas?

As well as identifying ethical problems in social research some investigators and many professional associations have attempted to find 'solutions' to the problems that have been identified. These include:

(a) *Collaboration.* Establishing working relationships and engaging in collaborative research has been suggested by several investigators especially in the study of education (*cf.* Woods and Pollard, 1988; H. Burgess, 1988). Yet this is not unproblematic as shown in the chapters by Raffe *et al*, Riddell and Troyna and Carrington. Researchers will therefore need to consider the implications of engaging in collaborative research given the power relationships involved in terms of access to knowledge.

(b) *Guidelines, codes and laws* have been the contribution made by professional associations and by governments to attempt to control research activity while protecting the respondents or 'subjects' of research investigation. Many professional associations in Britain and the USA have devised a statement or a code of ethics during the last thirty years. The term 'statement' more accurately reflects the state of the art in many professional associations as such documents offer guidance and provide a framework within which 'good' practice can be adopted. However, it is rare for professional associations to engage in the control of their members so that anyone breaking the 'code' will be ejected from the organization. Copies of some of the statements and codes developed in the USA by anthropologists are reprinted in Cassell and Jacobs (1987), while British material is available from the British Sociological Association (1982), the Market Research Society (1986), the Social Research Association (1986) and the British Educational Research Association (Elliott, 1989). In recent years individual research projects have also established ethical guidelines to demonstrate to participants the way in which they would work — a key example in education is the Pilot Records of Achievement in Schools Evaluation (PRAISE) project whose team include their statement of ethical principles in the final report (see Broadfoot *et al*, 1988), Many of the contributors to this volume discuss codes and statements to which they work (see, for example, the chapters by Sammons and Simons) but they are quick to point out that such statements are not universally applicable to all circumstances but have to be interpreted in relation to the project on which a researcher works.

Educational researchers, administrators and policy makers have also been concerned about the information that is available to those who participate in projects (see the discussion by Sammons) and more broadly to those who participate in the education service. In 1987 the Inner London Education Authority (ILEA) set up a committee to consider a freedom of information policy in education. The report (ILEA, 1987) advocates a policy of freedom of information based on principles concerned with access to information, the processing of information and the use of information (see Tomlinson, Mortimore and Sammons, 1988, pp. 14–15). Such recommendations, if adopted by local education authorities, schools and the education service generally will have implications for the quality of information that is available for the purpose of research in education. However, all individuals who collect and convey information are now subject to legal requirements in many countries as shown by Akeroyd in her review of data protection legislation in Britain and Overseas (Akeroyd, 1988). Those individuals who are engaged in the education services of the United Kingdom as participants or as researchers are subject to the Data Protection Act of 1984 (Data Protection Registrar, 1985, 1986, 1987) which will influence the kinds of data that are obtained, recorded, stored and used (see the chapter by Raffe *et al* for a discussion of its implications in survey research).

A common theme to all these suggestions for handling ethical dilemmas in research is the notion that there is no 'solution' to the problems identified by researchers. Such a situation means that researchers need to regularly reflect on their work so as to develop their understanding of the ethical implications associated with social and educational investigation. Inevitably, it will be found that ethical dilemmas and their 'solution' will be problematic, but as Bronfenbrenner (1952) remarked the only way to avoid this problem would be 'to refrain from doing research altogether' (p. 453). Certainly this is not advocated by the contributors to this volume. Instead, the chapters that follow are offered to help researchers in their reflections about the ethical issues associated with different methodologies in the conduct of educational research.

References

ADELMAN, C. (Ed) (1984) *The Politics and Ethics of Evaluation*, London, Croom Helm.

AKEROYD, A. (1988) 'Ethnography, personal data and computers: The implications of data protection legislation for qualitative social research', in BURGESS, R. G. (Ed) *Conducting Qualitative Research: Studies in Qualitative Methodology, Volume I*, London, JAI Press.

BARNES, J. A. (1979) *Who Should Know What? Social Science, Privacy and Ethics*, Harmondsworth, Penguin.

BRITISH SOCIOLOGICAL ASSOCIATION (1982) *Statement of ethical principles* (mimeo). (Available from British Sociological Association, 10 Portugal Street, London WC2A 2HU)

BROADFOOT, P. et al (1988) *Records of Achievement: Report of the National Evaluation of Pilot Schemes*, London, HMSO.

BRONFENBRENNER, U. (1952) 'Principles of professional ethics: Cornell studies in social growth', *American Psychologist*, **7**, 2, p. 452–5.

BULMER, M. (1980) 'Comment on "The ethics of covert methods" ', *British Journal of Sociology*, **31**, 1, pp. 59–65.

BULMER, M. (Ed) (1982) *Social Research Ethics*, London, Macmillan.

BURGESS, H. (1988) 'Collaborating in curriculum research and evaluation', in WOODS, P. and POLLARD, A. (Eds) *Sociology and Teaching: A New Challenge for the Sociology of Education*, London, Croom Helm.

BURGESS, R. G. (1984) *In the Field: An Introduction to Field Research*, London, Allen and Unwin.

BURGESS, R. G. (1985) 'The whole truth? Some ethical problems of research in a comprehensive school', in BURGESS, R. G. (Ed) *Field Methods in the Study of Education*, Lewes, Falmer Press.

BURGESS, R. G. (Ed) (1988) *Conducting Qualitative Research: Studies in Qualitative Methodology, Volume I*, London, JAI Press.

CASSELL, J. and JACOBS, S. E. (1987) *Handbook on Ethical Issues in A*
Washington, American Anthropological Association.

DATA PROTECTION REGISTRAR (1985, 1986 and 1987) *The Data P*
1984: Guidelines Series, Wilmslow, Office of the Data Protection Registrar.

DENZIN, N. (1968) 'On the ethics of disguised observation', *Social Problems*, **15**,
4, pp. 502–4.

DIENER, N. and CRANDELL, R. (1978) *Ethics in Social and Behavioural Research*,
Chicago, IL, University of Chicago Press.

ELLIOTT, J. (1989) 'Towards a code of practice for funded educational research',
Research Intelligence, 31, pp. 14–18

ERIKSON, K. T. (1967) 'A comment on disguised observation in sociology', *Social
Problems*, **14**, 4, pp. 366–73.

ERIKSON, K. T. (1968) 'On the ethics of disguised observation: A reply to
Denzin', *Social Problems*, **15**, 4, pp. 505–6.

HOMAN, R. (1980) 'The ethics of covert methods', *British Journal of Sociology*,
31, 1, pp. 46–59.

INNER LONDON EDUCATION AUTHORITY (1987) *Informing Education: Report of
the Committee of Inquiry into Freedom of Information*, London, ILEA.

MARKET RESEARCH SOCIETY (1986) *Code of Conduct*, London, Market Research
Society.

OXFORD ENGLISH DICTIONARY (1976) *The Concise Oxford Dictionary* (New
Edition), Oxford, Oxford University Press.

PUNCH, M. (1986) *The Politics and Ethics of Fieldwork*, Beverly Hills, CA, Sage.

REISER, S. J., DYCK, A. and CURRAN, W. (1977) *Ethics in Medicine*, Cambridge,
MA, MIT Press.

SOCIAL RESEARCH ASSOCIATION (1986) 'Social research association ethical
guidelines', Appendix B in *The SRA Directory of Members 1985–86*, London,
SRA.

TOMLINSON, J., MORTIMORE, P. and SAMMONS, P. (1988) *Freedom and
Education: Ways of Increasing Openness and Accountability*, Sheffield Papers in
Education Management 76, Sheffield, Sheffield City Polytechnic.

WOODS, P. and POLLARD, A. (Eds) (1988) *Sociology and Teaching: A New
Challenge for the Sociology of Education*, London, Croom Helm.

Part One
Ethical Issues and Research Methods

1
Ethics and Tactics: Issues Arising from an Educational Survey

David Raffe, Ivor Bundell and John Bibby

Introduction

Discussions of research ethics tend to focus on qualitative or experimental methods. Survey researchers probably consciously confront ethical problems less frequently than most other social researchers; respected textbooks of survey methods make no reference to ethical issues (Moser and Kalton, 1971; Hoinville and Jowell, 1978).

True, survey respondents typically experience less inconvenience and intrusion than the subjects of other research studies; and a survey respondent, buried in a large sample, may feel less threatened by the publication of results. But surveys too have their ethical problems. The collection, storage and linkage of personal databases contain at least the potential for abuse. And the greater external validity claimed for survey research makes the use of its results even more critical. As the Radical Statistics Education Group (1982, p. 3) has noted, 'the use of "statistics" and "computers" is often thought to lend an aura of infallibility to research results' which may be 'used to silence the legitimate concerns of those wishing to speak up for their own interests'.

The relative neglect of ethical issues in survey research may partly arise from the research process itself. Survey researchers, especially those using mail surveys, typically have little direct personal contact with their subjects; yet it is in the context of direct personal relationships that ethical issues are most often raised. In this chapter we discuss how ethical issues arise in the practice of survey research. This practice conditions whether or not an ethical principle is acknowledged in a particular case, how it is interpreted and how conflicts between principles are resolved. Our discussion is based on our own experience of conducting the Scottish Young People's Survey, formerly the Scottish School Leavers' Survey.

David Raffe, Ivor Bundell and John Bibby

The Scottish Young People's Survey (SYPS)

The Scottish School Leavers' Survey was first carried out by the Centre for Educational Sociology (CES) in 1971 (Burnhill, McPherson, Raffe and Tomes, 1987). It was then a postal survey of a sample of qualified school leavers in Scotland from the previous school session. There was another similar survey in 1973. Since 1977 the survey has been conducted biennially, and has covered all types of school leavers, including the unqualified. Sample fractions have ranged from 10 per cent to nearly 40 per cent.

Since 1985 (with a smaller pilot study in 1984) the survey has developed in two further ways. First, in addition to surveying the previous year's leavers, it now covers an overlapping sample of the previous year's fourth year (equivalent to the English fifth year), including both leavers and stayers. Second, this sample is followed up in subsequent surveys, currently extending to age 19. These changes coincided with the change of name (to the Scottish Young People's Survey) and with the introduction of the Youth Cohort Study in England and Wales, which drew on the Scottish experience (Clough and Gray, 1986). The SYPS continues to use postal questionnaires to collect both attitudinal and 'objective' data covering a range of topics, particularly concerning education and the labour market.

Initially funded by the Scottish Education Department (SED), the survey is now funded by the SED, the Manpower Services Commission (MSC), the Industry Department for Scotland and the Department of Employment. However the 1977 and 1981 surveys were also funded by the Social Science Research Council (SSRC, now the ESRC) as part of the Collaborative Research Programme (see below). The CES has received continuous SSRC/ESRC support since 1974, and may expect continuity for a further eight years from 1987 when it becomes a designated Research Centre of the ESRC. The balance between government and Research Council funding is an important ingredient of the CES's status as an applied but independent research body.

Throughout its existence the survey has obtained sample names and addresses from the SED. However, at a critical point in its development it needed to supplement these with names and addresses obtained from the local authorities. This arose from the desire to extend the coverage of the 1977 survey, and increase the sample size, in connection with the SSRC-funded Collaborative Research Programme which ran from 1975 to 1982 (Gray, McPherson and Raffe, 1983). This aimed to break down some of the boundaries between researchers, practitioners and others by helping non-professional researchers to influence the survey design and to analyze survey data. In the course of this programme the CES adopted a Code of Practice (McPherson and Raffe, 1979). Among other things this protected the confidentiality of data concerning individual sample members and schools; subject to this it provided for open access to the data which are stored in the Scottish Education Data Archive. Other clauses of the code, for example concerning wide consultation over the questionnaire, have fallen into abeyance with the termination of funding for collaborative research, but the principles of anonymity and public access to the data are preserved, for example in current contracts with government departments which refer to the code.

The survey is also subject to other regulatory codes. The Data Protection Act (1984) requires users of personal data held on computers to register with the Data Protection Registrar's Office established by the Act. Most medium or large surveys store personal data on computer and are thus covered by the Act; academic survey researchers usually register through their parent institution — in the case of CES, the University of Edinburgh. The broad aims of the Data Protection Act are embodied in eight principles. However data held for 'historical and research' purposes are exempted from the principle which gives individuals the right of access to personal data about themselves, provided the data are not made available in a form which identifies individuals. Research data also have partial exemption from two further principles, with the effect that such data may be held indefinitely and the use of the data for research purposes need not be disclosed at the time of data collection.

Of the principles which do concern research data, the two most important are probably the principle which states that personal data 'shall not be used or disclosed in any matter incompatible with' the purpose for which they are held, in this case research; and the principle which requires 'appropriate security measures' to be 'taken against unauthorized access to, or alteration, disclosure or destruction of' the data. A further principle, which many researchers might find troublesome, states that personal data should be 'accurate', although this is framed more to protect individuals against damage resulting from inaccuracy, than to enhance the validity of measurement in social research. The main effect of the Data Protection Act on the work of the CES has been to ensure a thorough review of current security practices regarding personal data, both on-line and off. The task of registering has also involved a considerable amount of extra work.

Since the CES uses government data, particularly in the construction of the sample, it is affected by the Code of Practice of the Government

Statistical Service (GSS, 1984). The main purpose of this code is to protect the confidentiality of data collected by government departments from 'statistical units' such as individuals, households or (in some cases) schools. There are only three circumstances under which these data may be subsequently transferred to other departments or organizations in a form which identifies individual respondents: if the transfer is specifically provided for by law; if the respondents have given their consent; or if the information is transferred to *bona fide* researchers and for statistical purposes only, and the transfer has prior written ministerial authorization. Before 1983 the SED only provided the CES with details of sample members if they had consented to take part — or, more precisely, if they had not withheld their consent. This resulted in a level of opting-out which, although not large in absolute terms, was skewed towards the less qualified. We discuss some of the implications of this below. Since 1983, ministerial authorization has been given for the transfer and sample members have not had a prior opportunity to opt out.

The thrust of the GSS code (1984) is to protect individual confidentiality, and not to restrict access to information. The transfer of anonymous data is specifically allowed for, and the preamble to the code notes that 'if proper safeguards on confidentiality are applied, it is to the general advantage if data collected for statistical purposes inside government are also available to outside analysts and researchers' (p. 4).

Some Ethical Principles

The above discussion of regulatory codes has raised ethical issues relating to accuracy, confidentiality, breadth of consultation, rights of access, and continuity of purpose. However, ethical principles range far wider than regulatory codes, including the CES's own Code of Practice. We do not attempt here either to review the literature or to propose a comprehensive ethical code for survey research. However we suspect that the following set of principles, or something similar, would attract fairly wide assent.

Ethical principles in survey research, we suggest, concern the proper conduct of relationships between researchers and three groups of people: resource-providers, data subjects, and a broad amorphous group that we shall call 'the public'. There is of course an overlap here: data subjects *are* key resource-providers in the research production process.

With respect to providers of resources, such as funders or employers, researchers should clarify their obligations in advance, and honour them honestly. As a general rule, resource-providers should not have rights of confidentiality; nor should any intellectual property rights allow them to inhibit publication of results. This latter is especially important for methodological aspects of the research, which should be explicated for dissemination and public appraisal. The prior existence of suitable codes of conduct can strengthen the researcher's hand in ensuring that these conditions are incorporated into any written contracts.

A particular group of resource-providers whose importance may be overlooked are the 'gatekeepers' who control access to sampling frames and/or sample members. Relationships between gatekeepers and researchers are often determined more by bargaining power and by the dictates of sound business practice than by any lofty ethical ideals. However, where the gatekeeper has a personal relationship with the data subject (for example, as proxy, parent, or teacher), researchers should be sensitive to the nature of that relationship, and to the private spaces which it maintains. This does not necessarily mean that one should accept the gatekeeper's word as final, especially where the gatekeeper is in a position of considerable power over the data subjects.

With respect to data subjects, researchers should be conscious of their intrusive potential, and should seek to minimize any intrusion; the confidentiality of data must be respected and protected by positive measures; and data subjects should be told the purposes of the research and should have adequate opportunity to withhold their cooperation. (This last is the principle of 'informed consent'.) 'Snooping' and 'voyeurism', and intrusive questioning which may merely reflect a hobby or passing interest on the part of the researcher, should be avoided (Huizer, 1973, p. 170).

With respect to the public, researchers should pursue openness, sensitivity, accuracy, honesty and objectivity in their choice of topic, methods, analysis and dissemination. This includes respecting the interests of different groups in society; avoiding research designs which preclude particular outcomes of the enquiry; disseminating findings fully, as well as widely; and facilitating the re-use of data.

In outlining these principles we have drawn upon a range of existing codes (British Sociological Association (BSA) 1973; International Statistical Institute (ISI) 1986; Market Research Society (MRS) 1986; Association des Administrateurs de l'INSEE, 1985) as well as upon recent and forthcoming statistical texts (Moore, 1985; Bibby and Moore, forthcoming). There are, of course, more general issues underlying most of these principles: many of them reflect the perception that 'knowledge is power' and enjoin a continuous resensitizing to power relationships, not only between researchers and data-subjects but also those involving resource-providers and the public. A corollary of this last point is that it is not only the researcher who should act ethically. The principles outlined above are, nevertheless, not comprehensive. Among other things they make no reference to relationships within a research team, which probably deserve close ethical scrutiny particularly given the currently limited opportunities and careers in research.

The application of these principles in any given situation will require judgment upon which two honest researchers could honestly disagree. In addition, several tensions in these principles are readily discernible:

— between principles and the feasible actions in any given situation;
— between different ethical principles; and
— between groups, as mentioned above, and other individuals or groups; for example, in emphasizing the 'right' of (randomly selected) data subjects to withhold consent, do we infringe the 'right' of groups to which they belong to be adequately represented in the data?

These tensions will be apparent in the following three sections, which reflect on ethical decision-making in the context of the CES surveys, and discuss the ways in which it is influenced by the practice or tactics of research. They describe how the practice of survey research may influence, respectively, whether an ethical issue is recognized in any particular context, how general principles are applied to particular situations, and how conflicts between principles are resolved.

Non-decision-making and Ethical Issues

We have discussed ethical principles in terms of the researcher's relations with three categories of people. For certain purposes these may be regrouped into two main groups. The first consists of all those on whom the researcher is dependent for resources or data; it includes the providers of resources and those data-subjects from whom data are collected directly. The second group comprises those on whom the researcher is not dependent for resources or data; it includes data-subjects from whom data are not collected directly, and most of the diffuse group that we have labelled 'the public'. The researcher's relationship with all members of the first group is one of negotiation. The relationship may be implicit, as for example when a researcher designs a questionnaire and its covering letter in a way that encourages a sample member to respond to a mail survey; the relative negotiating strengths may vary, as may the outcomes of the negotiation; but in all cases the negotiation process makes it more likely that the ethical aspects of the relationship will be consciously considered. Indeed the researcher may invoke ethical principles — notably those affecting confidentiality — as a tactic in the negotiation.

Conversely, for the second group, with whom the researcher has no relationship of dependence or negotiation, it is easier to overlook that any ethical issues arise. This group may be the victims of a kind of ethical non-decision-making.

The most obvious example concerns data-subjects from whom data are not directly collected. Many surveys collect information on 'third persons', such as the respondent's parents or spouse. It is of some interest that such persons do not have the status of data-subjects under the Data Protection Act, although since the information held on them still counts as personal data it is subject to much the same safeguards under the Act as other data held for research purposes.

Although by definition third persons do not negotiate with survey researchers, the respondents supplying data may negotiate on their behalf. In a limited sense this is true of the SYPS. We have asked several 'personal' questions, for example about earnings, mental health and sex education, that might have aroused the sensitivities of our respondents. We have also piloted an ethnic origin question, and plan to include it in future surveys. As far as we can tell, none of these questions has troubled our respondents. The questions that do prove sensitive, and are sometimes met with refusals, are those that ask about young people's parents and families. Our respondents seem happy to answer any questions about themselves but may be less willing to divulge personal information about others. In this respect our respondents may be said to be negotiating on behalf of third persons although as a general rule we suspect that these people still tend to be left out of the ethical account.

Many surveys obtain data on their main subjects or sample members from sources other than sample members themselves, for example school records. Some surveys obtain data exclusively from records; other surveys use such data to supplement information collected directly from sample members. We have, for example, used test scores supplied by local authorities, and employment data supplied by careers services, and linked them with questionnaire data on the same individual sample members. The principle of informed consent is rarely applied in such cases — probably because the researcher does not negotiate the data collection directly with the data-subjects, whose ethical claims are therefore more easily overlooked. We are asking our current sample members' permission to use data on their vocational qualifications held by the certifying body. In this we are anticipating the requirement of the body concerned; and even where the principle of informed consent is not enforced in this way those holding the data may act as trustees or guardians for the data-subjects concerned. The use of administrative data for research purposes without the data-subjects' knowledge or consent is permitted under certain conditions by both the Data Protection Act and the Government Statistical Service code. But the inconsistency remains. It is ironical that we hold personal data, from other sources, on survey non-respondents who, through not responding, have presumably exercised their rights under the principle of informed consent and withheld their consent.

Another example of ethical non-decision-making concerns those groups to whom our Code of Practice extends confidentiality. As we have mentioned, individual schools may not be identified on our data unless with their own consent; but (for example) individual careers services and further education colleges are directly or indirectly implicated by our data but receive no such protection. This inconsistency may arise at least partly because of the role which schools have played as gatekeepers to the sample. Whether this has been collected directly from schools or with the local authorities or SED as intermediaries, collecting the sample has always depended on the cooperation of the schools from whose administrative records it is obtained. This may have forced their ethical claims to the attention of the CES more strongly than those of other groups.

The practice of survey research may therefore encourage a kind of non-decision-making whereby ethical issues are less likely to be acknowledged in relation to those on whom the researcher is not dependent for resources or data. The Data Protection Act goes some way towards forcing the ethical claims of these people to the attention of the researcher, but its effect may still be partial. If this is true for a survey which has generated its own Code of Practice, and which was for a time funded precisely to explore such issues in relation to the research process, it is even more likely to be true for other educational surveys.

From the General to the Particular: Applying the Principles

Even if ethical principles are recognized as applying to a particular instance, some principles would, if implemented in full, require considerably greater resources than are normally available to the researcher. For example, it is very costly to make survey data publicly available in such a way that members of the public can easily use them. In practice publicly available data-sets are effectively only available to people with the knowledge, expertise and technical resources to make proper use of them — often, indeed, only to other professional researchers. In our collaborative research programme we sought to extend access to a wider public of teachers and other educational practitioners; but this was only possible because our funding enabled us to give direct support to our 'collaborators'. This funding has now ceased.

Even when there are no resource constraints, there may be considerable latitude in interpreting an ethical principle in a given situation. The principles tend to be expressed in very general terms.

This particularly concerns the principles governing a researcher's relations with the 'public'. For example, the principle of respecting the interests of different groups begs the questions: what groups? how are their interests defined? In the CES we have sought to allow for this problem through allowing groups access to the data, although we acknowledge that practical difficulties, combined with the different levels of resources available to different groups, make this a far from ideal solution. Our Code of Practice obliges us to draw the attention of all parties concerned to any partial uses that in our judgment are made of the data.

Ethical principles governing relations with data-subjects may also be vague. The data should be confidential to the research team — but who comprises the team? Like many large scale surveys we employ temporary staff to administer and code the surveys. It occasionally happens that a sample member is personally known to a coder; there is no way of preventing this, although we impress upon coders the importance of confidentiality and require them to sign the standard confidentiality declaration when they join the CES. They are part of the research team. On the other hand we organize the processing of data so that all personal identifiers are removed before questionnaires go for data-preparation. Staff involved in data-preparation therefore need not be regarded as part of the research team. A particular problem occurs in relation to studies which follow up our survey respondents — typically small studies which seek to interview groups of interest identified through the data. These can only be carried out if those doing the work can be counted as part of the CES research team.

Similarly, ethical principles, as well as the Data Protection Act, require researchers to protect the confidentiality of personal data; but efforts to do this may be more or less intensive. Routine measures to achieve confidentiality include the removal of all personal identifiers such as names and addresses from both physical and computer-held records, and their replacement with ID numbers. The 'key' which links ID numbers to the identifying information is then kept separate and secure. Often measures to protect confidentiality conflict with the practical requirements of data analysis; for example, within the CES we have experienced considerable inconvenience in merging or matching data-sets where respondent or school ID numbers have been scrambled as an additional safeguard. Nevertheless, it is impossible to achieve absolute security of data, as hackers have demonstrated on numerous other and more sensitive data-files. A problem in survey research is that individuals may be identified in the data through unique combinations of characteristics. To take a fictional example, our sample is unlikely to include more than one female apprentice baker from Dunfermline who left school in 1984 with four O grades and lives with her father and stepmother — yet such an individual could in principle be identified through data publicly available in our data-sets. We take some comfort from the fact that a malicious person would be unlikely to set out to identify such an individual in our data since she would have only a one in ten chance of being included; moreover correct identification presupposes perfectly accurate data! (A standard response to this problem is the 'random disturbance' or corruption of data either in data-sets or in published tables. We have not done this.) A more likely danger is that a school could be identified through its local authority division and other school-related variables in the public data-sets. Short of removing all school-level and school-related variables there is no way that the anonymity of schools can be guaranteed absolutely.

The anonymity of schools in the SYPS data raises a more specific problem. Our Code of Practice states that 'the anonymity of schools should be maintained except where the schools themselves and any associated individuals who might be identified through the data on a single school all give their consent'. Provided no such individual, for example a particular teacher, is identifiable, we have taken the agreement of the headteacher as sufficient token of a school's consent. The code could of course be interpreted much more rigorously and require the consent of a much wider range of people, but this would be extremely time-consuming for the researchers concerned. As in many other instances, ethics can be demanding in terms of resources.

The principle of informed consent provides another example of latitude of interpretation: just how fully should respondents be informed? and what opportunity should they be given to withhold their consent? The covering letter for the SYPS describes the survey's objectives in fairly general terms, for example:

A representative cross section of young people from all over

Scotland has been asked to take part in this survey. The results should help those who plan education and training to understand what it is that young people do, and what they want.

On the back of the questionnaire is a more formal description:

The Scottish Young People's Survey will provide information on the views and experiences of school leavers and school students to help improve education and related services. It is run independently by the Centre for Educational Sociology at Edinburgh University.

This is supplied with a full address and telephone number.

Like most large surveys, it would be impossible for us to give a full and detailed account of the purposes of the survey, precisely because most of the uses of the data are not known at the time of the survey. In this respect we reflect the spirit of both the Data Protection Act and the Government Statistical Service code, which accept 'statistical' purposes as a sufficient description of the objectives of data-collection. We do not identify our sponsors, mainly to minimize bias: a survey which was visibly identified with the SED and the MSC might yield biased answers about schooling or YTS. Only a few sample members use the phone number or write to enquire about the survey. Those who do so tend to ask who sponsors the survey, how we obtained their name and address or what use will be made of the data. We do not know whether the large majority who make no enquiry share their concerns.

What constitutes the opportunity to withhold consent? SYPS sample members currently have no prior opportunity to opt out of the survey (although when this opportunity existed it is very doubtful whether those who opted out were well informed about the survey). Non-respondents may expect to receive one or two reminder postcards and a second copy of the questionnaire. Reminder procedures of this kind are standard in all survey research. Their main purpose is to convince non-respondents that the exercise is more serious than a commercial mass mailing, and that their own individual response is valued. As such they attempt to persuade rather than coerce sample members to respond, although they obviously contain a minor nuisance value. We have considered telephone or interview follow-ups of non-respondents, and have been inhibited more by resource than by ethical considerations. (In 1986 we included non-respondents to our 1985 survey in our postal follow-up and achieved a nearly 40 per cent response. This confirmed that many non-respondents may change their minds after a period; the exercise also revealed that non-respondents were very different from the original respondents with respect to labour market experiences and other characteristics.) If sample members let us know explicitly that they do not wish to take part in the survey, or in future surveys, we abstain from all further contact.

The principle of informed consent is therefore, like so many other ethical principles, open to a wide range of interpretations. It is of some interest that the Data Protection Act specifically exempts research data from this principle. Data collected for other purposes may be used for research or statistical purposes without informing data-subjects or obtaining their consent, provided that the data are 'not used in such a way that damage or distress is, or is likely to be, caused to any data subject'.

Like most researchers we tend to respond to the latitude of interpretation of ethical principles by referring to the (perceived) expectations of others; in other words we attempt to respect the interests and rights of other groups as they themselves would define them. This response possibly reflects a lazy approach to ethics: we are in effect accepting the standards that prevail among those with whom we deal, but these standards may themselves be questioned on ethical grounds. For example prevailing notions of what is legitimately 'public' and 'private' — which tend also to be reflected in current legislation — may reflect the distribution of power and influence as much as any ethical code. Simply trying not to offend against other people's expectations may also discourage researchers from applying ethical principles when not forced to, a further example of non-decision-making. Above all, it tends to reflect tactical more than ethical considerations. For example, when we consider what information about the survey to give to sample members, maximizing response may be as important a motive as the principle of informed consent. We are anxious to reassure sample members that the survey has no commercial or marketing function and that it is not aligned with specific political or vested interests.

Resolving Conflicts between Ethical Principles

Few professional codes even begin to admit that there are inherent conflicts between technical and ethical considerations, and between different ethical considerations. . . . For instance, most codes contain some sort of exhortation to researchers to strive for the highest possible standards of accuracy. But few admit that it is precisely the ideal of high technical standards that is responsible for some of the worst breaches of ethical principles:

it is the pursuit of accuracy through high response rates and reduction of bias that produces the propensity to nag or cajole or deceive respondents, or to disclose as little as possible to them. (Jowell, 1982, p. 48)

This comment draws our attention to the conflict between technical and ethical considerations and the resulting temptation to interpret vague ethical principles in a way that least interferes with technical concerns. It also points to the conflicts which frequently arise between different ethical principles, conflicts that tend to be overlooked in many of the attendant debates. For example, much of the current concern to protect the privacy of data-subjects and the confidentiality of data may result in greater inconvenience to survey respondents, and thereby conflict with the ethical principle that intrusion and inconvenience should be minimized. Codes such as that of the Government Statistical Service which restrict transfer of data and linkage between data-sets may result in the duplication of data-collection activity, causing extra inconvenience to those supplying the data.

The openness of the research process — in the sense of disseminating findings, allowing access to data and, where possible, extending access to the control of the research — has been a continuing principle of the CES's research (Gray, McPherson and Raffe, 1983, ch. 17). Applying this principle to its fullest extent would require massive resources — being ethical can often be very expensive. Nevertheless, the ethical principle of openness may be easier to apply to surveys than to other kinds of research; typically survey data and the instruments by which they are generated are more easily made public. However, partly for this reason, partly because survey data typically have greater generality, and partly because surveys have greater resource requirements, they may come under greater political pressure than other types of research, particularly where government funding is involved. Pressure may be applied in different ways than in respect of other methods of research. We have observed that the relative 'objectivity' of survey data can make it difficult to suppress the results of survey research: they can less readily be dismissed as subjective or unsubstantiated. On the other hand pressure may be applied to prevent unwelcome data being collected in the first place; disputes, where they take place, tend to focus on survey design and on the content of questionnaires or interview schedules.

In the CES we believe we have had some success in persuading government that in the long term at least its interests are best served by promoting an independent and open research process. Our success may have been encouraged by the relative liberality of SED research policy, and our position is strengthened through funding from both the SSRC/ESRC and the UGC (McPherson, 1984). It is further strengthened by our own Code of Practice and by our ability to appeal to more general norms of academic research: an example of ethical codes having tactical value.

However, although these conflicts, or potential conflicts, involve ethical principles they are less obviously conflicts between ethical principles. One reason why data (and the data–generation process) can more easily be made public for surveys than for most other types of research is that confidentiality is less likely to be infringed in the process. However, even surveys may face conflicts between confidentiality and openness: in the SYPS the rule protecting the confidentiality of schools means, for example, that many TVEI projects cannot be identified without the consent of the headteachers concerned, inhibiting the use of data of clear public interest. The restriction was introduced partly to prevent misleading and injurious 'league tables' of schools from being produced on the data. Even here, the ideal solution would be to extend rather than restrict public access to data, so that schools unfairly treated in such rankings can show that a fairer use of data and controls will produce a different verdict. But in practice this may be less than ideal. The sensational if misleading newspaper headline usually receives far more attention than the correction published several weeks later.

It is common for surveys to appeal to the altruism and group identity of sample members. The SYPS encourages young people to respond in order to help improve things for other young people. This raises another area of conflict between principles: between those protecting the rights of the individual sample member and those protecting the rights of the group to which he or she belongs. By definition, samples are selected to represent larger groups. Whatever they may do about it in practice, researchers tend to be aware of the right of individuals not to participate in the research. Yet this may infringe the right of the group which those sample members were chosen to represent to be adequately and accurately represented. Up to the mid 1970s less qualified school leavers tended to be inadequately represented in the statistics and research on Scottish education. They were in a sense disenfranchised. This reflected the tendency for the education system to be designed for more academic pupils: the less qualified were, in more than one sense, 'children of no account' (Gray, McPherson and Raffe, 1983, p. 176). More immediately it reflected the deficiency of sampling frames for less qualified young people, and the prevailing view that surveys would not achieve a satisfactory response from them. In the event the CES and the SED have overcome these problems through a combination of pragmatic and technical improvements, and more recently by removing the prior opportunity to opt out of the survey, which less qualified school leavers had exercised disproportionately. Thus by marginally restricting the individual right not to take part, the collective right of the less qualified to be represented in the survey was more effectively realized. This collective right may have had some tangible value. The surveys have drawn attention to the position of the less qualified; to the extent that research ever has an influence on policy, the survey may have encouraged educational reforms affecting these young people and it has helped to enfranchise them within the educational polity (Robertson, 1984, p. 229).

Conclusion

We have attempted to illustrate, through the experience of the Scottish Young People's Survey, some ways in which ethical issues are raised in the practice of survey research. We have drawn attention to the element of 'non-decision-making' regarding many ethical issues, and to the varying levels of awareness that ethical principles are relevant in given situations. The way that generally worded ethical principles are applied in practice, and the way that conflicts between such principles are resolved, may reflect practical and technical as much as ethical considerations. They may also reflect the power relationships governing the research process and its context. There is a continuing dialectic of ethics and tactics.

In this chapter we have listed a brief set of ethical principles and taken this code as a fixed starting point in developing our argument. We conclude by noting that the very adoption by researchers of this or any other code may be for reasons of tactics more than of ethics. As Jowell (1982, p. 48) has pointed out:

Codes are generally written by professionals for professionals. To overstate only slightly, they advocate caution not so much to protect the public, more because overstepping the norms would tend to queer the pitch for other professionals.

Appendix: Extracts from the CES Code of Practice

The CES Code of Practice is relatively long, was drawn up in the specific context of the Collaborative Research Programme, and was first published as an appendix to a discussion paper with the rider that 'the spirit, intentions, and details of the code should be interpreted in the light of the paper to which it is an appendix'. The code is currently being revised, in an attempt to preserve the underlying principles but specify them in the current context. The following extracts cover the main points touched on in the chapter.

The Contents of the Main Survey

CES should consult widely over the contents of the main survey but not of any mid-cycle survey.

'Consultation' means the opportunity to influence the content of the main survey from the pre-pilot stage onwards. Questions for the surveys may be vetoed only by the CES.

Procedures for the Surveying and Sampling

The purposes of the survey and the procedures for its analysis should be adequately explained to the pupil both at school when his or her cooperation is being sought and in the questionnaire, when it is posted to the leaver; but brevity must be balanced with specificity.

The provision for seeking the cooperation of the pupil should be reviewed if cooperation rates are too low.

Leavers should have the opportunity to reply anonymously and should not be pressed, beyond three reminders, to make any reply.

Anonymity

Measures should be taken to preserve the anonymity of individual survey respondents at all times.

The anonymity of schools should be maintained except where the schools themselves and any associated individuals who might be identified through the data on a single school all give their consent. An open attitude on this matter ought to be encouraged.

Unnamed schools grouped into categories numbering at least five may be studied and discussed without permissions being sought.

These anonymity requirements are to be upheld by the CES through:

1 An undertaking to be signed by all users of the SEDA.
2 Schools and individuals are to be identified in the data only by numbers, and these numbers have themselves to be kept separate from publicly accessible data-sets.
3 Variables where values are low frequencies which might enable individuals to be identified are to be aggregated or suppressed in public data-sets.
4 Uses of the data are to be monitored.

Access

Access to the SEDA is open to all persons and limited only by the confidentiality restrictions described above. The CES will help users with SPSS and other technicalities of analysis as far as available time and resources permit; but if these are scarce it will favour those who show the greatest commitment of time and energy and are judged most likely to make constructive use of the data.

Product

Within the limits entailed by the anonymity of respondents and schools no category of analysis of the SEDA (Scottish Education Data Archive) should be proscribed.

The CES and other approved 'gatekeepers' to the archive have the right and responsibility to draw to the attention of the user factors that bear on the truth or reliability of claims that the SEDA is asserted to support.

The CES has the right and responsibility to draw to the attention of other parties whom it knows to have an interest in a situation under analysis, uses of the data by others that are believed to be partial.

References

ASSOCIATION DES ADMINISTRATEURS DE L'INSEE (1985) *Code of Statistical Ethics,* Paris (mimeo).
BIBBY, J. and MOORE, D. (forthcoming) *Thinking Statistically,* London, W. H. Freeman.
BRITISH SOCIOLOGICAL ASSOCIATION (1973) *Statement of Ethical Principles and their Applications to Sociological Practice,* London (mimeo).

BURNHILL. P., MCPHERSON, A., RAFFE, D. and TOMES, N. (1987) 'Constructing a public account of an educational system', in WALFORD, G. (Ed) *Doing Sociology of Education*, Lewes, Falmer Press.

CLOUGH, E. and GRAY, J. (1986) *Pathways 16-19: National Youth Cohort Study (England and Wales) 1985-1990*, Division of Education, University of Sheffield (mimeo).

DATA PROTECTION ACT (1984) London, HMSO.

DOCKRELL, W. B. (Ed) (1984) *An Attitude of Mind: Twenty-five Years of Educational Research in Scotland*, Edinburgh, Scottish Council for Research in Education.

GRAY, J., MCPHERSON, A. and RAFFE, D. (1983) *Reconstructions of Secondary Education*, London, Routledge and Kegan Paul.

GOVERNMENT STATISTICAL SERVICE (1984) *The Government Statistical Service Code of Practice on the Handling of Data Obtained from Statistical Inquiries* Cmnd. 9270, London, HMSO.

HOINVILLE, G. and JOWELL, R. (1978) *Survey Research Practice*, London, Heinemann.

HUIZER, G. (1973) 'The asocial role of social scientists in underdeveloped countries: some ethical considerations', *Sociologus*, **23**, 2, pp. 165–77.

INTERNATIONAL STATISTICAL INSTITUTE (1986) 'Declaration on professional ethics', *International Statistical Review*, **54**, 2, pp. 227–42.

JOWELL, R. (1982) 'Ethical concerns in data collection' in RAAB, C. (Ed) *Data Protection and Privacy*, London, Social Research Association.

MCCRONE, D. (Ed) (1984) *Scottish Government Yearbook 1984*, Unit for the Study of Government in Scotland, University of Edinburgh.

MCPHERSON, A. (1984) 'An episode in the control of research', in DOCKRELL, W. B. (Ed) *An Attitude of Mind: Twenty-five Years of Educational Research in Scotland*, Edinburgh, Scottish Council for Research in Education.

MCPHERSON, A., and RAFFE, D. (1979) 'A code of practice for collaborative research', *Collaborative Research Newsletter*, 6, pp. 84–6, Centre for Educational Sociology, University of Edinburgh (mimeo).

MARKET RESEARCH SOCIETY (1986) *Code of Conduct*, London, MRS.

MOORE, D. (1985) *Statistics: Concepts and Controversies*, 2nd edn, San Francisco, CA, W. H. Freeman.

MOSER, C. and KALTON, G. (1971) *Survey Methods in Social Investigation*, 2nd edn, London, Heinemann.

RAAB, C. (Ed) (1982) *Data Protection and Privacy*, London, Social Research Association.

RADICAL STATISTICS EDUCATION GROUP (1982) *Reading Between the Numbers*, London, BSSRS.

ROBERTSON, D. (1984) 'Education in Scotland in 1984', in MCCRONE, D. (Ed) *Scottish Government Yearbook 1984*, Unit for the Study of Government in Scotland, University of Edinburgh.

WALFORD, G. (Ed) (1987) *Doing Sociology of Education*, Lewes, Falmer Press.

2
Ethical Issues and Statistical Work

Pamela Sammons

Introduction

At first sight the links between the terms 'ethical' and 'statistical' are not self-evident and may appear at best tenuous. The Concise Oxford Dictionary defines statistics as 'Numerical facts systematically collected' and statistic as the 'science of collecting, classifying and using statistics'. In research, statistics commonly refers to the methods used to collect, classify and analyze quantitative data. The definition of ethics of course concerns morals — the 'science of morals, treatise on this, moral principles, rules of conduct, whole field of moral science'. Despite the apparent lack of association between statistics and ethics, the phrase 'rules of conduct' is I think the key to their connection. In this chapter it is intended to explore the nature of some of the rules of conduct which, it can be argued, should govern the uses of statistical work with particular reference to educational research. It is not my purpose, however, to attempt to provide a definitive set of rules. Indeed, I hope that the discussion will demonstrate that the application of a set of absolute rules would be both impractical and undesirable.

The role of statistical work in education, as in other areas of social research, has expanded enormously over the last thirty years — reflecting the growing range of statistical techniques, and the availability of sophisticated statistical package programs and increasingly powerful computers. Many courses in education and other associated disciplines (for example, psychology and sociology) include a component to familiarize the student with basic statistical ideas and methods. And many major educational journals contain a substantial body of articles based upon quantitative research, even though the nature and complexity of the techniques used, and the level of statistical expertise required to understand articles, varies considerably depending upon the main readership at which journals are aimed.

There has been considerable debate as to the appropriateness of statistical, quantitative and, in particular, scientific methodology in educational research (the same sorts of debates have occurred in various fields of social science, particularly in sociology). It is not intended to rehearse the detail of the arguments for and against using statistical methodology in educational research here. A useful summary is provided by Eggleston's (1979) discussion of the characteristics of educational research which examined some of the conceptual, technical and methodological problems to be faced in recognizing, '. . . the specificity of education as an object of investigation' (p. 1). He commended Langeveld's (1965) assertion that '. . . educational studies are a "practical science" in the sense that we don't only want to know facts and understand relations for the sake of knowledge, we want to know and understand in order to be able to act "better" than we did before!'. This clearly has moral overtones with its suggestion that the purpose of such research is to change and also improve educational practices. It highlights the need for particular consideration of ethical issues in educational research — because of its potential practical applications and the common intention of researchers in the field to influence policy makers, as well as practitioners and, in some cases, consumers.

Eggleston (1979) drew attention to the controversy surrounding the use of quantitative methods — particularly those statistical techniques developed in the physical and biological sciences. He commented, 'There are some researchers who are convinced that these powerful techniques can and should be used in educational research and others who advance cogent reasons why research in the social sciences (including education) cannot be conducted by these methods' (p. 8) and went on to argue, '. . . constant vigilance is required wherever any method is used to collect and examine data to test propositions for truth' (p. 8).

The use of experimental designs in educational research has been the subject of much criticism. Yates (1971) suggested that the search for generalizations (or empirical laws) in such research is misdirected because human behaviour is context dependent. However, such criticism is not always justified. As Eggleston (1979) concluded, '. . . demonstrating that the findings of physicists include invariant empirical laws in the matter-energy systems and pointing out that there are prior grounds for the belief that such laws will not operate in the educational process, does not demonstrate the futility of applying the methods of enquiry used in natural sciences in educational research' (p. 9). Instead it was argued that methods should be chosen according to their utility and judged on the basis of their results. Eggleston further noted, 'The syntax of mathematics facilitates a rigour of discourse unparalleled in other languages. Such hypothetical statements are examined for goodness of fit in the observable world. If, in pursuit of regularities in teacher–pupil behaviour, we find such models to apply only under certain specified conditions, then the use of these methods will be justified. I hope that we do not deny educational researchers access to these methods on doctrinaire grounds' (p. 9).

In the view of many involved in educational research the field has benefited from a multidisciplinary attack on a wide variety of problems. Statistical methods have a valuable part to play in the repertoire of those engaged in educational research. This is not to say that such methods are 'better' than other approaches — for example, qualitative methods. Some of the most fruitful research involves a combination of methodological approaches — for example, our understanding of classroom behaviour can benefit from statistical analysis of observational data collected by the means of systematic instruments, combined with higher inference observational techniques and qualitative analysis of perceptive fieldnotes.

The increased use of statistical methods in educational research is a development that some regret for other than philosophical reasons. In part this seems to reflect a widespread dislike or even fear of 'numbers' and 'maths'. The Cockroft Report (DES, 1982) has demonstrated that many individuals have difficulties even with fairly simple statistical concepts such as percentages or averages. Moreover, as the Radical Statistics Education Group (1982) observed, 'It is socially acceptable to be baffled and bemused by numbers' (p. 34).

There are, undoubtedly, serious problems in the extent to which large sections of society are able to properly understand and interpret many aspects of information which are of a statistical nature. This is a major stumbling block to the creation of an informed democracy, and therefore to greater public understanding of, and participation in, decision-making. Many of the current moves towards greater freedom of information I think inevitably will be of benefit to only a minority with the required skills to understand information, unless greater attention is paid to questions of presentation and communication. This issue has been considered in some depth by the ILEA's (1987) recent Freedom of Information Inquiry (The Tomlinson Report) with which I was involved. This inquiry was instituted to examine ways in which the ILEA could give greater public access to information about the education service it provides. In its remit the Committee of Inquiry was specifically asked to investigate access to information about individual schools. Attention was drawn to the need for all information to be presented in ways which are accessible to the public and consumers of the education service. This is particularly important for statistical information. Wake (1986) commented at a seminar arranged by the Inquiry: 'As to ability to handle information, this takes skills and experience, and, as we are all aware, some people are better placed to play the system than others. Moroever, . . . much of the population remains vulnerable to facts, figures and the power of the word when spoken authoritatively' (p. 4).

There is clearly a sense in which the purposes and processes of education relate to information — its creation, transmission and use. In defining the goals of education the Warnock Report (DES, 1978) included the enabling of a child to become an active participant in society and a responsible contributor to it, capable of achieving as much independence as possible. Accepting these goals the Tomlinson Report (ILEA, 1987) proposed that, 'Access to knowledge cannot be kept on ration but needs to be made as open as possible, both by sharing with the pupils what the teacher knows and by building the skills of research, enquiry and critical analysis so that the pupils can seek and understand for themselves' (para. 7.4).

If the purposes of education are to facilitate the individual's development, autonomy, self-awareness and capabilities so that he or she can participate in society, then abilities to understand and use information, including numerical and statistical information, need to be developed. Without these individuals are liable to misunderstand, or misinterpret much information which they need in order to make informed decisions and to hold to account those who make decisions which affect them. They are also vulnerable to the misuse and distortion of information by groups with a particular view to propound or axe to grind. It is a truism that information is about power, those who have information are in a position to withhold it, misuse or distort it, or to disseminate it selectively. Perhaps it is because the general level of confidence and expertise in handling statistical information (and even more in applying statistical methods) is lower than in other areas, that the need for awareness of ethical issues and recognized codes of conduct which can inform and guide both those who analyze, interpret and publish statistical data and those who use the results of such statistical analyses, is particularly acute.

Examples of Misuse of Statistical Information

A recent example of the misuse of statistical information about schools by the media, is provided by the publication of information concerning parental first and second preferences in their choice of secondary schools at transfer ('How parents mark the schools' *The London Standard,* 6 March 1986, p. 11). These figures apparently show marked differences between schools in their popularity with parents. However, what was *not* published was an accompanying set of figures of school size (in terms of number of places available at the school) which was closely related to the number of parents expressing a first preference, or figures on numbers of pupils in the relevant locality of the transferring age-group. Such additional data would have provided the necessary context for the interpretation of the raw figures on preferences.

An example of the need to use numerical information appropriately is provided by the legal requirement (under the 1980 Education Act) that secondary schools must publish their pupils' examination results. The stated aim of this legislation is to increase parents' access to information, and thus foster accountability through the mechanism of consumer choice. However, as Gray and Hannon (1986) note, the legislation does not require schools (or LEAs) to provide any interpretation of their raw examination results. The argument put forward by the supporters of the legislation was that 'examination results speak for themselves'. However, educational research suggests that this view is unfounded.

Mortimore and Byford (1981) suggested that the requirement to publish means that '. . . the methods of presenting examination results have become a matter of importance' (p. 32). Gray *et al* (1986) stated '. . . we are distinctly unimpressed by the form in which the 1980 Education Act required schools to publish their examination results. We know that our unease is widely shared, but unfortunately these expressions of concern do not as yet appear to have been translated into policies and action in more than a handful of LEAs' (p. 116).

There is much statistical evidence that schools vary considerably in the areas they serve and in the background characteristics of their pupils. (See The Plowden Report, Central Advisory Council for Education, 1967; Little and Mabey, 1972, 1973; Sammons *et al*, 1983; Cuttance, 1986.) There is also a wealth of research evidence of the existence of strong relationships between pupils' backgrounds and their educational outcomes (see, for example, Rutter and Madge, 1976; Marjoribanks, 1979; Essen and Wedge, 1982; Mortimore and Blackstone, 1982; Sammons *et al*, 1983; Mortimore *et al*, 1986). Due to awareness of such relationships, and knowledge that the composition of pupil intakes differ so markedly between schools, it is argued that comparisons of individual schools' raw examination results, without providing the *context* of pupil intake are misleading because they will inevitably favour schools with socio-economically advantaged intakes. For proper and fair comparisons it is necessary to take into account the characteristics of the pupil intake to schools. The dangers of statistical comparisons of examination results failing to compare like with like through neglecting to measure differences in intakes adequately have been illustrated in work by Marks *et al* (1983). The results of their study of examination performance were flawed because of inadequate control for the influence of pupil intakes.

Similarly, Gray and Hannon (1986) have indicated that the HMI's interpretation of schools' examination performance in the full inspection reports (made public since 1983), failed to consider the impact of intake in a systematic way. For this reason schools with advantaged intakes tended to receive more favourable HMI evaluations than those with disadvantaged intakes. In contrast, Gray *et al* (1986) commended the ILEA's method of computing schools' adjusted examination results. This uses statistical methods (multiple regression techniques) to control for relationships between examination results and intake characteristics and provides a measure which contextualizes schools' examination results (see Mortimore and Byford, 1981; South, 1986). Adjusted results have been published on an authority-wide basis in 1986 and 1987.

It is notable that the Secretary of State for Education has recently taken note of such statistical findings by acknowledging the importance of links between pupil intake and schools' outcomes. In arguing for the introduction and publication of national testing it is stated, 'LEAs will be better placed to assess the strengths and weaknesses of the schools they maintain by considering their performance in relation to each other, and the country at large, taking due account of relevant socio-economic factors' (DES, 1987, p. 5).

A Code of Practice for Statisticians

A committee was set up to see whether it was possible to produce a code of ethics for statisticians by the International Statistical Institute (ISI) in 1979. The ISI code was used by the Social Research Association's (SRA) Ethics Committee which worked in parallel with the ISI Ethics Committee, the SRA's guidelines are based on the ISI codes with minor adaptations to make them relevant for social researchers (SRA, 1986). This decision to work together, and the adoption of a very similar code of ethics (or ethical guidelines as the SRA termed them), reflects the close association of statisticians with those involved in various aspects of social research and the significant contribution of statistical techniques to the methodology employed by social researchers.

Jowell's (1981) discussion of some ethical and technical conflicts of introducing a code of practice for statisticians was influential in determining the content of the ISI's draft code. He noted that there are two very different views about the need for and value of a code of conduct:

> Most professionals are genuinely ambivalent about both the desirability and the utility of codes of conduct. They recognize that, to accommodate the diversity of practice, methods and approaches represented within a profession, such codes may end up embodying only the lowest standards; they fear that rigid regulation of practice would inhibit rather than promote concern about, and discussion of ethical issues; and, perhaps most important, they regard ethical behaviour as a matter for the individual, not to be imposed by a body such as the ISI or even a national society.
>
> On the other hand, many professionals concede that a suitable code would have demonstrable benefits. At the very least, it would help to expose flagrant examples of malpractice; it would provide a framework within which individual ethical decisions could more easily be made (p. 167).

Jowell suggested that any code adopted should seek to inform and guide practice rather than to regulate it. This point was reiterated in the ISI's draft code (1983). The basis adopted in the ISI code (and later by the SRA) is that ethical matters are for the individual to determine rather than for the profession to impose. The aim is '. . . to enable ethical judgments to be informed by shared values and experience. It therefore seeks to document widely held principles of statistical inquiry' (ISI, 1983, p. 530). Both the ISI code and the SRA guidelines are prefaced by a statement which recognizes that they are not a set of absolute rules, and that on occasion the operation of one principle may impede the operation of another. It is made clear that the guidelines cannot resolve such choices or prioritize the various principles. The ISI stated, 'The code is intended as a framework within which the conscientious statistician should be able to work comfortably. When departures from the framework of principles are contemplated, they should be the result of deliberation rather than of ignorance' (p. 530).

Jowell (1981) reported that, '. . . a code of practice would, I suggest, be valuable as long as it was, "an enabling rather than an intimidating medium of influence" (Levy, 1974, p. 208), a distillation of experience, convention and collective wisdom' (p. 171). He went on to summarize the views of Ladd (1979) that, '. . . organized rules of ethics are an intellectual and moral absurdity, and that the proper function of a professional association is to encourage frequent discussion, debate and publication of ethical issues' (p. 171). He contrasted two broad classes of potential codes of practice — aspirational codes (which contain high and worthy ideals), and regulating codes (which seek to legislate on specific aspects of professional conduct). He rejected both classes and instead proposed a third — an *educational* code which would specifically structure its provisions to illuminate issues rather than to pronounce on them. Jowell concluded, 'An educational code would start from the premise that deliberate malpractice is largely uncontrollable and that the main function of a code is to enable the diligent professional better to understand the ethical components of his or her work'. (p. 173)

The ISI draft code and the SRA's ethical guidelines share a common intention to be informative and descriptive rather than authoritarian or prescriptive. Both also note that neither the principles nor the commentaries attempt to reiterate general written or unwritten rules or norms, such as compliance with the law or the need for probity.

Even though designed as a guide to action, it is unlikely that consideration of the ISI code of conduct would affect the behaviour of the tiny minority of researchers who engage in the deliberate deception or falsification of results. Perhaps the classic example of deliberate misuse of methods of statistical inquiry is the research of the late Cyril Burt in which IQ data for twins it now appears was fabricated, a deception which went undiscovered for many years. The latter's results were influential in the shaping of education provision into a tripartite system in the 1944 Education Act. They provide a clear demonstration of the need for critical examination of statistical research results, especially those which may have a potential practical impact upon policy choices.

Honesty is a basic principle which all researchers (whether or not they engage in statistical inquiry) must be expected to adhere to scrupulously. No general code of conduct can be expected to guard against the actions of those who do not subscribe to this fundamental unwritten rule of behaviour. As was noted by Burgess, as long ago as 1947, 'Above all better statistics depend . . . on more sensitive individual consciences and more statistical zeal' (Jowell, 1981; quoting Burgess, 1947, p. 282). The comment by Burgess neatly links two aspects which I think are of particular relevance to the consideration of ethics and statistical work. The first is the idea of conscience — which of course is fundamental to the application of a code of conduct which depends upon the individual to regulate his or her own behaviour by making appropriate ethical choices. The second is the idea of statistical zeal, which to my mind draws together the ideals of accuracy in the collection and analysis of data, appropriate selection of techniques for the analysis, and careful interpretation and reporting of results. The latter are all relevant to the examination of the technical aspects of statistical work.

However, although the ISI code is to be recommended for the general ideas embodied in its various principles and discussion of associated issues, there is some justification for criticizing its lack of attention to the technical aspects of statistical inquiry. These are as important for ensuring high standards of statistical research work as the sensitivity of the conscience of the individual researcher. For this reason, after a discussion of the principles embodied in the ISI code, a further section is included which addresses some of the technical issues and conflicts which are also of relevance for a full consideration of a code of conduct, or guidelines for those engaged in statistical work.

The ISI Draft Code

The code considers the statistician's obligations to different groups — society as a whole, funders and employers, subjects involved in research work, and colleagues. Although produced specifically for statisticians, it is as a code designed to *inform* debate about ethical issues in statistical work that the code is worth considering by all those engaged in research involving the collection, analysis and interpretation of quantitative data. Because it is a non-prescriptive, educational code, it may prove particularly appealing to those engaged in educational research.

Obligations to Society

1.1 *Widening the scope of statistics* – Statisticians should use the possibilities open to them to extend the scope of statistical inquiry, and to communicate their findings, for the benefit of the widest possible community (p. 531).

The code observes that it is the role of statisticians to develop and use concepts and techniques for the collection, analysis or interpretation of data, and that they should attempt to influence even if they cannot determine the way in which their data are ultimately disseminated and used.

The code contrasts the position of academics, who usually possess a greater degree of autonomy over the scope of their work and dissemination of their results, with that of those employed in the public sector, commerce or industry, where the final decisions about the publication of findings or use of data may rest with the employer or client. Nonetheless, such pressures can also be felt by those in the academic world who often tender for funds to undertake research projects. The code advises, '. . . statisticians are most likely to avoid restrictions being placed on their work when they are able to stipulate in advance the issues over which they should maintain control' (p. 532).

> 1.2 *Considering conflicting interests* – In planning all phases of an inquiry, including publication of findings, statisticians should weigh the likely consequences for society at large, groups within it, respondents or other subjects, and possible future research (p. 532).

Those involved in educational research as well as those who engage in statistical inquiry share a belief that greater access to accurate information will be of ultimate benefit to society. The code comments, 'The fact that information can be misconstrued or misused is not a convincing argument against its collection and dissemination ... Nonetheless, the statistician has to be sensitive to the possible consequences of his or her work and should, as far as possible, guard against predictably harmful effects' (p. 532).

An example of such conflicts in educational research is the examination of the attainment and progress of pupils from different ethnic or social groups. Evidence of lower attainment by those of certain ethnic or social class backgrounds (for example, Caribbean pupils or those with parents in manual occupations) than those of other groups (for example, ESWI or Asian or those in non-manual occupations) may contribute to or reinforce the development of negative stereotypes of members of such groups — or the attribution of blame to certain family lifestyles. Yet without research documenting the existence of inequalities in attainment or progress it is unlikely that pressure and interest would have developed to establish the *reasons* for such differences in the outcomes of education, and to identify ways of changing the system to prevent the underachievement of significant groups of pupils.

The ISI concludes its consideration of obligations to society as follows:

> Statisticians are not in a position to prevent action based on

statistical data. They can attempt to preempt predictable misunderstandings or to counteract them when they occur. But to guard against the use of their findings would be to disparage the very purpose of much statistical inquiry (p. 533).

1.3 *Pursuing objectivity* – While statisticians operate within the value systems of their societies, they should attempt to uphold their professional integrity without fear or favour. In particular, they should not engage or collude in selecting methods designed to produce biased results, or in misrepresenting statistical findings by commission or omission (p. 533).

The code acknowledges that science can never be entirely objective, and statistics is no exception. Cultural and personal values may influence the researcher's interests and choice of research questions, while the employment base and source of funding may impose particular priorities, obligations and prohibitions. Nevertheless, the statistician still has

. . . a responsibility to pursue objectivity and to be open about known barriers to its achievement. In particular, statisticians are bound by a professional obligation to resist approaches to data collection, analyses interpretation and publication that are likely (explicitly or implicitly) to misinform or to mislead rather than to advance knowledge (p. 533).

Given this obligation to undertake statistical research as objectively as possible, the researcher should try to make his or her values explicit at all stages of the research inquiry. In addition, in reporting results reference to any ethical conflicts and resulting choices occurring during the research design or conduct of the inquiry would be helpful. This would inform other researchers about the influence of such issues and the way they were resolved.

Obligations to Funders and Employers

2.1 *Clarifying obligations and roles* – Statisticians should clarify in advance the respective obligations of employer or funder and statistician; they should, for example, refer the employer or funder to the relevant parts of a professional code to which they adhere. In reports of the findings, they should (where appropriate) specify their respective roles.

2.2 Assessing alternatives impartially – Statisticians should consider the available methods and procedures for addressing a proposed inquiry and should provide the funder or employer with an impartial assessment of the respective merits and demerits of alternatives.

2.3 Preempting outcomes – Statisticians should not accept contractual conditions that are contingent upon a particular outcome from a proposed statistical inquiry.

2.4 Guarding privileged information – Statisticians are frequently the custodians of information that the funder or employer may legitimately require to be kept confidential. Such confidentiality should not apply to the statistical methods and procedures that have been utilized (p. 534).

The code elaborates these principles by noting that a common interest exists between funder or employer and statistician as long as the aim of statistical inquiry is to advance knowledge. It is argued that relationships between statisticians and their funders or employers involve mutual responsibilities.

The funder or employer is entitled to expect from statisticians a command of their discipline, candour in relation to limitations of expertise and of their data, openness about the availability of more cost-effective approaches to a proposed inquiry, discretion with confidential information. Statisticians are entitled to expect from funder or employer a respect for their exclusive professional and technical domain and for the integrity of the data (p. 535).

Obligations to Colleagues

3.1 Maintaining confidence in statistics – Statisticians depend upon the confidence of the public. They should in their work attempt to promote and preserve such confidence without exaggerating the accuracy or explanatory power of their data.

3.2 Exposing and reviewing methods and findings – Within the limits of confidentiality requirements, statisticians should provide sufficient information to colleagues to permit their methods, procedures, techniques and findings to be assessed. Such assessments should be directed at the methods themselves rather than at the individuals who selected or used them.

3.3 *Communicating ethical principles* – To conduct certain inquiries statisticians need to collaborate with colleagues in other disciplines, as well as with interviewers, clerical staff, students, etc. In these cases statisticians should make their own ethical principles clear and take account of the ethical principles of their collaborators (p. 536).

It is suggested that statisticians derive their status and certain privileges of access to data in part because of their professional citizenship. Therefore, statisticians have certain responsibilities towards their professional colleagues. The good reputation of statistics is seen to depend upon the professional conduct of individual statisticians. Because of this 'In considering the methods, procedures, content and reporting of their inquiries, statisticians should therefore try to ensure that they leave a research field in a state which permits further access by statisticians in the future' (p. 537).

The principle that all research work should be open to scrutiny, assessment and possible validation by colleagues is generally accepted by academics. The code makes a specific mention of the difficulties inherent in the task of ensuring that potential future users of data are made aware of the limits of their reliability and applicability by the statistician. It is suggested that statisticians should avoid either overstating or understating the reliability or generalizability of data. It concludes that general guidelines cannot be given, '. . . except for a counsel of caution. Confidence in statistical findings depends critically on their faithful representation' (p. 537).

Obligations to Subjects

4.1 *Avoiding undue intrusion* – Statisticians should be aware of the intrusive potential of some of their work. They have no special entitlement to study all phenomena. The advancement of knowledge and the pursuit of information are not themselves sufficient justifications for overriding other social and cultural values (p. 538).

It is suggested that the greater use of secondary data analysis is one way of reducing intrusion by researchers. However, it also needs to be remembered that, '. . . subjects who have provided data for one purpose may object to its subsequent use for another purpose without their consent. This is particularly sensitive in the case of identified data.

Decisions in such cases have to be based on a variety of competing interests and in the knowledge that there is no "correct" solution' (p. 538).

4:2 *Obtaining informed consent* – Statistical inquiries involving human subjects should be based as far as practicable on their freely given informed consent. Where participation by subjects is required by law, statisticians should point out the terms of the relevant law and try to ensure that participation is as informed as possible. Where participation is voluntary subjects should be made aware of their right to refuse in advance for whatever reason or, in the course of their involvement, to discontinue cooperation and to withdraw data just supplied.

4.3 *Protecting of the interests of subjects* – Neither consent from subjects nor the legal obligation to participate absolves the statistician from considering the subject's interests, especially in relation to potentially harmful effects of participating. In the relationship between statisticians and subject, both parties have special interests. To enable subjects to protect their interests, statisticians should routinely furnish information that would be likely to affect a subject's decision to participate. They should also attempt to supply additional information requested (p. 539).

The principle of informed consent is heavily dependent on unstated assumptions about the amount of information and the nature of consent required to constitute acceptable practice, although a subject should be adequately informed about the purpose and nature of an inquiry, the code concludes that no universal rules can be framed, and that the quality of the information provided is as important as the quantity. Statisticians are advised to assess what items of information are likely to be material to a subject's willingness to participate. A variety of items should be considered including: the purpose of study; policy implications; identity of funder(s); anticipated uses of the data; data storage arrangements, degree of security, etc.; method by which the subject has been chosen; and degree of anonymity and confidentiality. Several modifications to the principle of informed consent are also proposed (see clause 4.4.).

The principle of informed consent is, in essence, an expression of belief in the need for truthful and respectful exchanges between statisticians and human subjects. It is clearly not a precondition of all statistical inquiry. Equally it remains one of the most important and widely practised professional norms which is overridden only at considerable risk (p. 541).

It is also pointed out that sometimes subjects can be harmed by research because they belong to a particular group or section of society (see clause 1.2).

An example of a case where it might not be possible fully to inform all participants in advance of the exact purpose of a research study is the field of teacher expectation. As part of a recent longitudinal study of junior schooling, teachers were asked on a regular basis to rate the ability of all pupils in their class individually. The main purpose of the study was to examine school effectiveness and to study the attainment, progress and development of pupils through the years of junior schooling (Mortimore *et al*, 1986). However, one issue of interest, given well documented differences in attainment for girls and boys, and those of different social class and ethnic groups, was to investigate whether there was any evidence of teacher underrating the abilities of certain groups. Explaining this aspect of analysis *prior* to obtaining teacher ratings could have had an impact upon the way teachers rated children, and therefore have prevented the examination of bias in teachers' expectations. Given the importance of teacher assessment in education, the potential significance of the research question was thought to override the principle of providing a detailed explanation of this aspect of the study at the inception of the investigation.

For all social researchers some inquiries involve a conflict of principles where a belief in openness in obtaining fully informed consent has to be weighed against a belief in accuracy and discovery.

4.5 *Maintaining confidentiality* – Statistical data are unconcerned with individual identities. They are collected to answer questions such as 'how many?' or 'what proportion?', not 'who?' The identities and records of cooperating (or non-cooperating) subjects should therefore be kept confidential (whether or not confidentiality has been explicitly pledged), unless informed consent to release them has been granted.

4.6 *Preventing disclosure of identities* – Staticians should take all reasonable measures to prevent their data from being published in a form that would allow any subject's identity to be disclosed or inferred.

4.7 *Utilizing identified data* – On occasions, access to identified data (for example, medical or administrative data, or other research material) is granted by their custodian to statisticians for a new or supplementary inquiry. In deciding whether or not to utilize such material, statisticians should take into account the likely sensitivity and interests of subjects. It is the statistician's responsibility, not only the custodian's, to consider the subject's entitlement to anonymity and informed consent (pp. 544–5).

The ISI explains that, 'Statistical analysis is often based on data initially collected for administrative purposes; even when it is not, the individual (or organization) is often the initial source of data. Nonetheless the link between name and characteristics can usually be dispensed with' (p. 545). Although there is no failsafe method of guarding against breaches of confidentiality, many procedures can be used to reduce their likelihood, the best and simplest of which is anonymity. Even so, it must be remembered that anonymity is not always a guarantee of confidentiality. 'A particular configuration of attributes can, like a fingerprint, frequently identify its owner beyond reasonable doubt' (p. 545).

There are many well developed computer systems specifically designed to maintain individual confidentiality. In dealing with sensitive personal data relating to named individuals, researchers have a duty to ensure that they make proper use of such systems to protect their data. The assumption should be that a guarantee of confidentiality has always been given or implied unless it has been explicitly waived in advance.

Some Technical Considerations

The use of statistical techniques and approaches to data analysis are not limited to statisticians alone, even if they were that would not remove the need for careful examination and explanation of the technical aspects of their application in any given piece of research. Midzuno (1981) has noted '. . . malpractices in the course of designing, implementing and processing enquiries, inadequate uses and interpretations of methodologies and results elsewhere, to mention just a few. All of such undesirables are damaging statistics' (p. 196). There is, however, a particular need for care in the application of statistical techniques by those who have not been specially trained in the field of statistics.

Wood (1986) criticized the abuse of correlation methods in educational research, '. . . statistical practice in educational and psychological research is generally a degraded version of what statisticians know' (p. 249). While this is undoubtedly an overexaggeration of the practice of non-statisticians engaged in statistical inquiry, it is a useful reminder of the need to apply such techniques with appropriate care and consideration of their theoretical bases. Whatever the problem chosen for research any empirical work should be preceded by a full consideration of the research problem, data requirements and limits of different statistical techniques. It is in posing a particular research question and designing a study that choices as to the appropriate methodology should be made. If a quantitative approach is selected it is at this early stage that questions about the ethics of statistical work should be raised.

a) Functions of statistical methods

Statistical methods are commonly used for one of two different functions. It is important that in presenting results the distinctions between these two purposes are made explicit. One purpose is to describe or summarize data in a useful way; the second is to make inferences from the data. For example, in studying pupil attendance it is useful to reexpress the 'raw' figures (for example, number of half-days absence for each pupil) or change their form so that variations and interesting patterns may be more easily identified. This is commonly done by calculating a variety of simple descriptive statistics such as percentages, averages, standard deviations, etc. In addition tables, diagrams or graphs may be used to illustrate characteristics of the data, and measures of association be calculated to assess the strength of the relationships between variables.

The second function of statistics is to derive estimates and to draw inferences about the characteristics of the *population* based on information obtained by measuring aspects of samples(s) drawn from a total population (the complete set of objects under study). Inferential statistics are needed to allow the researcher to generalize from information obtained from his or her sample(s). Statistical inference can be used to estimate population parameters and also to test statistical hypotheses. Using the attendance example — one might wish from a pupil sample to estimate the average or standard deviation for a total population of pupils. Having examined some relationships in the data (for example between parents' social class and pupil attendance) one might also wish to test the probability that the differences found in the sample are typical of differences in the population using a statistical test of significance.

b) Levels of analysis

The appropriate level(s) of analysis also need to be specified at the start of an investigation. Problems can arise in interpreting results if attempts are made to use one kind of sample to answer a question which should be examined at a different level. Robinson (1950) has described the problem of the 'ecological fallacy' which involves the mistake of attempting to generalize the results of analyses conducted at one level (the area) to another level (the individual). Such generalizations can prove misleading, as was demonstrated in Robinson's calculation and comparison of correlations of illiteracy and race at two levels, individual and territorial.

More recently Goldstein (1984) conducted a review of several statistical studies of school or LEA examination results in which he argued that misspecification in the level of analysis influenced the conclusions which could be properly drawn. On occasion the use of multilevel models may be required to ensure that data are analyzed at the most appropriate level (see Burstein, 1980). In the analysis of school-effectiveness the levels of the pupil, the class and the school should be examined. Goldstein (1986) has described a multilevel model which was applied in the analysis of school effectiveness in a recent study of junior schooling (Ecob, 1985; Mortimore *et al*, 1986).

c) *Providing technical details*

An explicit reference to the nature of the sample used (or information concerning the availability of such technical details) and relating to the levels of analysis used at different stages of an investigation assists the proper interpretation of statistical work in educational research. The rationale for the particular choice of methodology used in the analysis of data should also be given. The ISI (1983) code suggests that statisticians should aim to provide sufficient information for the proper interpretation of their results. Details such as sample size, response rates and where possible and appropriate, sampling errors help to provide such context.

In the case of questionnaire and interview studies the exact questions used can aid the interpretation of results, as there is evidence that replies can be very sensitive to minor changes in phrasing. Of course, where a questionnaire is long (or several are used) it might prove impractical to publish in full. However, the researcher should be prepared to make available copies of all non-published instruments used in a study on request.

Where possible information about the reliability and validity of instruments used should be provided. With any test or measurement procedure used to collect research data, there is a need for reliability and validity. Reliability concerns '. . . The degree to which results are consistent across repeated measurements' (Carmines and Zeller, 1979, p. 15). Reliability is therefore an empirical issue. In contrast, validity '. . . is usually more of a theoretically-oriented issue because it inevitably raises the question, "valid for what purpose?" ' (p. 15). Carmines and Zeller stress the importance of establishing the construct validity of measures used in quantitative research, and argue that 'Construct validation focuses on the extent to which a measure performs in accordance with theoretical expectations' (p. 27).

d) Choice of statistical techniques

The choice of appropriate statistical techniques should be determined by research judgment, the purposes of the study and the nature of the various data-sets used in the study.

Non-parametric or distribution-free statistics (which make no assumptions about the nature of the population from which samples are drawn) traditionally have been used in educational research where data of an ordinal or nominal level of measurement are available. Rules developed by Stevens (1946), linking scales of measurement with the use of specific types of statistical test, have been accepted in the majority of texts on statistical analysis, and many researchers in the social sciences have accepted the use of the 'measurement statistics rule' (Siegal, 1956). More recently, however, researchers in sociology, psychology and education have adopted more sophisticated and powerful parametric tests, traditionally reserved for use only with interval or ratio level data, in analyses of lower level data. Such use of parametric tests has become particularly popular for analysis of data forming ordinal scales (see Baker *et al*, 1966; Labovitz, 1970, 1972).

The ordinal–interval controversy has implications for social science research practice. Those who consider it legitimate to use parametric tests on interval level data adopt a 'pragmatic' rather than a 'purist' approach. Labovitz (1970) argued the advantages of the pragmatic approach and used parametric rather than non-parametric tests on ordinal data. He suggested that many parametric techniques are robust with respect to violations in the parametric assumptions, particularly that of normality in the data.

Although it is possible to transform data to ensure normality some researchers do not adopt this practice, since many parametric tests (analysis of variance, product moment correlation and regression) are relatively robust to violations of the normality assumption. A disadvantage of the use of transformed data is that the results of any tests used apply to the transformed and not to the original data. Thus, interpretations and conclusions drawn from the results should properly refer only to the transformed data. Moreover, it has been suggested that blanket transformations of all variables are required in order to preserve the original patterns of relationships within the raw data. Yet, if this is done, sometimes, the effect can be to adversely affect the distributions of as many variables as have their distributions improved.

A 'pragmatic' approach to statistical investigations may be riskier than a 'purist' approach; however, it can prove fruitful especially when research is exploratory or heuristic in nature. The researcher should draw attention to his or her approach in such circumstances.

Avoiding Abuse of Statistical Techniques

Nie *et al* (1975) have drawn attention to the advantages of using computer packages in the process of inductive social research. They note that high speed computers and easy to use statistical packages have yielded an explosion of statistical capability. This has had the enormous advantage for researchers of enabling them to test theory with data files containing large numbers of cases and variables which previously it would have been impractical to consider and analyze. Nonetheless, this capacity for statistical analysis can sometimes lead to misuse and misinterpretation of data and statistical techniques. Nie *et al* note two particular forms of potential abuse: (i) ease of access often means overaccess; (ii) uninformed use of the available statistical techniques.

Researchers may sometimes overanalyze their data. Thus Nie *et al* criticize those who conduct ' "grand fishing expeditions" substituting the crudest form of empiricism for the careful interaction of concepts, hypotheses and data analysis — a problem of the overproduction of information' (p. 3). Whilst it is undoubtedly useful, particularly in the early stages of analysis, for researchers 'to get to know' their data by calculating simple descriptive statistics and utilizing some of the graphical options for presenting data, this *exploratory* analysis should not be allowed to become an alternative to the testing of hypotheses based on pre-existing or developing theory or the results of past research. Nie *et al* recommend a useful rule-of-thumb, 'to request only those tables, coefficients, etc. for which you have some theoretical expectations based upon the hypotheses in your research design' (p. 3).

In connection with the second form of abuse (uninformed use of techniques), it is sometimes the case that fairly complex statistical techniques are utilized by those who do not understand their underlying assumptions or their statistical or mathematical bases. Nie *et al* propose a second rule-of-thumb that, 'a user should never attempt to use a statistical procedure unless he understands both the appropriate procedure for the type of data and also the meaning of the statistics produced' (p. 3). Both these rules-of-thumb provide useful additions to the rules of conduct which should govern the use of statistics in educational, and other aspects of social research. They are an essential part of the notion of greater statistical zeal referred to earlier.

In addition, it is advisable for researchers to discuss their use of statistical procedures with other researchers involved in the relevant field of inquiry, and with qualified statisticians. Such discussions will be helpful both during the course of designing a study, and again at the analysis stage. This is particularly important when controversy exists as to appropriate methods of analysis or when methodological developments are occurring. In publishing the findings, the researcher should refer to the reasons for the choice of particular statistical approaches in the study, and note why any alternative approaches were rejected.

Such a strategy was adopted at the inception and during the course of the study of junior education referred to earlier (Mortimore *et al*, 1986). The research team (of which I was a member) benefited from preparing a paper describing some of the statistical issues involved in the data analysis, and outlining provisional decisions concerning the most appropriate methodology to use in investigating the existence and size of school effects on pupils' educational outcomes. This strategy assisted us in two ways, by clarifying our own thoughts, and by allowing us to ask other researchers involved in investigating school effectiveness for their views and comments on our proposals. The members of the Association of Child Psychiatry and Psychology sponsored School Differences Study Group provided a useful forum for discussion of these issues.

Assessing 'Statistical Responsibility'

The Radical Statistics Education Group (RSEG) (1982) has produced a critical guide to educational research designed to provide consumers of educational research with guidelines to enable them to evaluate the results of statistical studies. The guide provides examples of appropriate statistical criticism through an examination of three major and controversial pieces of educational research which had all employed fairly sophisticated statistical techniques.

In a discussion of the use and abuse of statistical methods the authors note that it is not always possible to assume there is only one correct statistical approach to any research question. But they acknowledge that statistical methods can sometimes be applied inappropriately, and put forward a number of questions which should be used in the proper evaluation of such research. These they suggest 'can be seen as defining, in a rather loose way, the idea of statistical responsibility. These questions are essentially technical ones' (RSEG, 1982, p. 11).

In developing the concept of statistical responsibility the RSEG acknowledges that essentially technical issues require rules or guidelines to behaviour. The set of eight questions they ask of quantitative research studies can be viewed as guidelines for statistical research practice in addition to providing a basis for critical appraisal of published studies. The group notes 'We also think these questions could usefully be considered by those engaged in educational research, particularly when they are writing up their results' (p. 12). I suggest that the questions posed by the RSEG serve an educational function and form a useful technical supplement of guidelines for statistical decisions to the more general issues covered by the ISI's draft code of ethics.

Before listing the RSEG's technical questions for evaluating statistics in educational research, it is also worth drawing attention to their comments concerning the proper conduct of statistical criticism. It '. . . should aim to clarify rather than obscure the issues underlying the research in question' (p. 11). In my view, this recommendation can be equally applied to the presentation of research results. The researcher should accept a responsibility to present his or her data and results in a way that explicitly refers to the theoretical and methodological issues underlying the research, the various choices made during the design of the study, collection and analysis of data, and interpretation of results, and the reasons for those choices. This should enable more informed and fruitful debate of the findings, and thus assist the development of the particular field of research.

The RSEG refers to Bross' (1960) proposal that a statistical critic should present a counter-hypothesis to the one advanced in the research. This counter-hypothesis should be plausible theoretically and be confirmed empirically by the data under discussion, or by some other relevant data. The RSEG notes that for this to occur critics must make explicit the concept and theories that they are working with, and that for empirical confirmation the researcher must make his or her data available publicly.

Most would support the contention that researchers should make their data available wherever this is possible without infringing the rights to confidentiality of the subjects of research whether these be individuals or, if confidentiality has been promised to them, institutions or groups (ISI, 1983, code clauses 3.1 and 3.2). In addition, this proposal also relates to the principle of informed consent. In some cases individuals and institutions may have agreed to become involved in a research project and provide data to a research group or institution in which they have confidence. They might be less willing to become involved if they knew that the data were at a later stage to be made publicly available, possibly to groups whose interests (or in some cases motives) they might not approve (*ibid*, clauses 4.2, 4.3). These considerations must be borne in mind by the researcher, and sometimes difficult choices will need to be made where the interests of subjects and of colleagues conflict.

Questions Suggested for a Critical Examination of the Technical Aspects of Statistical Research in Education (RSEG, 1982, pp. 12–13).

1 Are the measures or indicators chosen to represent the underlying concepts of the research appropriate? In other words, do they have *construct validity*?

2 Have the researchers taken into account the effects of sampling error on their conclusions? In other words, is it likely that they would have come to the same conclusions if, by chance, they had selected a different sample? If critics can demonstrate that the results can in fact be explained by chance then they are, in our view, presenting a tenable counter-hypothesis. This is the issue of *statistical conclusion validity*.

3 Are there alternative explanations involving 'third variables' that could invalidate the findings and that have not been taken into account or 'controlled'? This is the question of *internal validity*.

4 Is the sample properly described and are unjustified generalizations made about populations which were not sampled? This is the question of *external validity*.

5 Is the analysis conducted at the *right level*? Is it pupils, classes or schools or some other level that is of interest? Would the

results be affected by an analysis at a different level or by an analysis which explicitly took account of more than one level?

6 Are the statistical procedures *properly explained* so that non-statisticians can come to their own conclusions, however tentative, about whether the chosen methods were in fact appropriate to answer the research question posed?

7 Are there *discrepancies* between careful interpretations and qualifications in chapters giving results, and wide claims in the conclusions?

8 Is there any firm evidence of *fabrication* of data or deception in the way the results are presented? If so, this must be exposed whatever the consequences for the research.

Other Considerations

As a supplement to the ISI code of ethics and the more technical issues discussed above, two further aspects should be considered by the researcher involved in statistical work. Finney (1983) argued that the ISI's code ignored one potentially important matter

... the responsibility of a statistician for preserving, uncontaminated and unmodified, data entrusted to his care. This is in no way restricted to human data; the data may relate to production of individual cows or trees or potato plants, or lengths of life of electronic components, but if the original data are placed in my hands for analysis I must show responsibility towards the original 'owner' while I am their custodian (p. 553).

The duty of preserving intact the data used in research is worth acknowledging. Of course constraints of storage space, resources, the movement of researchers between institutions and jobs, and allocation of time for the painstaking task of cataloguing, labelling, recording and filing research data, instruments, computer output and working papers, all create practical difficulties in adhering to this principle. Nevertheless it remains an ideal to which all scrupulous researchers should aspire. Loss or destruction of data and inadequate maintenance of research records and working papers may frustrate the possibilities of later secondary analysis of the data, or prevent proper evaluation of the original research.

The final aspects which all educational researchers should consider seriously are the provision of feedback to participants in research, and the wide dissemination of findings in a form accessible to different types of audience who might have an interest in the results.

Having worked in a research group which operates a clearing system for external researchers wishing to undertake studies in inner London institutions, it is surprising that many researchers fail to observe one of the conditions upon which access had been granted, namely providing the Authority with details of their results and copies of articles, etc. This problem has been commented upon by a former Director, 'It was as if researchers were not interested in dissemination and had little idea of the courtesies of research. Teachers are not paid to help research. They should at least be given first sight of the results' (Shipman, 1980, p. 22).

Whenever possible during research, and certainly after its completion, those who have participated in a study should receive an account of the findings. This is a matter which frequently does not receive the careful attention it merits. Of course, feedback during the course of a piece of research may not always be possible if it might influence the latter collection of data (as in a longitudinal study). However, it is still often practicable to provide some information at an early stage. In the study of junior school effectiveness (noted earlier) the research design did not permit the feedback of results *prior* to the completion of data collection and analysis (Mortimore *et al*, 1986). However pupils' test and assessment results were provided for class teachers on a regular basis. At a later date, as results on differences in effectiveness became available, meetings were arranged to present the early findings. Staff of all schools involved were invited to attend to discuss the results and their interpretation (the confidentiality promised schools was strictly observed). After the meetings a draft report was sent to all schools summarizing the findings. Prior to the publication of the final report of the study, advance copies were sent to participating schools.

In addition, in order to allow wide dissemination of the results they were presented in a variety of forms so that they were more readily accessible to different audiences. A four volume main report containing many detailed discussions of the data and methodology, a short non-technical summary report, a book, and both long and short journal articles covering different aspects of the findings were prepared. Equally important was the dissemination of results through talks for teachers and heads on in-service and management courses, HMI and the ILEA Inspectorate, elected LEA members, students at teacher training institutions, as well as academics. From our experience in this study, researchers have much to gain from presenting their results to, and discussing them with, a variety of audiences. In addition, such activity is valuable because it may promote cooperation in later work due to greater awareness of the results of previous studies and evidence of their application. This may be helpful also in promoting greater understanding of the role and uses of statistical inquiry in educational research.

Summary

As in other areas of educational research there is a need for those engaged in statistical work to be aware of the ethical issues which affect their activity. An informative educational, rather than a regulatory or aspirational code is required. Ethical decisions are properly made by the individual researcher, but should be informed by the values and experiences of others engaged in statistical work. While it is acknowledged that there is no complete set of principles which provide guidance on ethical choices in statistical work, the code proposed by the ISI is worth consideration by all who use statistical techniques in educational research.

Attention to technical matters is also a necessary prerequisite for the proper application of statistical techniques and the interpretation of research results. Given this, there is a need for those using statistical techniques to seek appropriate advice prior to beginning an investigation, and to discuss methodological issues with other researchers. It is also advocated that researchers who use statistical methods should make a practice of including information concerning their research design, data collection and selection of methods of analysis when publishing results. Proposals for developing statistical responsibility put forward by the Radical Statistics Education Group provide a summary of some of the more important technical issues which affect the interpretation of statistical research in education, and it is suggested that greater attention paid to ensuring statistical responsibility by those using statistical methods would improve the quality of educational research. Overall, a combination of statistical zeal and a sensitive individual conscience is required for the proper conduct of statistical inquiries.

References

BAKER, B. O., HARDYCK, C. D. and PETRINOVICH, L. T. (1966) 'Weak measurement versus strong statistics: An empirical critique of S. S. Steven's prescriptions and statistics', *Educational and Psychological Measurement*, **26**, pp. 291–309.

BROSS, I. (1960) 'Statistical criticism', *Cancer*, **13**, pp. 394–400.

BURGESS, R. W. (1947) 'Do we need a "Bureau of Standards" for Statistics?' *Journal of Marketing*, **11**, pp. 281-2.

BURSTEIN, L. (1980) 'The role of levels of analysis in the specification of educational effects', in: DREEBEN, R. and THOMAS, J. A. (Eds) *The Analysis of Educational Productivity, Vol. 1: Issues in Micro Analysis*, Cambridge, MA., Ballinger.

CARMINES, E. G. and ZELLER, R. A. (1979) 'Reliability and validity assessment', *Sage University Paper: Quantitative Applications in the Social Sciences Series*, No. 17, Beverly Hills, Sage Publications.

CENTRAL ADVISORY COUNCIL FOR EDUCATION (1967) *Children and Their Primary Schools, Vols 1 and 2* (The Plowden Report), CACE (England), London, HMSO.

CROSS, M. (Ed) (1980) *Social Research and Public Policy: Three Perspectives*, Amersham, Social Research Association.

CUTTANCE, P. (1986) *Effective Schooling: A Report to the Scottish Educational Department*, Centre for Educational Sociology, University of Edinburgh.

DEPARTMENT OF EDUCATION AND SCIENCE (1978) *Special Educational Needs*, (The Warnock Report), London, HMSO.

DEPARTMENT OF EDUCATION AND SCIENCE (1982) *Mathematics Counts*. Report of the Committee of Inquiry into the Teaching of Mathematics in Schools (The Cockcroft Report), London, HMSO.

DEPARTMENT OF EDUCATION AND SCIENCE (1987) *The National Curriculum 5-16: A Consultation Document*, July, London, HMSO.

DONNISON, D. and EVERSLEY, D. (Eds) (1973) *London: Urban patterns, problems and policies*, London, Heinemann.

DREEBEN, R. and THOMAS, J. A. (Eds) (1980) *The Analysis of Educational Productivity, Vol. 1: Issues in Micro Analysis*, Cambridge, MA., Ballinger.

ECOB, R. (1985) 'Multilevel mixed linear models and their application to hierarchically nested data'. Paper read to the Fourth European Meeting of the Psychometric Society and Classification Societies, Cambridge, July.

EGGLESTON, J. (1979) 'The characteristics of educational research: mapping the domain' *British Educational Research Journal*, **5**, pp. 1-12.

ESSEN, J. and WEDGE, P. (1982) *Continuities in Childhood Disadvantage*, London, Heinemann.

FINNEY, D. J. (1983) 'Contribution to the discussion of the ISI code of ethics draft', *Bulletin of the International Statistical Institute* (Proceedings of the 44th Session), **L(50)** p. 553.

GOLDSTEIN, H. (1984) 'The methodology of school comparisons', *Oxford Review of Education*, **10**, pp. 69-74.

GOLDSTEIN, H. (1986) 'Multilevel mixed linear model analysis using iterative generalized least squares', *Biometrika*, **73**, pp. 43-56.

GRAY, J. (1981) 'A competitive edge: Examination results and the probable limits of secondary school effectiveness', *Educational Review*, **33**, pp. 25-35.

GRAY, J. and HANNON, V. (1986) 'HMI interpretations of schools' examination results', *Journal of Education Policy*, **1**, pp. 23-33.

GRAY, J., JESSON, D. and JONES, B. (1986) 'The search for a fairer way of comparing schools' examination results', *Research Papers in Education*, **1**, 91-119.

INNER LONDON EDUCATION AUTHORITY (1987) *Informing Education*, Report of the Committee of Inquiry into Freedom of Information (The Tomlinson Report), London, ILEA.

INTERNATIONAL STATISTICAL INSTITUTE (1983) 'ISI Code of Ethics (Draft)', *Bulletin of the International Statistical Institute* (Proceedings of the 44th Session), **L(50)**, pp. 527–53.

JOWELL, R. (1981) 'A professional code for statisticians? Some ethical and technical conflicts' *Bulletin of International Statistical Institute* (Proceedings of the 43rd session), **XLIX(49)**, pp. 167–93.

LABOVITZ, S. (1970) 'The assignment of numbers to rank order categories', *American Sociological Review*, **35**, pp. 515–24.

LABOVITZ, S. (1972) 'Statistical usage in sociology, sacred cows and ritual', *Sociological Methods*, **1**, pp. 13–37.

LADD, J. (1979) 'The quest for a code of professional ethics: An intellectual and moral confusion'. Paper prepared for the AAAS workshop on professional ethics, November.

LANGERVELD, M. J. (1965) 'In search of research', in: *The European Year Book of Educational Research*, Vol. 1, Amsterdam, Elsevier.

LEVY, C. S. (1974) 'On the development of a code of ethics', *Social Work*, **19**, 207–16.

LITTLE, A. and MABEY, C. (1972) 'An index for designation of educational priority areas', in SHONFIELD, A. and SHAW, S. (Eds) *Social Indicators and Social Policy*, London, Heinemann.

LITTLE, A. and MABEY, C. (1973) 'Reading attainment and social and ethnic mix of London primary schools', in DONNISON, D. and EVERSLEY, D. (Eds) *London: Urban Patterns, Problems and Policies*, London, Heinemann.

MARJORIBANKS, K. (1979) *Families and Their Learning Environments: An Empirical Analysis*, London, Routledge and Kegan Paul.

MARKS, J., COX, C. and POMIAN-SRZEDNICKI, M. (1983) *Standards in English Schools*, London, National Council for Educational Standards.

MIDZUNO, H. (1981) 'Contribution to the discussion of a professional code for statisticians: Some ethical and technical conflicts', *Bulletin of the International Statistical Institute* (Proceedings of the 43rd session), **XLIX(49)**, pp. 195–7.

MORTIMORE, J. and BLACKSTONE, T. (1982) *Disadvantage in Education*, London, Heinemann.

MORTIMORE, P. and BYFORD, D. (1981) 'Monitoring examination results within a local education authority', *Bedford Way Papers 5 Publishing School Examination Results*, University of London Institute of Education.

MORTIMORE, P., SAMMONS, P., STOLL, L., LEWIS, D. and ECOB, R. (1986) *The Junior School Project Main Report*, Research and Statistics, London, ILEA.

NIE, N. H. *et al* (1975) *Statistical Package for the Social Sciences*, New York, McGraw-Hill.

RADICAL STATISTICS EDUCATION GROUP (1982) *Reading Between the Numbers: A Critical Guide to Educational Research*, London, BSSRS Publications Ltd.

ROBINSON, W. S. (1950) 'Ecological correlations and the behaviour of individuals', *American Sociological Review*, 15, 351–357.

RUTTER, M. and MADGE, N. (1976) *Cycles of Disadvantage*, London, Heinemann.

SAMMONS, P., KYSEL, F. and MORTIMORE, P. (1983) 'Educational priority indices: A new perspective', *British Educational Research Journal*, **9**, pp. 27–40.

SHIPMAN, M. (1980) 'A view from experience in local government' in CROSS, M. (Ed) *Social Research and Public Policy: Three Perspectives*, Amersham, Social Research Association.

SHONFIELD, A. and SHAW, S. (Eds) (1972) *Social Indicators and Social Policy*, London, Heinemann.

SIEGAL, S. (1956) *Non parametric statistics for the behavioural sciences*, New York, McGraw-Hill.

SOCIAL RESEARCH ASSOCIATION (1986) 'Social Research Association ethical guidelines', Appendix B to the *SRA Directory of Members 1985–86*, London, SRA.

SOUTH, L. (1986) *Looking at School Performance*, RS 1058/86, Research and Statistics, ILEA.

STEVENS, S. S. (1946) 'On the theory of scales of measurement', *Science*, **103**, pp. 677–80.

WAKE, R. (1986) 'Access to information — the public interface from a practitioner's perspective'. Paper presented to the ILEA's Freedom of Information Inquiry Seminar, County Hall, London, 31 October.

WOOD, R. (1986) 'Think before you square correlations — or do anything with them', *British Educational Research Journal*, **12**, pp. 249–55.

YATES, A. (Ed) (1971) *Role of Research in Educational Change*, Palo Alto, CA, Pacific Books.

3
Grey Areas: Ethical Dilemmas in Educational Ethnography

Robert G. Burgess

At the heart of the ethnographic enterprise is the relationship between researcher and researched for many commentators (*cf.* Hammersley and Atkinson, 1983; Burgess, 1984) have remarked on the way in which ethnographic data are based on close relationships in the field. This has lead some researchers to point to the importance of understanding the dynamics of the relationship between the researcher and the researched (*cf.* Casagrane, 1960; Burgess, 1985a) and in turn the relationship between the researcher, the research, the process of researching and the results that are disseminated (*cf.* Peshkin, 1982). But we might ask: What are the characteristics of this relationship between those who research and those who are researched?

The lynchpin of this relationship has been well summarized by Punch (1986) when he states:

> For more so than with other styles of social research, then this approach [fieldwork] means that the investigator engages in a close relationship during a considerable period of time with those he or she observes. This is of vital significance, because the development of that relationship is subtly intertwined with both the outcome of the project and the nature of the data (p. 12).

He continues:

> Pivotal to the whole relationship between researcher and researched for instance is access and acceptance (p. 12).

Such a position contains a number of ethical implications about openness, trust, commitment and confidentiality. In short, the relationship implies a respect for the rights of the individual whose privacy is not invaded and who is not harmed, deceived, betrayed or exploited. However, as

Klockers (1979) has shown, fieldwork in urban locations forces researchers to examine critically the realities of their relationships where ethical dilemmas frequently occur. Indeed, Cassell (1980) has argued that some of these day-to-day problems need to be examined as she remarks:

> When only outstanding and scandalous cases are defined as matters for ethical concern, then the daily perplexities, interactions and decisions occurring in the field may well be perceived as merely 'personal'. Ethics then becomes an academic subject, consisting primarily of abstract concepts counterposed by shocking violations (p. 42).

It is, therefore the purpose of this chapter to focus on some of these issues in educational ethnography.

Yet one might wonder whether ethical problems are of any *real* significance in educational research in general or in ethnographic research in education in particular. A brief glance at the second edition of Cohen and Manion's (1985) basic text on educational research methods reveals that there is no reference to ethical issues, while Verma and Beard (1981)[1] address the question *What is Educational Research?* with only a brief mention of research ethics in one paragraph.[1] Finally, those researchers engaged in case study research and ethnography have not done much more[2] as in a book devoted to ethnography in educational research, Woods (1986) only provides a four page outline on 'the psychology and ethics of observation'. Here, Woods begins by advising the reader to head for perfection as he argues that when doing fieldwork:

> as guest, visitor, supplicant, one must behave with tact, discretion and decorum, and flawless recognition of proprieties at all times (p. 56).

However, he does go on to outline two basic ethical problems. First, the morality of doing educational research and secondly, the classic debate about the ethics of covert as opposed to overt observation[3], a situation that he indicates is a 'grey area' in research. It is by focusing on these grey areas in ethnographic study that we can begin to focus on ethical issues, for it is important to relate an abstract discussion of ethical principles to the particular ways in which they are worked out in day-to-day practice (Pring, 1984). We turn, therefore, to a discussion of some ethical dilemmas that I have confronted in an ethnographic restudy of a co-educational Roman Catholic comprehensive school that I have called Bishop McGregor School[4].

Robert G. Burgess

The Research Context

My research in Bishop McGregor started in 1972 when I was a postgraduate student. Here, the research focused on work with teachers and pupils and included a number of ethical problems that had to be handled during the fieldwork (*cf.* Burgess, 1984, 1985b). Many of these problems were related to the context in which I worked in classrooms and staffrooms and to my own status as a postgraduate student who had taken the role of part-time teacher.

When I returned to McGregor School in the 1980s, some ten years after the initial fieldwork had been done, I came back to the same general location but there were changes in the social context. Some teachers were no longer in the school, some held higher status positions than they had ten years previous and many were new to the school since my first study had been conducted. At the level of research relationships I had to begin again to establish my credibility. In part, this was helped by staff who had previously been in the school, who knew me and my previous study and who were prepared to introduce me to other teachers. However, it did not end there. Differences were also apparent as a consequence of the social and economic circumstances – in the early 1980s unlike the 1970s there were few opportunities for promotion and for change so few teachers were able to leave the school. Furthermore, with falling school rolls the possibility of redeployment was presented to staff each summer. Finally, McGregor School was also going through a period of development and expansion in the field of adult and community education as it was designated a community college (*cf.* Burgess, 1987).

In these circumstances the focus of the research was upon teachers. In part, this allowed me to follow up some of the themes that I had identified in part one of my initial study (Burgess, 1983) where I had examined relationships between the head and his staff and between the teachers working in the pastoral system and those in departments. However, I had been critical of this study as there were areas of senior management to which I had not been granted access and there were also specific situations such as teacher job interviews to which I did not have access. I decided therefore that in the restudy I wanted access to both these areas.

While some researchers such as Lofland (1971) have indicated that ethnographic work is an activity for the young, others such as Punch (1986) have highlighted the advantages of age and status in gaining access to areas of senior management in organizations. Certainly, the headteacher indicated that he was prepared to grant me access to the school and to the staff once again due to the relationship we had established in the past. However, he also indicated that he was prepared to get the governors to agree to me being present at all their meetings including those for teacher appointments. It appeared that doors were opening partly as a result of my age and contact with members of the school over a ten-year period and partly as a result of my status as the head indicated that he thought my position in the university and my experience of education could be of advantage to the school.

Within a week of being back in McGregor School I was invited along to a governors' meeting and within a month I found that I had access to a series of teacher job interviews. Here my passage was being eased by the head and I now had access to areas that I had always wanted to research some ten years earlier. However, it was these areas that were to prove problematic in terms of the politics and ethics of McGregor School and of the research.

At the first governors' meeting I attended I was introduced to the chairman by the head which merely resulted in my presence and my purpose being announced by the chairman when new governors were welcomed to the meeting. Here, the first ethical problem arose. Certainly, it could not be said that the members of the governing body were unaware of me or of my research intentions; especially as I sat throughout their meetings with a notebook and pen taking down almost verbatim statements of what was said. But, in this setting there was no opportunity to negotiate permission to use material — it was automatically assumed that I was using the meetings for research but it was also apparent that people had little idea about the format of my notes. Many comments seemed to suggest that I was doing little more than keeping my own set of minutes of their meeting.

My problems did not end there. When the representative of the National Union of Teachers (NUT) heard that I was sitting in on job interviews she approached me on behalf of her members. First, she asked who had granted me permission to sit in on these interviews. Secondly, she was interested in what I was going to do with the information. She explained that job interviews were associated with much confidential information and she wanted to know what would happen to this material. In reality, I could not provide a direct answer to this question as I did not know how the material could be used. However, I argued that it was important that I should be allowed to continue to be present at job interviews so that teachers could get to know what transpired. This answer seemed to provide some satisfaction and I was assured that there would be no objections from the NUT about my presence at interviews.

While it was evident that access to some new social context was problematic I did not anticipate any problems with areas to which I had access in the past. Certainly, this was the case with the staff common room. As in the previous study, I was welcomed back into the common room and made a member of the Common Room Association which entitled me to attend all social occasions including the staff social at the end of term. In the past, this social that took place after school on the last day of term had mainly been the opportunity for a bout of drinking when those teachers who were leaving were given presents. However, I found that in the 1980s staff were accustomed to a 'comic' routine from some of their colleagues. I had read about Hammersley's difficulties with staffroom relations; especially racism in the staffroom (Hammersley, 1984) but I had no experience of such situations. While I appreciated the difficulties for other researchers I did not anticipate that this would be a problem for me. Nevertheless, when a West Indian teacher was leaving McGregor his 'friends' stood up and made short speeches in which they made racist remarks about the teacher 'swinging from trees', and 'being thrown bananas'. In addition, comments were also made about his teaching: 'He's great with the kids — except when he fancies eating them!'[5] To my horror, many teachers found these insults entertaining. However, it was fortunate that I could distance myself from these comments with a number of teachers with whom I was sitting. It was apparent from the expression on the head's face that he was also deeply embarrassed. Indeed, at one point in the proceedings I found him looking directly at me. I could only imagine that he, unlike some teachers, realized that all these remarks were destined for my fieldnote book and ultimately for publication. Yet this could not necessarily be the case for all the teachers. I was present as another member of the Common Room Association, but I was also a researcher who was not merely socializing but also researching. The question that remains is whether my presence constitutes 'spying' at least from the point of view of some staff.

Certainly, my research and my research activities were open rather than closed. But it can be asked, had their consent been obtained?

Gaining Access and Informed Consent

All codes of ethics and statements of ethical principles (American Anthropological Association, 1971; British Sociological Association, 1982) place the principle of informed consent at the centre of ethical research activity. According to this principle:

The voluntary consent of the human subject is absolutely essential. This means that the person involved should have legal capacity to give consent; should be so situated as to exercise free power of choice, without the intervention of any element of force, fraud, deceit, duress, overreaching or any other ulterior form of constraint or coercion; and should have sufficient knowledge and comprehension of the elements of the subject matter involved as to enable him to make an understanding and enlightened decision. (Nuremberg Code, 1949, reprinted in Reiser *et al*, 1977, pp. 272–3).

However as Diener and Crandall (1978) indicate problems can arise even when consent is obtained. Certainly, in my study teachers had been informed that research was taking place but it was not possible to specify exactly what data would be collected or how it would be used (*cf.* Jorgenson, 1971). In this respect, it could be argued that individuals were not fully informed, consent had not been obtained and privacy was violated. Often this is discussed in relation to extreme examples (*cf.* Humphreys, 1970). However, my examples are taken from a staff social and from teacher job interviews to which we now turn.

On gaining access to teacher job interviews I reached an agreement with the head whereby he would either introduce me to all candidates or he would give me an opening to do this for myself. However, I soon found that this rarely happened in a systematic way. In the first job interviews that I sat in on the head gave me the opportunity to introduce myself to candidates and to ask if they had any objections to me being present. Needless to say, neither of the candidates indicated any objection nor for that matter have any candidates since. However, it is dubious whether this kind of situation can be regarded as constituting informed consent given the power relations involved in the situation. What candidate would risk having me ejected from an interview when it was apparent that the head and the governors had invited me into the situation?

However, there were also situations where I was not given an opportunity to introduce myself nor did the head provide any introduction. Then there were other occasions when the head met all candidates who were on interview for a post. Here, I was introduced in the following way:

This is Mr Burgess from Warwick University. He's doing some research with us and will be sat in the interviews. He's a sort of 'fly on the wall'.[6]

While this statement might have satisfied the head, it could hardly be regarded as informed consent. Indeed, a teacher who subsequently came to McGregor School told me that when I had been introduced in this way there had been speculation among the candidates as to what I was really doing. In a similar way, local authority advisers who sat in on interviews were rarely any better informed. As McGregor is a Catholic school they were present as the guests of the governing body. Often different advisers arrived to conduct interviews. On several occasions they were late and unless specifically asked there was no opportunity to introduce myself or my project unless it was specifically raised by the head or by a governor during an interlude. On this basis, it could be argued that data collection took place under different conditions concerning the relative 'openness' of my research activity. However, it is not possible within such formal situations to make an announcement about research activity prior to each interview. Nevertheless my research activities could not be regarded as covert to those people involved in interviews as I sat with notebook and pen and openly made notes throughout each interview session. As a consequence the topic of my research or as the chairman of governors called it, my 'minute taking', became a topic of conversation which made it very public to all concerned. But it was doubtful whether all of the people in the interviews had a similar understanding of the research.

My problems did not end there. Part of my agreement about sitting in on job interviews related to my own activities. I agreed that I would not take any part in the proceedings nor would I divulge any information to teachers about what transpired in the interviews. However, I soon found that this was far from straightforward. When the first group of informal interviews occurred for a post I joined the head. All went well until lunchtime when we were joined by a governor. The governor began by asking the head to rank the candidates that we had seen in order of preference for the formal interviews in the afternoon. Once the head had responded the governor turned to me 'And what do you think?' he asked. I explained that I was not there to pass comments on the candidates. 'But I'm interested in what you think' he said. I still persisted, saying that I was not there to make judgments, but he taunted me with the comment 'Why don't you think?' At this point I remarked that I had a moral position to keep up to which the governor replied: 'I'm not worried about your moral position'. Clearly, it was not going to be easy to be 'a fly on the wall'. In subsequent interviews I was asked questions by governors about candidates and about references. Usually, I tried to deflect these questions by means of a non-committal response so that I would not directly influence the decisions that were made. However, I did break with this convention on one occasion when in the middle of meeting candidates and interviewing them one governor turned and asked me what the post was about for which they were interviewing. It was the kind of question that was unexpected but I felt obliged to address it.

Over the two-year period that I sat in on job interviews I became accustomed to deflecting questions about candidates. In turn, when internal candidates approached me in the common room with remarks that attempted to obtain comments on their interviews I avoided them. However, there were occasions when this was not possible. For a set of interviews for the post of coordinator of adult religious education, candidates were seen by eight separate groups who were to decide on the final shortlisting for the formal interviews. I sat in on one group where I could maintain my position of observer as I was not asked for any comment. But things did not proceed that easily. When all the groups met in the middle of the day I found that I was approached by several people who wanted to know my ranking of the candidates. I decided that a useful tactic would be to return the question and get these individuals to provide their own ranking. When this was done I promptly agreed with the ranking that they had provided. While this ensured that I did not influence which candidates were finally interviewed it was deceptive. Nevertheless, I would maintain that this was justified in gaining data (*cf.* Punch, 1986) and in turn in respecting the rights of individual candidates without harming them. The situation is as Punch indicates:

> some elements of covert research ('the betrayal of trust, deception, the invasion of privacy, damage to field relations and the reputation of social research', Homan and Bulmer, 1982, p. 121) are not exclusive to covert methods. (Punch, 1986, p. 40)

But as Punch indicates, the questions to be considered are:

How far should you go in deception? Should you avoid harm?

It is these questions that can be addressed through further examples from job interviews.

Handling Deception

We have already seen how ethnography involves spending time among the people who are studied and taking part in their activities. Often, researchers write as if they are the only individuals who take part in illegal or deceptive activities. However as Polsky (1967) remarks in relation to his studies of criminal communities:

> If one is effectively to study adult criminals in their natural settings, he [the researcher] must make the moral decision that in some way he will break the law himself. He need not be a 'participant' observer and commit the criminal acts under study, yet he has to witness such acts or be taken into confidence about them and not blow the whistle. That is the investigator has to decide that when necessary he will 'obstruct justice' or have 'guilty knowledge' or be an accessory 'before or after the fact, in the full legal sense of those terms' (pp. 139–40).

Often it is extreme cases, such as criminal activity, that are taken as ideal examples of 'guilty knowledge', yet even the world of teacher job interviews presents a similar situation.

For one set of job interviews at Bishop McGregor School six candidates had been called to attend for interview for the whole day. Informal interviews were to take place in the morning followed by formal interviews in the afternoon. However, after a series of informal interviews the head decided that he was no longer interested in two of the candidates. Yet he considered that the governors were under an obligation to see all the candidates in the afternoon as they had been invited for the whole day. Accordingly, it was decided that all the candidates would be seen by the governors and that those teachers who were not suitable for the post would be given an equivalent amount of time to those candidates in whom they still had an active interest. I was present at these discussions and whether I liked it or not I was also a party to the decision that had been made. Here, some measure of deception was involved.

Throughout all teacher job interviews I regularly kept notes of the questions and the responses that were made. However, I knew that in two of the interviews which were to take place neither the questions nor the responses were of any consequence to the selection panel − or so at first sight it appeared. In these circumstances I seriously contemplated not keeping any fieldnotes when these candidates appeared. Yet I was also caught in a dilemma. The candidates all knew from their informal interviews and from the explanation that had been given that I was a researcher who sat and took notes − would they not think it unusual if I did not take any notes? Furthermore, as I did not say anything in the interviews it meant that if I did not take any notes it would raise further questions about my purpose and my role in the job interviews. Whether I liked it or not I was a party to these 'mock interviews'. I decided that as I was involved I would also maintain the deception by taking notes but by just keeping a record of the questions that were asked and not the answers. This way I thought I would not convey anything to the candidates about what was really happening.

In the majority of interviews, keeping a near verbatim record involved continuous writing. However, I soon found that by just keeping a note of the questions I did not have enough to do. I decided, therefore to write a note about this problem to myself. An entry in my fieldnotes reads as follows:

> My problem here is what I am to do. In this instance (while an interview is in progress) I am usually taking notes but here it is pointless in the sense that I know that what this candidate says is not going to be of any consequence for appointment as the head and the deputy head (community) have already squared the others that they are not interested in this candidate. I have decided to handle this situation by just writing questions.

While this was a strategy that was designed to fill in the time, my brief notes also highlighted the fact that the questioning strategy which was used was different. Each of the people posed slightly different questions which were very general and which only required short answers. The result was that the panel not only asked questions but also started answering them and holding a discussion with the candidate. It soon became evident to the candidate that this was not a 'normal' pattern for an interview. However, he did not say anything explicit but at the end of his 'interview' he said a formal goodbye to the panel and wished them well in establishing the community college. The governors looked very embarrassed. But they now had a further interview to conduct where they had no interest in the candidate.

In the second case the situation was slightly different. The head had invited the candidate to interview before all the references had arrived. However, one reference was far from complimentary and therefore the candidate was no longer regarded as a serious contender for the post. The questioning strategy in this instance was similar to the previous candidate but here I decided to keep a complete record of not only questions but also answers and comments from governors as it gave me an example of how such situations were handled. Nevertheless, I was still party to some deception on the part of the governors and handled it by continuing to write notes — a strategy that I decided would result in no 'clues' being given by me about the status of these interviews.

During the course of teacher job interviews I have been in receipt of much confidential information: the way decisions are reached, the curriculum vitae of the candidates and the references that are marked confidential and which have been written for the head in connection with the selection process. But we might ask: what constitutes confidentiality?

Issues of Confidentiality

It is not just sociologists who debate questions of confidentiality for I soon found that the participants in my study talked about confidentiality. Indeed, when I circulated a note to staff indicating that all responses would be confidential one teacher asked me: 'How confidential is confidential?'. She explained that she wished to make some critical comments about the activities of another teacher but did not wish to be identified in my final report with such comments against her name. I assured her that I would be using pseudonyms in my report in order to protect the identity of individuals. However, as Barnes (1979) remarks:

> confidentiality is at risk from the very moment when the scientist
> is told or allowed to see something that would normally be hidden
> (p. 145).

Nevertheless, circumstances arise when confidential documents are passed to a researcher — some of which are not suitable for publication. For example, the head of Bishop McGregor School now passes me material some of which is confidential for certain periods of time before it is released more widely, while other material is marked 'not for publication'. As Barnes (1979) indicates there is a risk involved here but the head has indicated that he trusts me not to use this information. While I would not use information that is clearly marked as not being suitable for publication I do nevertheless use the material to assist in my analysis and understanding of social situations — it is taken into account during my work (*cf.* Woods, 1986).

There are situations during interviews when individuals tell me things that are 'just between ourselves' or 'in confidence' when the tape-recorder is still on. In other instances I have been asked to switch the tape-recorder off. In the period that follows an individual provides an account of a situation that they do not wish to be made public. Yet in these circumstances one might ask: if the information is confidential why am I being told? In a Catholic school such interviews are often likened to confessions which imply an opportunity for individuals to unburden themselves. However, it is really a transfer of a burden from them to me. Again, these are circumstances where the information cannot be used directly but where my understanding is used in other situations that are disseminated and published.

The Dissemination of Data

Many commentators (*cf.* Becker, 1964; Barnes, 1979; Fetterman, 1984) have remarked on the problems associated with the production of ethnographic reports. However, I would argue that problems arise at an earlier point when findings are 'fed back' to informants. At Bishop McGregor School I have an agreement that I will feed into the school system parts of my analysis that will be relevant for educational practice prior to publication as the head has indicated in discussion with me that it is too long to wait to know what went wrong in a school until a study is published. It is also touched upon in a letter handwritten by the head and sent to me on exercise book paper after reading a previous paper on the ethical issues surrounding the teaching of Newsom pupils in Bishop McGregor School (*cf.* Burgess, 1985b). He wrote as follows:

> Dear Bob,
>   This is like one of those Russian dolls. Outer is Newsom. Inside is you teaching and discussing Newsom pupils. Inside again is your seven year writing up of the fieldwork and discussing it in draft with me. Inside that again is your account of that discussion and inside again is my writing to you having last evening read for a second/third (?) time your chapter in *Field Methods*.
>   But never forget that while for you at the centre of the almost infinite model is an elusive quality called truth. While for me at the centre are youngsters, although perhaps at the centre for both of us are two powerful and slightly (?) self satisfied egos.
>   Now comes the question. Thinking this and believing it a) do I send it and if so do I sign it.
> [Signed in   or Geoff [pseudonym]
> his real name]
> You choose.
> P.S. I play fair — this is the only copy.

Perhaps by quoting this I have continued the cycle a stage further. However, I feel it also illustrates the importance of understanding the educational activities at McGregor School from my work.

On this basis the restudy has included periods when I have spent time talking to the head about some aspects of my analysis. This was the case when several members of the community team had obtained posts in other schools. Here, I offered an analysis of the divisions between school and community (Burgess, 1986) although I was also careful not to identify individuals with the positions that I had portrayed.

Within days the head issued a paper entitled 'Community in Crisis' which was based on various discussions with people within and beyond McGregor School. No parts of the document were attributed to individuals. However, after spelling out some practical problems the following section appeared.

> A slight philosophical piece which can be skipped by pragmatists (another school of philosophy). Perhaps the mistake [of going community] was made by me some nearly three years ago when as we set up the community exercise, either not knowing, or wilfully choosing not to know, I set up the Deputy Head positions (and at that time I had two to fill). I indicated that the school position would be 100 per cent school and the community position should be 100 per cent community. I failed. Of course! As both occupants of both posts will tell anyone who holds a microphone under their noses I was bound to fail. It doesn't work like that. Life doesn't work like that.[7]

I had not seen this document when it was first issued as it came out from the head's office on a day when I was not in school and when I was away from the University. However, one teacher on reading this material became concerned about the oblique reference to me conducting tape-recorded interviews in the school. He decided to telephone me but instead obtained the Sociology Department secretary at Warwick University. When he discovered that I was not available he dictated the following message for me:

> (Name of teacher) rang from (real name of school) and left this message:
>
>> 'I am quite distressed at a letter which has been circulated, but I don't know to whom by (the head) which has certain implications with regard to tapes which you have made in the school. If possible I would like my tapes back.'[8]

As this secretary did not work on the project she did not, until that phone call, know the location of my research school — while attempting to protect himself this teacher had blown my cover in my own department!

When I saw this message I was not sure what it referred to. I decided to telephone one of my informants (*cf.* Burgess, 1985a) to find out what letters had been circulated by the head. As soon as I was told about the 'Community in Crisis' document and that there was a phrase in it about tape-recording I realized what had occurred.

I decided to begin by obtaining a copy of the document before going to talk to the teacher concerned. Having read through it and identified the paragraph I went to see that teacher to discuss the problems involved. Inside the teacher's room was another teacher but it was indicated that I could talk in front of them both — indeed, it rapidly became clear that they both knew what I had come to talk about.

I explained that I had seen the 'Community in Crisis' document and I appreciated how it appeared that I had been talking to the head about tapes that I had made. The teacher who had made the telephone call said 'How did you get a copy of the document? How did you come to see it?' I explained that I always received copies of all documents written by the head. Both teachers shook their heads and looked horrified. They both indicated that they profoundly disagreed with this aspect of the head's policy, as in their view it was far too lax. The teacher who had made the phone call then continued by saying that it seemed as if tapes were being handed over to the head to listen to. The other teacher agreed. I indicated that this had never happened nor would it ever occur. I emphasized that the only person who listened to the tapes was the secretary who worked on the project and I also took the opportunity to remark that had it not been for the phone call the department secretary would not have known the location of the project. Finally, I restated my commitment to both these teachers and emphasized my long term commitment to them and to the school.

It was a difficult ten minute meeting when questions were raised about loyalty, trust and confidentiality. Here, I confronted a real problem concerning data dissemination. On the one hand I had summarized trends that I had perceived in the school so as to link in with the head's request for some input into policy and practice. But this had been the source of my difficulties. I had made no comments that were attributed to individuals but this had been 'read into' the head's remarks by the two teachers. Certainly, this incident highlights how data dissemination while being seen as a virtue by some is seen as problematic by others. The situation is as Barnes (1979) indicates, one where although privacy and confidentiality is not breached it is not always welcomed by those who will be shown to be less than perfect. But we might ask what are the implications for the ethnographer?

Robert G. Burgess

Some Implications for Fieldwork Practice

Professional associations have attempted to come to terms with these 'grey areas' by outlining 'codes' of ethics (American Anthropological Association, 1971; British Sociological Association, 1982). While it is relatively easy to prescribe a set of abstract principles it is less easy to apply them or to enforce them. Many researchers have indicated the difficulties of working with codes of ethics when engaged in fieldwork (*cf.* Barnes, 1977, 1979; Burgess, 1981; Punch, 1986).

This does not mean that such researchers are automatically in favour of covert research with all the implications of deceit and betrayal. Instead, they take account of the situational elements of fieldwork which codes fail to resolve. Nevertheless, it is apparent as Punch (1986) states:

> the fieldwork often has to be interactionally 'deceitful' in order to survive and succeed (p. 71).

Yet this is qualified in terms of the responsibility and accountability of the fieldworker in different social settings. It does imply as Barnes (1979) has indicated that fieldwork involves compromise and negotiation — not only on the part of the researcher but also between researcher and researched (*cf.* Simons, 1984). Fundamentally, it means that a review of ethical problems and dilemmas should be at the heart of reflexive practice by those ethnographers who are working in the field.

Acknowledgment

The restudy of Bishop McGregor School that is reported here was made possible by grants from the University of Warwick Research and Innovations Fund and by the Nuffield Foundation to whom I am very grateful. I would also like to record my thanks to the teachers of Bishop McGregor School for their help and assistance.

Notes
1 See Verma and Beard (1981), p. 32.
2 An exception is a detailed treatment of ethical issues in educational evaluation by Adelman (1984).
3 This topic has been given centre stage in the ethics literature. See, for example, Bulmer (1982) for major papers on this topic in Britain and the USA in the 1970s and 1980s.
4 For a discussion of the study and restudy see Burgess (1987).

5 Extract from fieldnotes.
6 *Ibid.*
7 Extract from 'Community in Crisis' document written by the head in May 1986.
8 Recorded telephone message.

References

ADELMAN, C. (Ed) (1984) *The Politics and Ethics of Evaluation*, London, Croom Helm.
AMERICAN ANTHROPOLOGICAL ASSOCIATION (1971) 'Statements on ethics: Principles of professional responsibility' reprinted in WEAVER, T. (Ed) *To See Ourselves: Anthropology and Modern Social Issues*, Glenview IL., Scott, Foresman and Company.
BARNES, J. A. (1977) *The Ethics of Inquiry in Social Science*, Delhi, Oxford University Press.
BARNES, J. A. (1979) *Who Should Know What?*, Harmondsworth, Penguin.
BECKER, H. S. (1964) 'Problems in the publication of field studies', in VIDICH, A. J. *et al* (Eds) *Reflections on Community Studies*, New York, Harper and Row.
BRITISH SOCIOLOGICAL ASSOCIATION (1982) 'Statement of ethical principles and their application to sociological practice'. Originally published in 1968, revised 1970 and 1973.
BULMER, M. (Ed) (1982) *Social Research Ethics*, London, Macmillan.
BURGESS, R. G. (1981) 'Ethical "codes" and field relations'. Paper presented to the 41st Annual Meeting of the Society for Applied Anthropology held at the University of Edinburgh, April.
BURGESS, R. G. (1983) *Experiencing Comprehensive Education: A Study of Bishop McGregor School*, London, Methuen.
BURGESS, R. G. (1984) *In the Field: An Introduction to Field Research*, London, Allen and Unwin.
BURGESS, R. G. (1985a) 'In the company of teachers: Key informants in a comprehensive school', in BURGESS, R. G. (Ed) *Strategies of Educational Research: Qualitative Methods*, Lewes, Falmer Press.
BURGESS, R. G. (1985b) 'The whole truth? Some ethical problems of research in a comprehensive school', in BURGESS, R. G. (Ed) *Field Methods in the Study of Education*, Lewes, Falmer Press.
BURGESS, R. G. (1986) 'School and community: It's so close together you can't see the join', *Journal of Community Education*.
BURGESS, R. G. (1987) 'Studying and restudying Bishop McGregor School', in WALFORD, G. (Ed) *Doing Sociology of Education*, Lewes, Falmer Press.
CASAGRANDE, J. (Ed) (1960) *In the Company of Man*, New York, Harper and Row.
CASSELL, J. (1980) 'Ethical principles for conducting fieldwork', *American Anthropologist*, **82**, 1, pp. 28–41.
COHEN, L. and MANION, L. (1985) *Research Methods in Education*, 2nd edition, London, Croom Helm.

DIENER, E. and CRANDALL, R. (1978) *Ethics in Social and Behavioural Research*, Chicago, IL, Aldine.

FETTERMAN, D. M. (1984) 'Guilty Knowledge, dirty hands and other ethical dilemmas: The hazards of contract research', in FETTERMAN, D. M. (Ed) *Ethnography in Educational Evaluation*, Beverly Hills, CA, Sage.

HAMMERSELY, M. (1984) 'Staffroom news', in HARGREAVES, A. and WOODS, P. (Eds) *Classrooms and Staffrooms: The Sociology of Teachers and Teaching*, Milton Keynes, Open University Press.

HAMMERSELY, M. and ATKINSON, P. (1983) *Ethnography: Principles and Practice*, London, Tavistock.

HARGREAVES, A. and WOODS, P. (Eds) (1984) *Classrooms and staffrooms: The Sociology of Teachers and Teaching*, Milton Keynes, Open University Press.

HOMAN, R. and BULMER, M. (1982) 'On the merits of covert methods: A dialogue', in BULMER, M. (Ed) *Social Research Ethics*, London, Macmillan.

HUMPHREYS, L. (1970) *Tearoom Trade*, London, Duckworth.

JORGENSON, J. (1971) 'On ethics and anthropology', *Current Anthropology*, **12**, pp. 321–34.

KLOCKERS, C. B. (1979) 'Dirty hands and deviant subjects', in KLOCKERS, C. B. and O'CONNOR, F. W. (Eds) *Deviancy and Decency: The ethics of research with human subjects*, Beverly Hills, CA., Sage.

LOFLAND, J. (1971) *Analyzing Social Settings*, Belmont, CA., Wadsworth.

PESHKIN, A. (1982) 'The researcher and subjectivity: Reflections on an ethnography of school and community', in SPINDLER, G. (Ed) *Doing the Ethnography of Schooling: Educational Anthropology in Action*, New York, Holt, Rinehart & Winston.

POLSKY, N. (1967) *Hustlers, Beats and Others*, Harmondsworth, Penguin.

PRING, R. (1984) 'Confidentiality and the right to know', in ADELMAN, C. (Ed) *The Politics and Ethics of Evaluation*, London, Croom Helm.

PUNCH, M. (1986) *The Politics and Ethics of Fieldwork*, Sage University Papers Series on Qualitative Research, Methods, Volume 3, Beverly Hills, CA., Sage.

REISER, S. J., DYCK, A. and CURRAN, W. (1977) *Ethics in Medicine*, Cambridge, MA, MIT Press.

SIMONS, H. (1984) 'Principles and procedures for the conduct of an independent evaluation', in ADELMAN, C. (Ed) *The Politics and Ethics of Evaluation*, London, Croom Helm.

SPINDLER, G. (Ed) (1982) *Doing the Ethnography of Schooling: Educational Anthropology in Action*, New York, Holt, Rinehart and Winston.

VERMA, G. K. and BEARD, R. M. (1981) *What is Educational Research?* Aldershot, Gower.

VIDICH, A. J., BENSMAN, J. and STEIN, M. R. (Eds) (1964) *Reflections on Community Studies*, New York, Harper and Row.

WALFORD, G. (Ed) (1987) *Doing Sociology of Education*, Lewes, Falmer Press.

WEAVER, T. (Ed) (1973) *To See Ourselves: Anthropology and Modern Social Issues*, Glenview, IL, Scott, Foresman and Company.

WOODS, P. (1986) *Inside Schools: Ethnography in Educational Research*, London, Routledge and Kegan Paul.

4
Exploiting the Exploited? The Ethics of Feminist Educational Research

Sheila Riddell

Introduction

In the early stages of my research I expected that I would spend most time pondering over weighty matters of theoretical interpretation. In fact, the aspect of the research which has caused me most soul searching has been to do with the ethical issues which have constantly arisen. On the subject of the Girls into Science and Technology (GIST) action research project, Kelly (in this volume) comments that while the research was actually being carried out, those who were involved were more concerned with actually getting on with the work than agonizing over the ethical issues which it raised. The analysis which she gives of the ethics of the research is, then, retrospective. As she points out, one of the problems with this is that three years after a research project has finished, memories of what actually happened and what it felt like at the time will have blurred. In contrast, my involvement with the ethical issues of the research has been ongoing, and continues today, one-and-a-half years after the final set of interviews were completed. This is not because I am a particularly moral person, but rather, I think, because I was trying to deal not only with the ethical demands of mainstream sociology, but also with those of feminist sociology which, as I discuss in this chapter, were sometimes at variance with each other. I also discuss the specific ethical questions I encountered with regard to feminist research. These tended to concern definitions of honesty, power relations between researcher and researched and the degree of responsibility which the researcher has for those who participate in the research. I will consider how problems associated with these issues recurred throughout the research process, looking particularly at ethical issues associated with choice of methods, negotiating access, dealing with power relations in fieldwork, analyzing and interpreting data and finally disseminating findings.

Sheila Riddell

The Research Project

The data reported here were gathered from parents, pupils and teachers in a predominantly rural county in the south-west of England between March 1983 and July 1986. The research project, which is being written up as a doctoral thesis (Riddell, 1988), was based in two comprehensive upper schools, and concerned the gender and class divisions which arose when pupils made their subject option choices. A major focus was to analyze the way in which the process of option choice is influenced by the messages concerning masculinity and femininity transmitted by the school organization, teachers, parents and pupil peer groups. Class differences in the construction of masculinity and femininity in these different locations were also explored. A variety of research methods was used, including lengthy periods of observation in both schools, interviews with parents, pupils and teachers and questionnaires administered to parents and pupils. Data gathered by qualitative methods were used to interrogate quantitative data and vice versa, thus broadening the scope of the enquiry and enabling general statements to be made about these particular populations with a reasonable degree of confidence. Sieber (1973, reprinted in Burgess, 1982) has argued strongly for the dissolution of the boundaries between the qualitative and quantitative traditions in the interests of improving strategies of social research. He lists ways in which field research can help in the collection and interpretation of survey data. Perhaps one of the most important points he makes is that the use of ethnography in conjunction with quantitative methods may help the researcher to avoid abstracted empiricism. This was certainly one of my major concerns in using a range of research techniques.

Ethics and Choice of Methods

The debate about feminism and the ethics of research starts as soon as a decision has to be made about which methods to use. As I have already indicated, I was attracted to the idea of using both qualitative and quantitative research methods so that the complex picture of the social world which can be provided by interviews and observation could be counterbalanced by the potential for wider generalization provided by quantitative methods. However, the question of what constitutes acceptable working methods for feminists has been hotly disputed. It was some time before I was able to convince myself, through trying out various approaches in the field and reflecting on these experiences, that there was nothing either intrinsically pro- or anti-feminist in any of these methods, and what mattered above all were the values implicit in the conduct of the research.

First, however, I would like to give a brief picture of the sort of objections which have been raised. Some feminists, notably Stanley and Wise (1983), have been particularly critical of much feminist sociology which, they say, reflects an essentially positivistic masculinist world view. They argue that whereas feminism insists on the validity of every woman's experience, positivism searches for patterns of causation and universally applicable theories, and therefore the two are irreconcilable. The work of marxist feminists, for example Coward *et al* (1976) and the Centre for Contemporary Cultural Studies (CCCS) (1978), with their implicit or explicit use of the concept of false consciousness, is found to be particularly at variance with a belief in the validity of every woman's experience. The marxist feminist approach, Stanley and Wise maintain, is patronizing of other women and should be deeply offensive to all feminists. Instead of there being one objective social reality, they subscribe to the view that there are 'competing views and realities competently managed and negotiated by members of society'. The only valid research project, then, is to attempt to understand how personal reality is constructed, starting with one's own, and they contend that no attempt should be made to move towards larger scale theory.

I disagree with Stanley and Wise's attack on attempts to offer explanations for women's oppression in terms of describing patterns and connections between variables. First of all, if structural accounts are to be rejected, it is not clear how the oppression of women is to be explained, nor how it is to be combated. It is hard to imagine how a programme for political change might emerge from the view that all accounts of reality have equal validity. However, Stanley and Wise insist that it is no use telling a battered mother of six that she is oppressed if she thinks she is not. All that can be done is to understand how she constructs her reality. Whilst I would agree that it is necessary to explore people's accounts of their experience, it is also important to be clear that objectively this woman is oppressed whether she thinks she is or not. I do not think that Stanley and Wise are right to completely reject the notion of false consciousness, because I do feel that sociologists may have access to interpretations which are not immediately accessible to the actors themselves. This is not to claim god-like status for sociologists, for, as McRobbie (1982) reminds us, no interpretation can take account of the full complexity of social reality, and must therefore be partial. Although Stanley and Wise insist that no conception of the world is 'better' than another, they in fact lay claim to interactionist theory and ethnomethodological approaches as the only ones which are consistent with feminist thought and practice. In their terms, then, my research would clearly be methodologically unacceptable.

Most feminist writers, however, are much less prescriptive about the methods which researchers should adopt, and do not accept Stanley and Wise's view that it is anti-feminist (and therefore, by implication, unethical if the researcher sees herself as a feminist) to attempt to identify consistent patterns and to move from empirical data to general theory. Duelli Klein (1983), says that the basic demand of feminist research ethics is that the work should be not simply *on* women, but also *for* women. She feels that the model of feminist action research developed by German women such as Mies (1983) is particularly useful. In this particular project, sociologists collaborated with women in a battered women's refuge through all the stages of research. However Duelli Klein does acknowledge that this model may not be appropriate for all research, and what matters most is how the research is conducted and the purposes for which the findings are used. Some feminists, such as Jayaratne (1983), point out that quantitative methods may be extremely useful in bringing about political change because of their ability to demonstrate the generalizability of findings and to produce the sort of data likely to convince both the public and those in power. The view that qualitative work is intrinsically more feminist is challenged by Morgan (1981) and Scott (1984). Morgan explains that quantitative data may be seen as 'hard' and qualitative data as 'soft', but the image of the intrepid male ethnographer bringing back news from the mean streets may have distinctly macho connotations. Scott also criticizes the assumption that all qualitative data is somehow more feminist, pointing out that qualitative sociologists may be just as critical of feminist bias and lack of objectivity as those who use quantitative methods.

In summary, then, I initially had a very hard task convincing myself that my choice of methods was not at variance with feminist research. Ultimately, however, I felt that my use of quantitative as well as qualitative methods could be justified on the grounds that, far from being mutually exclusive, they could be used in a complementary fashion. Data gathered by the use of multiple strategies can be both sensitive to people's lived experience, and enable more generalized statements about relationships between variables to be made. The use of interview and observation in conjunction with questionnaires also ensures that what has been termed 'hit and run' research is avoided. Ultimately, I decided, no particular research method is intrinsically more feminist that any other. What matters is how the research is conducted and whether it is likely to be helpful or unhelpful to women. I will now go on to consider the ethical dilemmas I encountered in the next stage, gaining access.

The Ethics of Access

During the ongoing process of negotiating access, I frequently encountered ethical problems, particularly with regard to honesty and power. At the first school where I did my research, Millbridge, I had previously worked for over six years as a teacher. This meant that politically and personally I was well known, so I could express quite openly my interest in gender. I suspected that this would make teachers much more circumspect in revealing their true opinions. However, particularly during interviews, many male teachers did not seem at all deterred from expressing sexist opinions to me. This point was illustrated very clearly when I was sitting in the marking room while Mr Tiller, the head of maths and Mr Francis, the head of English, were discussing allocation of pupils to maths and English groups for the coming year. Mr Tiller was arguing that it was important to include more boys than girls in the top maths group because even though girls did well in the third year exams, their performance generally deteriorated during the fourth year. The fact that I might be taking note of the sexist nature of this conversation had apparently dawned on them, but the continued undeterred. The conversation finished thus:

> *Mr Tiller:* That'll work out well because otherwise we'll have too many girls in the top set — Oh, I shouldn't really say that because Sheila's here.
> *Mr Francis:* Don't worry, Sheila isn't really frightening.

Like Cecile Wright (1987), who found that, when she interviewed teachers about their attitudes to black pupils, they did not attempt to disguise their racism, I can only conclude that I was simply not perceived as a threat.

At Greenhill, the second school where I carried out research, and where I had not previously worked as a teacher, I wanted to look at the effect of reactivity by seeing the similarities and differences between the data I collected here and at Millbridge. This of course raised all sorts of difficult questions about how honest I should be about the purpose of the research. I was reasonably sure that if I placed too much emphasis on gender I would simply not be allowed into the school. I therefore decided that in my initial letter and subsequent meeting with Mr East, the Headmaster of Greenhill, I would explain my research project in terms of an investigation into the operation of the option choice system in the school. I would certainly mention that gender and class were among the variables that I wanted to look at, but I would not dwell on the precise focus of the research any more than was necessary. Since the headmaster clearly had a view of educational research as neutral and objective, it would have been catastrophic to introduce myself as a feminist. After my first term in the school, Mr East retired and a new headmaster, Mr Theobald, took over. Although I introduced myself to him, he was clearly much too busy establishing himself in his new job to take much notice of me, and it was not until I asked to interview him near the end of the research that we had a proper chance to talk through its aims. In this way, I was certainly not adopting a covert role, but, on the other hand, it could be argued that I was not fully explaining the purpose of my research to my sponsors, as the British Sociological Association (BSA) statement on the ethics of research (1982) recommends. Early encounters with other important gatekeepers, all of whom were men, raised not only the question of honesty, but also of how a woman researcher should present herself to those whose sponsorship she needs. I was always conscious of how easy it would be to project stereotyped female qualities in order to allay fears and flatter male egos. Hammersley and Atkinson (1983) postively recommend this strategy when they say:

> In some circumstances it may be easier for females to present themselves as socially acceptable incompetents, in many ways the most favourable role for the participant observer to adopt in the early stages of fieldwork (p. 85).

This may make the task of gaining access easier, but unfortunately for women, many are never regarded as anything more than socially acceptable incompetents, and whether it is ethically acceptable to project negative female stereotypes to facilitate access is a moot point. Also, the life of a woman researcher in an institution where she has initially presented herself as vulnerable and in need of male protection could be very difficult. At one point during the research at Greenhill, I had to actively distance myself from one of the more senior staff, who, because he had provided me with some initial information about timetabling, felt that he then had a right to ask me thinly veiled questions about what was happening in particular teachers' classrooms.

Although my caginess about the aims of the research served some useful purpose in gaining access to Greenhill and enabling me to make comparisons with the Millbridge data, it became clear fairly soon that there were not only ethical but also practical problems in adopting what might be termed a semi-covert role. The teachers had simply been told by the headmaster that I was doing research on option choice, so, unless I provided them with this information, they would have no idea that I was also interested in gender. As I got to know particular individuals, the subject of sex-stereotyping in the curriculum inevitably arose. First of all, I suffered considerable anxiety trying to remember exactly what I had said to particular people, and I often ran through conversations in my head wondering if I had given away too much. Sometimes I left the school quite convinced that I would be asked to leave the next day on the grounds that I had gained access under false pretences. Eventually, my interest in gender became apparent through a number of specific incidents. One rather cold day, for instance, I turned up in trousers instead of the usual skirt and jumper, and a conversation ensued with a number of women teachers about the rules governing their appearance and behaviour. It transpired that although the wearing of trousers was not banned, if a women teacher did wear them 'it didn't exactly do her any good'. I was able to convey something of my views in a fairly casual way, and from this point on they became much more open to me about their position in the school, and I found the work less stressful as I was able to be more open. Against the increased openness of these women teachers, I had to balance the fact that two senior women teachers tended to avoid me from this point, always being too busy to be interviewed. Greater honesty, then, made me more relaxed and improved my relationship with at least some of the teachers. For once, considerations with regard to ethics and field relations were not at variance with each other.

Power Relations in Interviews

Much feminist writing on the ethics of research has focussed on the nature of power relations within the research process, and the potential which exists for exploitation and abuse. Oakley (1981) was one of the first to criticize the standard textbook account of interviewing, with its injunction to establish rapport, but deflect respondents' questions for fear of influencing their response. Her objections are both practical and ethical. First of all, she says, it is an impossible task for the interviewer to establish warmth and trust without revealing anything of her own personality and concerns. Secondly, the quality of the data will be much higher if the person who is being interviewed feels that they are participating in a real conversation and being treated as a person of equal status by the interviewer. And finally, it is morally indefensible for a feminist researcher to participate in a process which seeks to objectify the experience of other women. In her own research on transition to motherhood, Oakley says she answered questions as fully as possible, referrerd women to helping agencies where appropriate and kept in touch with some of the women for some time after the research was over. Finch (1984) has also criticized the notion of the objective interview as a hollow sham, and has described the richness of the data which is likely to be obtained when a female researcher interviewing another woman abandons the mystified role of researcher and instead presents herself as an ordinary woman with many of the same concerns as the woman she is interviewing. However, Finch takes the discussion a stage further by pointing out the ease with which one woman may exploit another. The reason that women talk so openly in interviews is because of their social powerlessness. They are the group whose opinions are least likely to be listened to, and in the closeness of the interview a woman may reveal more than she may wish to about herself. Further, she has only the researcher's word that this information will be treated as confidential. Similarly, data may be used by the researcher or by others to support theories and policies which are against the interests of women as a group. Scott (1985) has gone even further in her questioning of the ethics of a woman researcher interviewing women who are usually less privileged than herself because of the unequal power relations which are being exploited. She argues for more research by women on men so that masculinity rather than feminity is problematized. She does acknowledge, however, that carrying out such research is likely to be a far less comfortable experience, and it may be difficult for the researcher to encounter sexism in her work as well as in the rest of her life. Measor (1985), on the other hand, argues that being a woman interviewer is an advantage since both women and men are much more likely to talk about personal aspects of their lives than they would be with a male researcher. She does not indicate that playing on this willingness to talk, particularly when the person being interviewed is a woman, is in any way problematic.

There was, then, a difficult decision for me to make about whether my interviewing was going to focus on males or females, and in particular, how I could justify doing interviews with women. I was sceptical of the arguments put forward by some writers such as Oakley and Finch that if the interview is carried out on a woman to woman basis then it is somehow justified. This argument is not really convincing because even if the interviewer does reveal something of herself, she is still the one who walks away with the tapes at the end of the interview. The woman who is interviewed may enjoy talking about her life, but unless the research is used in some way to change the position of women in society, then she is not going to be any better off. Looking back now on the notes I made about the conversation which went on before the start of the interviews, it is certainly the case that I tended to reveal a lot more about my private life when I was interviewing women by themselves. I would talk about my own school-age daughter, and since I was pregnant at the time this would also sometimes come into the conversation. Were these confidences a manipulative strategy in order to give the woman the impression that she and I had equal control over the interview, whereas in the last analysis this was clearly not the case? Or was I simply responding in a sympathetic way to another woman, and telling her something about myself in return for what I hoped she was going to tell me about herself? Certainly, if this strategy was manipulative, it was not consciously so, but the central dilemma remains. By interviewing women and girls, was I falling into the trap of interpreting female behaviour as essentially problematic, and providing data about a less powerful group to be used by the more powerful? Ultimately, I attempted to avoid this by focusing equally on the experience of women and men, so that masculinity and femininity could be seen as constructed in relation to each other, and masculinity would not be upheld as the norm. With teachers, I interviewed slightly more men than women, but with parents, more women were interviewed than men. The reason for this was that when I rang parents to arrange an interview, I did not specify which parent I wanted to meet. As a result, thirteen of the interviews were with mothers only, fifteen were with both mother and father, and only three were with fathers only. With pupils, I carried out more interviews with girls than boys and during the period of observation, spent more time with them. This was a reflection of the fact that the world of the boys was much more tightly insulated against my entry into it.

At this point I should say something about the interviews and observation which I carried out with girls, since the power relations and ethical problems were similar to those I encountered when interviewing mothers. When I first started the fieldwork at Millbridge and Greenhill, I worried in case none of the pupils would want to talk to me. Certainly in the case of the girls, nothing could have been further from the reality. At Greenhill in particular, I was often approached by small groups of girls who asked if they could meet me at lunchtime. This was possibly because chatting was better than being banished to the Youth Centre. Nevertheless, their eagerness posed problems for me about how far our discussions should go into their private lives. Although I always stressed to them that they were under no obligation to talk to me, I felt that their consent to participate in the research was not the same as, for example, that of a teacher. The teacher would be much more able to evade or refuse to answer uncomfortable questions, and would also have more of an idea about what agreeing to take part in a research project actually entailed. Although pupils asked me some questions about the research, for instance, why on earth I should choose to be in school and whether I was being paid, they were certainly not in a position to place conditions on their participation. I therefore had to impose these limits myself. Like Fuller (1979), I decided that the toilets were the girls' own territory and I never carried out any observation there. I also sometimes felt that when I approached a group of girls in the lunch hour, even though they were always polite to me, I might be intruding on their private space. I decided that the only way to avoid this was to wait until the girls approached me. In conversations, too, I was aware that I had some responsibility for preventing them from giving away more than they might want to. For instance, we often talked about girlfriends and boyfriends, but I was wary of asking them to discuss their developing awareness of sexual relationships. Clearly, I could have no control over who was going to have access to the research report, and girls' accounts of sexual relationships might well be read in a voyeuristic or salacious way. This would hardly be helpful to either this particular group of girls or women as a whole. Looking back on the research, I am glad that I acted on these feelings of protectiveness towards the girls. Generally, I found that the boys were likely to talk in a less intimate way about their lives, and so the issue of consent did not arise in the same way.

As I have already mentioned with regard to gaining access, a range of ethical problems arose concerning power relations which exist for a female researcher interviewing men. Whether I was interviewing male teachers or fathers, an attempt would often be made at the start of the interview to establish their superior status. Quite often this would take the form of some comment on my physical appearance. When I interviewed Mr Short, a Greenhill physics teacher, we were sitting at opposite sides of a laboratory bench. He lent forward and touched one of my earrings, commenting, 'They're lovely. Do you know how they were made?' I was then in the difficult position of having to object to this teacher using a gesture which was intended to convey an invasion of my body space, thus establishing my subordinate position, or wrecking the interview by objecting. When I interviewed fathers in their homes, I would be reminded in a number of ways that I was only there on sufferance. The following exchange between myself and Mr Rennick, a Greenhill plant hire foreman, illustrates this:

> *S.R.:* Do you mind if I ask you what you do?
> *Mr Rennick:* I don't mind what you ask me. I'm not saying I'll tell you the truth.

Other men asked me about my teaching experience and my qualifications for doing the research, and I was treated to a number of diatribes about the irresponsibility of teachers since many of the interviews were carried out while teachers were taking industrial action. After talking to one particular mother and father for nearly an hour and a half, I was trying to bring the interview to a close with what I thought was a fairly innocuous question. I asked:

> Are you generally happy with the education Stephen's getting?

Mr Gammage, a policeman, replied:

> Well apart from this bloody irresponsible strike that's been going on . . .

Instead of bringing the interview to a calm conclusion, this resulted in a half hour's denunciation of the entire teaching profession. Analyzing how I responded to male attempts to establish power in the interview, I found that I generally backed off from conflict, and often found it difficult to probe for more detailed answers when what they said was very brief. Although I did not probe the women's responses either, they certainly offered me a far more intimate view of their lives. Of the three fathers whom I interviewed by themselves, one blocked my questions completely and gave yes/no responses to everything, and another answered very briefly. The headmasters whom I interviewed also provided proficient examples of school politics in operation, spending a very long time avoiding my questions.

As I have already mentioned with reference to access, the fact that men felt themselves in a position of superiority meant that they did not feel obliged to conceal their real thoughts, and at times seemed to have little regard for how I might be reacting to what they were saying. Mr Straw, the head of physics at Greenhill, for example, had this to say about the operation of the option choice system:

> I'm saying this to you even though I know it may go down the wrong way. In physics, we're lucky to avoid the drippy girls, the girls who really are perfectly pleasant and decent as long as

you don't try to make them work at anything, when they can get very nasty. Whereas the boys tend to have a different temperament. If you force them to work they'll generally respect you for it in time and knuckle down to it even though they don't want to to start with.

Another example of this was an account given by Mr Sluggett, a Greenhill history teacher, of why there were so few women in positions of responsibility in the school:

I don't like feminists or feminism very much. I'm a great believer in equality and people using their talents in whatever sphere. So them not being represented in the higher echelons of education isn't necessarily a reflection on them. It's just that I don't think there are necessarily as many of them of comparable ability as men and they have other strengths and go elsewhere. They become mothers and that sort of thing. You probably disagree with me very profoundly.

Far from wanting to argue with him, I remember feeling quite pleased that this teacher was prepared to express his sexism in such a blatant and undisguised fashion during a taped interview. In this way, I was protecting myself from hurt by reducing what this man was saying to useful data.

It is also important to note that there were significant class differences in the extent to which the person being interviewed attempted to take control of the interview process. Just as ethical issues arose with regard to the danger of exploiting women's eagerness to talk, so the same problems arose with regard to working class parents. Whereas middle class men often interrogated me, sometimes in quite an aggressive fashion, about my underlying assumptions and what I was going to do with the data, working class parents asked me very few questions about the research itself. One particular father, Mr Roberts, a technical college lecturer, had me greatly disconcerted when he asked me about my sampling procedure and why I had selected him for interview. I told him that I had selected parents on the basis of sex of child, class and place of residence. He immediately told me that he thought it was appalling that I should be able to find out about the class of parents, and he intended to contact the school to ask exactly what they were keeping in their records. In retrospect, I do not think he intended to contact the school, but was simply reminding me that he had no intention of taking on the role of passive respondent, and would not hesitate to ask me to leave his house if my questions became too personal and intrusive. Middle class mothers often asked about my research as well, but generally in a supportive way, and often related their own experiences of trying to improve their academic qualifications after having children. Working class women were the group least likely to question what I was doing. Scott (1984) also found that in her work on postgraduate sociology, gender and status were used by those she interviewed to either prevent her from asking the questions she wanted to or to control the course of the interview. As I have indicated, I feel that ethical issues are bound up in the way in which the researcher deals with these attempts by men to control the terms of the interaction. She can either acquiesce and hope that she will be perceived as non–threatening, or she can challenge what is happening and thereby risk being told nothing at all. In many ways, the format of the interview, with the woman listening and providing the man with conversational cues is very like the normal pattern of male/female conversation described by Fishman (1978), and as such may be objectionable to many feminists. Ethical problems arise, then, whether a woman is interviewing either other women or men. However these are resolved, the experience of interviewing women is almost certainly going to be more pleasant, although perhaps this should not be the deciding factor.

Quite apart from the problem of whether to focus the research on women or men, there were also difficult decisions concerning the raising of problematic issues between mothers and fathers when they were interviewed together. The interviews with parents covered not only which subjects the pupil was taking and why, but also what the parents expected them to do in terms of work and parenthood. This very often led to a discussion of the sexual division of labour and the position of women and men in the workplace and the family. Clearly, amongst many parents longstanding disagreements in these areas existed. One woman complained to me, in her husband's presence, that he still forgot that he had a fourth daughter, witnessed by the fact that he always brought home the wrong number of fish and chips on a Friday night. Sometimes conflict was resolved in a fairly humorous way. For example, in one particular family one man held forth at great length about how he regarded knitting and sewing as being female areas of work whereas it was his job to do decorating, gardening and mending the door locks. There was a pause and then he admitted: 'Except she doesn't do any knitting and crocheting,' and his wife added: 'And he don't do a lot of painting.' Everybody laughed. Sometimes, however, there was much less good humour, as this conversation between Mr and Mrs York illustrates:

S.R.: When Sally starts work d'you think she'll have equal opportunities with the men she'll be working with?

Mrs York: I don't think she will.

Mr York: I think she probably will.

[said at the same time]

Mrs York: No, there's still . . .

Mr York [talking over her] I think by the time she's in a work situation . . . I've seen attitudes change quite substantially over the last four or five years. Really, I mean that sincerely. There's a lot more acceptance of women in men's jobs. I see it much more than you would in a school situation . . . you're in a fairly cloistered environment. But out in the commercial world and I think by the time Sally is working it'll be more so. And in ten years, there won't be any differences. I really believe that.

S.R. D'you think that? [to Mrs York]

Mrs York: I'd like to think it, but I still think that women are put down.

Mr York [sounding very angry] I think nowadays the only women who are put down are the ones who allow themselves to be put down.

Mrs York: No . . .

Mr York: And the women who are prepared to allow themselves to be put down are decreasing all the time . . .

Although conversations such as these provided me with important insights into power relations in these particular families, I was troubled by the ethics of raising highly charged topics and then walking out leaving them unresolved and offering no solutions. Also, was it right for me to remain the detached observer, or should I become involved in the disagreement and take the woman's side? I am sure that I conveyed my support non-verbally, but I decided against direct intervention because this might cause arguments to escalate rather than subside, and I certainly did not want to be responsible for some violent episode after I had left the house. I would always try to steer the conversation back to more neutral ground before leaving. The undeniable presence of power struggles in interviews, then, raised a number of serious ethical questions, often with no easy answers.

Analysis and Interpretation of Data

Much feminist writing on the ethics of research has emphasized the importance of issues surrounding the control and interpretation of data.

Stanley and Wise, as we have already seen, berate feminist researchers who, they say, claim the right to interpret other women's experiences for them. A further issue closely connected with this concerns who the data actually belongs to. Mies (1983) and her co-workers, whose research I described earlier, were working on the assumption that the data belonged to the women who were living in the refuge rather than the sociologists, and this perhaps represents feminist research at its purest. As a model, it would probably only be feasible when researchers and researched were in complete agreement over the ultimate aims of the research, and it is very difficult to imagine how men and women could agree on the interpretation of data from a feminist educational research project. Burgess (1984) suggests a more modest form of collaboration. He gave the headmaster of Bishop McGregor School the right to comment on the chapters of *Experiencing Comprehensive Education,* and included as a footnote some of the headmaster's comments when their interpretations differed. There is a problem here concerning power relations, because it is not clear why the headmaster's opinion should be given preferential treatment over that of more lowly members of staff. Also, whether it is possible to do this will again depend on how those who have participated in the research are likely to react to the findings. Although I discussed my data with some women teachers and girls in the school, it would have been quite impossible for me to work out a collective interpretation with many of the boys and male teachers because of their hostility towards feminist ideas. This was made abundantly clear to me when I was asked to attend a physics department meeting at Greenhill to explain why only eight out of over 100 pupils opting for physics were female. Mr Straw, the head of department, delivered the invitation in the fashion of throwing down of the gauntlet:

> I hear you've got lots of interesting ideas about why girls aren't choosing physics so I hope you'll come and enlighten us.

The department was all male apart from one female part-timer, and from observation and interview it seemed to me that the sexism of Mr Straw, the head of department, and two of the other teachers, was very much at the root of why so few girls saw physics as an appealing option. Mr Straw had recently written a reply to a criticism made by HMI of the lack of girls in the department, and had argued that there was not a problem since the number of girls doing physics at Greenhill was about the same as the national average. Beforehand, I thought long and hard about how I was going to tackle this situation. I certainly was not going to offer an explanation which blamed the girls for their non-participation in physics, although I felt that this would have been very acceptable. The meeting proved as tense as I had anticipated, as the following extract from my notebook reveals:'

> The whole thing was extremely nerve-wracking — not helped by the fact that Mr Lill came in at the start, asked me if I was going to say anything different from what he'd heard already, and then walked out. Mr Short tried to ease the situation by making a few chatty comments about his own experience and was told by Mr Straw: 'Can you be quiet for the moment. We're here to listen to what Sheila's got to say, not to hear your anecdotes'.

After discussing the problem generally, I suggested, tactfully I hoped, that such practices as dismissing girls before boys and injunctions to the boys to 'let the ladies get the equipment first' might be implicated in establishing the subject's masculine image. At this point, things were clearly getting too controversial for Mr Straw, and he intervened:

> Hang on a minute, we're now talking about social mores, not educational matters, aren't we?

Clearly, in these particular circumstances it would have been very difficult to work out a shared interpretation of the data. Ultimately, I felt that they had consented to take part in the research, and I had agreed to protect their identities and feed back some of the findings. Having done that, I felt that I had the right to control the interpretation of the data.

Another very complex ethical issue concerns the extent to which a feminist researcher should adopt a value-free stance, or whether her personal and political convictions should be involved in her data analysis. I have found Janet Finch's (1986) analysis very helpful here. She points out that there is a long tradition within the social sciences of recognizing that no work could be entirely value free. This was acknowledged in the Rothschild Report (DES, 1982), which was commissioned by Sir Keith Joseph to investigate allegations of political bias within the social sciences. It found that only highly quantitative areas of work, such as demography, could aspire to neutrality. Referring to Becker (1970), Finch makes the point that bias is only alleged when the researcher takes the perspective of the subordinate group in a hierarchical relationship. To guard against the dismissal of feminist work as biased, Finch recommends that high standards of academic rigour should be employed. Furthermore, the researcher should ensure that both her research design and reporting are reflexive, making explicit the way in which her political commitments have influenced both her selection of problems, her conduct of the research and her interpretation of data. Ethical problems might well arise if a feminist researcher found data which were potentially damaging to the women who were being researched. As an example of this, she cites her own research into pre-school playgroups (Finch, 1985). Her observations of playgroups in working class areas revealed that these ranged from the disorganized to the over-organized, diverging widely from the Pre-school Playgroups Association model. For some time, she felt unable to write about her findings for fear of perpetuating the damaging stereotype of the working class woman as an inadequate mother. Ultimately, she analyzed her data in terms of the inappropriateness of imposing middle class patterns of childcare on working class women who were much less privileged in their living conditions and access to educational resources. By thinking about her findings in this way, Finch felt that she arrived at a more subtle interpretation, and was not obliged either to suppress data or to suggest an analysis which might have been damaging to the women who had helped her do the research.

I encountered a number of similar problems to that described by Finch in interpreting some of my data. For example, I found that working class mothers of girls, compared with middle class mothers, were often apparently not directly involved with their daughters' choice of subjects, and were certainly not encouraging them into non-traditional areas of the labour market. This might have been used as evidence of working class sexism, but closer analysis of quantitative and qualitative data revealed that with regard to general issues of gender equality, working class women were just as radical as middle class women, and their mistrust of their daughters moving into non-traditional areas of the curriculum stemmed from their perception of what jobs were actually available in the local labour market.

The question also arises of whether the ethical considerations involved in the interpretation of data on women should also apply to men. As I have already mentioned with reference to Mr Sluggett, I felt pleased that some of the men expressed their sexism so clearly. Although this admission certainly undermines the image of the impartial social observer, I suspect that few researchers respond to their data with total neutrality. However, becoming aware of these feelings made me even more careful to fully represent the diversity in both men's and women's attitudes, and to avoid depicting all men as demons and all women as angels. Although I was pleased that I had access to data which clearly showed the extent of the problem confronting women and girls in schools, I felt it very important to be clear about how representative each person's view actually was. If anything, my awareness of the ease with which feminist research can be accused of bias led me to interpret my data even more carefully and fairly. It is perhaps also important to consider what it might mean if someone were to argue that their research were value free. This would suggest to me that they either did not realize the implications of their position, or else they were trying to conceal their political viewpoint.

Disseminating Research Findings

The process of disseminating research findings raises ethical questions particularly concerning the balance between responsibility to those who have participated in the research and the wider audience who will finally read or listen to accounts of the work. Perhaps the question of who the research is for is particularly difficult for a first-time researcher to address. At the beginning of my own research project I found it very difficult to imagine ever being in the position to have anything sufficiently clear to say and therefore did not seriously consider the ethical implications of publication until the research was well underway. Thinking now about who my own research is intended for, it seems to me very difficult to justify unless it can be of some interest to a wider group of people than those who participated in it. Having said this, I feel it is very important to ensure that participation in the research should not be a damaging experience. Researchers in rural areas such as Chamberlain (1983) have made it clear how disastrous it can be if research findings can be directly linked to a particular community. When her oral history *Fenwomen* was published, the *News of the World* published a front page article headlined 'Why Mary unveiled a village's love secrets' and subtitled, 'There'll be red faces down on the farm when this book comes out.' This, she said, completely destroyed the promises of anonymity she had given to the women, and the research finished on a note of great bitterness. Bearing in mind experiences like this, I have tried hard to disguise the location of the research and the identity of the particular individuals involved. Having said that, it is surely impossible for anyone doing educational research to be able to give an absolute guarantee of anonymity. A teacher from a school where research has been carried out would probably be able to identify some individuals quite easily from the published report. For instance, how does anyone conceal the identity of the headmaster? This seems to me to be an insuperable problem, and it still concerns me.

In particular, it would cause me great sadness if any of the women teachers who confided in me about the injustices they experienced during the course of their careers were identified and punished yet again for daring to criticize their school. The only justification for publishing data of this sort is in the hope that it will be read by other women teachers who will see that many of their problems are structural and not due to their personal failings.

Problems still remain about what I will finally give the schools in the way of feedback. I have already talked to groups of teachers at both schools and to some groups of pupils. I also promised that when I finished my thesis I would submit a final report to the schools. Whereas there will be no problem talking about parents' and pupils' attitudes, it will be much more difficult to talk to the teachers about their own attitudes and practices. Hammersley and Atkinson (1983) tell the would-be ethnographer that in managing successful field relations it is important to ask: 'Am I being so nice to my hosts that I *never* get them to confront any troublesome or touchy topics?' (p. 104). For me this dilemma has persisted to the bitter end. If I fail to say to the teachers that their attitudes are part of the problem, am I evading an important issue? On the other hand, by arousing controversy that I am not there to deal with in the long term, am I simply making life more difficult for women teachers, some of whom will be there until retirement?

One final but very important point for a feminist writing about her research concerns style and accessibility. The Leeds Revolutionary Feminist Group (1979) have argued that feminist academics exploit the energy of the women's movement, transforming the movement's ideas into language which is incomprehensible to most women for the sake of advancing their reputation. There is a serious point to be answered here. If the object of feminist research is to help to understand and change the position of women in society, it is difficult to see how this can be achieved if only a small group of the initiated can understand what has been written. Some writers, like Oakley (1974a and 1974b), have attempted to tackle this problem by producing two books of their findings, one aimed at an academic audience and one at a wider reading public. In some ways, this seems to be quite a good solution to the problem, since it is likely that not everyone will want to read about, for example, methodological issues. My personal solution is to try at all times to write as simply and clearly as possible. Some ideas are difficult in themselves, but this does not justify deliberate mystification, which seems to be based on the belief that if nobody quite understands what you're saying they cannot criticize it.

Conclusion

This discussion of ethical issues arising during the various stages of my research indicates that the main moral dilemma I encountered concerned the balancing of responsibilities to those who the research is on, against the need to present the findings in an uncompromising way to a wider audience. Ethical problems begin with the choice of research methods, although I have argued that no method is intrinsically more or less feminist, and what matters is how the research is carried out and the data interpreted. Once the research is underway, issues of honesty in field relations are constantly encountered. Of course, the problem of what to tell people about the research cannot be neatly resolved by any researcher, since the precise focus often does not become clear until the project is well underway. There are, however, particular problems for feminists and others who undertake committed research, since access to the field may well depend on partial concealment of the purpose of the research. As well as this, there are ethical problems in dealing with unequal power relations during the initial negotiation of access and in carrying out the research. Responsibilities to women and men who participate in the research is a further problem for feminists. Official guidelines recommend that all respondents should be treated identically, but a feminist will undoubtedly feel greater commitment towards reaching a sympathetic interpretation of the female rather than the male perspective. A difficult distinction has to be made here between acceptable commitment and the sort of bias which would invalidate the research. Finally, in disseminating the findings, a feminist researcher has to make difficult judgments between what will be acceptable to those who have provided the data, and the need of a wider audience to hear the whole story. Having collected and interpreted the data as sensitively as possible, I have taken upon myself responsibility for its publication.

Davies (1985) has this to say about the ultimate benefit of her research for the girls who participated:

> I feel a sense of waste now: while highlighting the general lower status of females in a school I did nothing to promote these specific girls. They cannot, as I can, look at a book and say, 'I wrote that' or 'that was my idea'; they cannot even see their names in print and say 'that's me'. If ethnography is so technical or so mysterious that it cannot be shared out among all concerned, is it worth doing? (p. 94).

To some extent, I share her feelings. My own research might well have been truer to feminist principles if it had been more of a collaborative process. One of the problems was that by the time I had built up close enough relationships and had enough confidence in what I was trying to do, very little time was left to transform the project into one where the participants were taking a more active role. If I ever embark on another ethnographic research project, I would like to spend longer thinking about how such collaboration can be achieved right from the start. Ultimately, the ethics of feminist research demand that the work should be useful to women. Whether my research can be seen in this way is difficult to say. Perhaps the best that any one person can do is hope that some contribution, however small, has been made to understanding the position of women in society.

References

BECKER, H. S. (1967) 'Whose side are we on?' *Social Problems*, **14**, pp. 239–47.

BECKER, H. S. (1970) *Sociological Work*, Chicago, Aldine.

BELL, C. and ROBERTS, H. (1984) *Social Researching: Politics, Problems, Practice*, London, Routledge and Kegan Paul.

BOWLES, G. and DUELLI KLEIN, R. (Eds) (1983) *Theories of Women's Studies*, London, Routledge and Kegan Paul.

BRITISH SOCIOLOGICAL ASSOCIATION (1982) *Statement of Ethical Principles and Their Application to Sociological Practice*, London, BSA (mimeo).

BURGESS, R. G. (Ed) (1982) *Field research: A Sourcebook and Field Manual*, London, George Allen and Unwin.

BURGESS, R. G. (1984) *In the Field: An Introduction to Field Research*, London, George Allen and Unwin.

BURGESS, R. G. (Ed) (1985a) *Field Methods in the Study of Education*, Lewes, Falmer Press.

BURGESS, R. G. (1985b) *Issues in Educational Research: Qualitative Methods*, Lewes, Falmer Press.

BURGESS, R. G. (Ed) (1985c) *Strategies of Educational Research: Qualitative Methods*, Lewes, Falmer Press.

CHAMBERLAIN, M. (1983) *Fenwomen: A Portrait of Women in an English Village* London, Routledge and Kegan Paul.

CENTRE for CONTEMPORARY CULTURAL STUDIES (1978) *Women Take Issue*, London, Hutchinson.

COWARD, R., LIPSHITZ, S. and COWIE, E. (1976) 'Psychoanalysis and patriarchal structures' in WOMEN'S PUBLISHING COLLECTIVE (Eds) *Papers on Patriarchy*, London, WPC/PDC.

DAVIES, L. (1985) 'Focusing on gender in educational research' in BURGESS, R. G. (Ed) *Field Methods in the Study of Education*, Lewes, Falmer Press.

DEPARTMENT OF EDUCATION AND SCIENCE (1982) *Enquiry into the Social Science Research Council* (The Rothschild Report), London, HMSO.

DUELLI KLEIN, R. (1983) 'How to do what we want to do: The ethics and politics of interviewing women' in BELL, C. and ROBERTS, H. *Social Researching: Politics, Problems, Practice*, London, Routledge and Kegan Paul.

EGGLESTON, J. *et al.* (1986) *Education for Some*, Stoke-on-Trent, Trentham Books.

FINCH, J. (1985) 'Social policy and education: problems and possibilities of using qualitative research' in BURGESS, R. G. (Ed) *Issues in Educational Research: Qualitative Methods*, Lewes, Falmer Press.

FINCH, J. (1986) *Qualitative Research and Social Policy: Issues in Education and Welfare*, Lewes, Falmer Press.

FISHMAN, P. (1978) 'Interaction: The work women do', *Social Problems*, **25**, 4, pp. 397–406.

FULLER, M. (1979) *Dimensions of Gender in a School*, unpublished PhD thesis, University of Bristol.

HAMMERSLEY, M. and ATKINSON, P. (1983) *Ethnography: Principles in Practice* London, Tavistock.

JAYARATNE, T. E. (1983) 'The value of quantitative methodology for feminist research' in BOWLES, G. and DUELLI KLEIN, R. (Eds) *Theories of Women's Studies*, London, Routledge and Kegan Paul.

KELLY, A. (1978) 'Feminism and research', *Women's Studies International Quarterly*, **1**, pp. 225–32.

KELLY, A. (1986) 'Education or indoctrination? The ethics of school-based action research'. Paper presented to the British Educational Research Association Conference, University of Bristol, 4–7 September.

LEEDS REVOLUTIONARY FEMINIST GROUP (1979) 'Every single academic feminist owes her livelihood to the WLM'. Unpublished paper presented to Women's Research and Resources Summer School, Bradford.

MEASOR, L. (1985) 'Interviewing: A strategy in qualitative research' in BURGESS, R. G. (Ed) *Strategies of Educational Research: Qualitative Methods*, Lewes, Falmer Press.

McROBBIE, A. (1982) 'The politics of feminist research: Between talk, text and action', *Feminist Review*, **12**, pp. 46–59.

MIES, M. (1983) 'Towards a methodology for feminist research' in BOWLES, G. and DUELLI KLEIN, R. (Eds) *Theories of Women's Studies*, London, Routledge and Kegan Paul.

MORGAN, D. (1981) 'Men, masculinity and the process of sociological enquiry', in ROBERTS, H. (Ed) *Doing Feminist Research*, London, Routledge and Kegan Paul.

OAKLEY, A. (1974a) *The Sociology of Housework*, Oxford, Martin Robertson.

OAKLEY, A. (1974b) *Housewife*, Harmondsworth, Penguin.

OAKLEY, A. (1981) 'Interviewing women: A contradiction in terms' in ROBERTS, H. (Eds) *Doing Feminist Research*, London, Routledge and Kegan Paul.

RIDDELL, S. (1988) *Gender and Option Choice in Two Rural Comprehensive Schools*. Unpublished PhD thesis, University of Bristol.

ROBERTS, H. (Ed) (1981) *Doing Feminist Research*, London, Routledge and Kegan Paul.

SCOTT, S. (1984) 'The personable and the powerful: Gender and status in sociological research' in BELL, C. and ROBERTS, H. (Eds) *Social Researching: Politics, Problems, Practice*, London, Routledge and Kegan Paul.

SCOTT, S. (1985) 'Feminist research and qualitative methods: A discussion of some of the issues' in BURGESS, R. G. (Ed) *Issues in Educational Research: Qualitative Methods*, Lewes, Falmer Press.

SIEBER, S. D. (1973) 'The integration of fieldwork and survey methods', *American Journal of Sociology*, **78**, 6, pp. 1335–59, reprinted in BURGESS, R. G. (Ed) *Field Research: A Sourcebook and Field Manual*, London, George Allen and Unwin.

STANLEY, L. and WISE, S. (1983) *Breaking Out: Feminist Consciousness and Feminist Research*, London, Routledge and Kegan Paul.

WOMEN'S PUBLISHING COLLECTIVE (Eds) (1976) *Papers on Patriarchy*, London, WPC/PDC.

WRIGHT, C. (1986) 'School processes: An ethnographic study' in EGGLESTON, J. *et al. Education for Some*, Stoke-on-Trent, Trentham Books.

5
Education or Indoctrination? The Ethics of School-Based Action Research

Alison Kelly

Introduction

For four years, from 1979 to 1983, I was co-director of the Girls Into Science and Technology (GIST) project.[1] GIST was an action research project which attempted to research the reasons for girls' under-involvement in science and technology, and simultaneously to take action to remedy the situation. The project and its results have been described in detail elsewhere (Kelly *et al*, 1984; Whyte, 1986; Kelly, 1989) and I do not intend to do more than outline its main features here. This chapter will concentrate on the ethical issues raised by working in this way within schools.

The GIST project followed 2000 children from the time they entered secondary school aged 11 until they made their option choices three years later. During this time the project team co-operated with teachers in eight action schools to devise and implement strategies designed to encourage more girls to continue with physical science and technical craft subjects when these became optional. A wide range of different interventions were used, largely depending on the teachers' preference and enthusiasm. These included visits from women working in scientific and technical jobs who could provide positive role models for the girls; development of curriculum materials utilizing girls' interests; attitude-changing sessions with teachers; observation of classroom interaction with feedback to teachers; and careers advice to the children on the consequences of dropping scientific and technical subjects in third year. Outcomes were small but positive in subject choice; they were more distinct in attitudes, where children in action schools became markedly less sex-stereotyped and more willing than children in control schools to accept that males and (especially) females could cross traditional boundaries if they wanted to.

In addition to the aim of encouraging more girls to choose science and craft subjects, GIST was also concerned to explore the reasons for girls' avoidance of these subjects. Both quantitative and qualitative research methods were used. A range of attitude tests were administered to the children, and the development of their attitudes to science and to sex roles over the first three years of secondary schooling was traced; classroom observation was employed to establish some of the ways in which science comes to be seen as a masculine subject; teachers' opinions and behaviour towards girls in science and technology were explored through formal and informal interviewing. Numerous articles have been published in the research literature, and a follow-up study is currently investigating the links between children's attitudes and choices in the early years of secondary school and their post-school destinations.

In an earlier article I have labelled this project as simultaneous-integrated action research (Kelly, 1985a). The distinctive feature of this approach is that action and research are integrated and proceed simultaneously. As researchers we were not neutral outsiders, observing and recording the participants' views; on the contrary we were actively engaged with the situation we were studying. We were concerned both to change the current position in the schools we were working in, and to research and explain the existing situation. We did not have separate research and action workers; the whole project team was involved in both activities, often at the same time. On a single visit to an action school we might, for example, introduce a woman scientist who was speaking to the children, discuss with the teacher some piece of sex-differentiated behaviour he had observed in his pupils, and take notes on the reactions of teacher and pupils to the visitor's presentation[2]. The advantages and disadvantages of working in this way were discussed in the earlier chapter.

Action Research and Values

Simultaneous-integrated action research, such as the GIST project, involves various ethical dilemmas. Some of these concern the explicitly value-laden nature of the project. As Barnes (1979) says

in advocating change, values have to be made explicit, whereas values can more easily be taken for granted, or never made explicit, when studying the reproduction of the present state of affairs.

Many social scientists would now accept that there is no such thing as value-free, objective or neutral research. What is seen depends on the spectacles which are worn when looking. An approach which lacks any explicit value commitment generally entails tacit — often unconscious — support for the status quo. To say that all research is value-laden does not entail a disregard for traditional criteria of reliability and validity. On the contrary it takes them one step further. Many politically committed researchers now make a point of stating their own position in their reports so that the reader can take this into account when assessing the findings.

These issues take a rather different form when we consider action research. Here the researchers are concerned, not just to view their data in a particular light, but to alter the world in accordance with their values. In the GIST project the research team operated from a feminist standpoint, which was not necessarily shared with either the pupils or their teachers. We aimed to change girls' option choices and career aspirations because of our perception that girls were disadvantaged by traditional sex-stereotypes. We saw action in schools as one small part of a mosaic of action to ameliorate women's subordinate position in society as a whole. But there are legitimate alternative views — that women and men should have separate but equal roles in society, that men are naturally dominant, that women are not currently disadvantaged, that girls will find it too much of a strain to attempt non-traditional roles. I happen to disagree with these positions, but I do not deny their legitimacy. And I am sure they were held by some of the teachers, pupils and parents with whom we worked on the GIST project.

This raises the question of what right we had to intervene on one side of the debate. As citizens we obviously had the same right as any other citizen to participate in a debate about the purpose of schooling. We felt strongly that it was important — indeed that it was ethically right — to encourage more girls into science and technology, and we argued our position. But our participation in the debate was privileged over that of many other interested parties by our position as action-researchers. We were associated with prestigious institutions such as the university and the polytechnic, and our work was labelled 'research', with its connotations of objective and disinterested study. Moreover the view that women's position in society is a cause for concern currently enjoys at least some official endorsement, as witnessed by the Sex Discrimination Act and the support which our project received from several semi-official funding bodies.

However I do not want to rest the case for our right to intervene on the support which our viewpoint enjoyed from the establishment.

Quite apart from my contention that our aim of changing women's position in society goes far beyond their desire for equal opportunities, there is a more serious objection. In a pluralist society it is important that a range of alternative viewpoints should be represented in debate and action. I would argue that our right to intervene rested upon our ability to convince teachers and other interested parties that our ideas were valuable, that they were in the best interests of their pupils and that they were worth a try. Our right to take action was dependent upon negotiation.

As Barnes (1979) has pointed out

> the idea of negotiation makes sense only when the parties involved
> have different interests; it makes better sense when they have some
> limited power over one another and when they are not playing
> a zero-sum game, so that all can gain from a successful outcome
> to the bargaining.

The official endorsement of the GIST project may have made it difficult for teachers to express any overt disagreement with our aims — and indeed we encountered no outright dissent. But this does not mean that our interests were identical with those of teachers, or that no negotiation had to take place. Putting aside any divergence over the aims of the project, teachers are more concerned than researchers with issues of classroom control and management. Some of our suggestions for ways of increasing girls' involvement in science classrooms amounted to deskilling teachers — their traditional ways of coping with classroom behaviour were being criticized. Our wish to arrange special sessions with women visitors disrupted the timetable (although it also provided welcome variety). On the issue of power the balance was probably on the side of the teachers: they could ruin the project by non-co-operation. We had only the moral force of pushing for equal opportunities and full development of potential for all pupils — although these are powerful concepts in the teaching profession. Teachers could gain from involvement in a successful research project, which in several cases enhanced their career prospects. Researchers too could gain professionally from a successful outcome to negotiation (witness invitations to write chapters such as this).

Our case for intervening in schools clearly rested — as does most educational activity — on our assessment of what is in the children's best interests, even if they may not recognize it themselves. What if we were wrong? What if the changes which we thought would advantage pupils turned out not to do so? This question can be approached at the level of the individual or at the level of the group. At the individual level it is possible that some girls could have been persuaded to take physics 'O' level by the GIST project, and failed, whereas if they had taken history instead they would have passed. I do not necessarily accept that they will have been disadvantaged in this situation, but they might well feel that they have been. Does the right of the group (in this case women's right to technical training) outweigh the harm to the individual (of getting one less 'O' level)? I think the answer has to be 'yes', that we are principally concerned with the rights of groups (while trying to minimize any harm to individuals).

There is also the possibility that the intervention may prove counter-productive for the group as a whole. For example, there is evidence that some anti-sexist and anti-racist projects have actually increased sexism and racism among the dominant groups, so presumably increasing problems for the oppressed groups (Guttentag and Bray, 1976; Jeffcoate, 1981). This did not happen with GIST, but it could have done. It would be nice if we could guarantee success before we begin, but unfortunately that is not possible! Action-researchers here are in the same position as any other innovators — our intentions, and high ethical principles of benefiting children, may not be realized in practice. Again the concept of negotiation is useful in justifying change. In order to work in schools, we have to convince professional teachers that our aims and our methods are acceptable. We do not — and should not — have the power to impose our views on them unless they are convinced. And part of the researcher's job should be to monitor the progress of innovations, so that if they backfire they can be swiftly reconsidered.

This sort of negotiation between teachers and researchers, with similar but not identical interests, and small amounts of power over each other is probably not uncommon in educational settings. Much of the ethical agonizing that feminist researchers, in particular, have been prone to, has involved the issue of power, and the assumption that researchers are more powerful than the people being researched (for example, Stanley and Wise, 1983). In working with teachers this is, at most, a half-truth. But teachers are not the only participants in educational action research. The pupils are also involved, and to a lesser extent their parents. Pupils in particular, have far less power in schools. Are they to be involved in the negotiations? Is this desirable, and is it practicable?

In the GIST project pupils were not involved in negotiating the aims of the action or its implementation. This was partly a matter of expediency and partly a matter of policy. We did not have the resources to conduct meaningful negotiations with 2000 children and their parents. But even if it had been feasible it might not have been desirable to involve the pupils in this way. There are legitimate and illegitimate ways of achieving a desired outcome. Clearly the children knew they were involved in a project, but we decided not to spell out to them its aims because of the uneven balance of power. If we had told them that for the project to succeed we needed many more girls to continue with physical science in fourth year, and we needed a particular pattern of answers on the attitude tests, this would undoubtedly have affected the results. Whether we would have got more conformity or more defiance is debatable, but the option choices would probably have changed. Neither we nor the teachers felt that we should put such pressure on the children — even if the outcome would in fact have been in their own interests.

We did however encourage teachers to discuss sex stereotyping with their pupils, and to raise issues with them which we hoped would lead to less stereotyped behaviour. In this we were treading a narrow and familiar line between education and indoctrination. Perhaps we trod too cautiously. Teachers frequently try to change pupils' behaviour, and in this they have much more power than educational researchers. Pupils are taught at school about the dangers of taking heroin, and no-one seriously suggests inviting pushers into school to put their case, or that teachers shouldn't tell pupils what outcome they want. This is an extreme example, with an overwhelming weight of opinion on one side. Smoking may be more relevant. Many teachers smoke themselves, but nevertheless schools preach about the dangers of tobacco. They rarely put the argument about free choice, or the relaxing effect of a quick puff. Presumably the rationale here is that teachers truly believe that what they are doing is in the best interests of their pupils; and that out-of-school they are frequently exposed to a culture where smoking is accepted or even encouraged. By putting one side of the argument only, schools are seen as counteracting publicity from other, informal sources.

This was the argument we made with respect of sex stereotyping. Out-of-school (and indeed inside school) children are immersed in a sexist society where men and women are expected to do different things and have different attributes. A bit of countervailing propaganda within class can only have a limited effect. Indoctrination occurs when one approach is so monolithic that other possibilities became invisible. This could not possibly be said to be true of the limited GIST interventions — in fact it is easier to argue that the non-traditional option is invisible. Nevertheless in at least one school the careers teacher became concerned about the one-sidedness of only inviting women in non-traditional jobs into school, and arranged for visits from women nurses and hairdressers 'for balance'.

This episode illustrates the concern that some teachers felt about the transmission of values. Eraut (1984) suggests that teachers

> may handle values in three different ways: (1) by assuming them
> or taking them for granted (implicit transmission); (2) by
> advocating them or refuting them and taking up a definite value
> position (explicit transmission); or (3) by making them the subject
> of his or her teaching with the intention of promoting pupils'
> value awareness while still preserving their autonomy (explicit
> discussion). Promoting value awareness as a teaching goal implies
> that values should be explicitly discussed but not imposed by the
> teacher, but this aim is difficult to achieve in practice. So we have
> to consider a further possibility, that of the unintentional
> transmission of values.

Our intention in the GIST project was to move beyond implicit
transmission to explicit discussion. Some of the teachers felt that we were
advocating explicit transmission (of non-traditional values) and were not
prepared to be a part of this. The anti-racist movement in education, and
some anti-sexist projects (for example Developing Anti-Sexist Initiatives
(DASI)) certainly do take this stance. In the present situation this actually
serves to promote explicit discussion, by contrast with the prevailing
racist and sexist society. But it can produce a backlash by teachers and
pupils who feel they are being indoctrinated.

Educational action research of the kind described by Ebbutt (1985)
aims to support teachers who are becoming more reflexive about issues
that concern them. The teacher's perspective is taken as central. But this
severely limits the range of problems which can be considered, and
implicitly accepts the status quo. Simultaneous-integrated action research,
as in the GIST project, aims to increase teachers' awareness of issues that
they may not previously have considered. By so doing it has a more
explicit political purpose. At first sight it also has greater ethical problems,
as it attempts to change teachers' values. But this is not necessarily
unethical, unless it is considered ethical to unquestioningly support the
status quo.

Eraut (1984) argues that

> if values are so embedded in the culture of a community that they
> are taken for granted by all its members, it is not the responsibility
> of a teacher working within that community to be uniquely aware
> of them. But if values are only shared by one section of the
> community, and the teacher is not aware of this, there is a problem
> ... I call it value complacency.

Many teachers are complacent about traditional sex roles. They do not realize that they are transmitting values that are increasingly disputed in our society. Part of the aim of the GIST project was to make teachers more aware of this point — and thus to make them better teachers. Professional competence demands thinking about issues such as the values that are being transmitted in teaching, and projects such as GIST, by bringing a different perspective into the schools, can assist in this. The ethical responsibility of a researcher includes promoting the right to think and the right to know by exposing practitioners to alternative viewpoints.

The final issue related to values in action research that I want to raise is that of unpalatable results. All researchers have a duty to think about the implications of their results, and the way they may be used in political debate. Action researchers have perhaps more of a duty than others, as the perceived success or failure of their project may affect the distribution of further funds for action in this area. The GIST project was not as successful as we would have liked in changing girls' option choices, and we suffered from a piece of irresponsible journalism which gave the impression that GIST had failed to alter teachers' attitudes or behaviour (Wilce, 1984). Our own account of the project stressed both positive and negative outcomes, and explored the factors which we felt might have inhibited its progress. This has been reasonably well received by most commentators, who have appreciated the difficulties under which we worked. But I have heard it suggested, by teachers who have read the newspaper report and nothing else, that since GIST was unsuccessful in altering girls' options the sex difference was clearly genetic, and no more action should be taken to counteract girls' under-representation in physical science. I certainly do not want to argue for suppression or distortion of results to avoid this sort of reaction. That would negate the job of researcher, and, to the extent that knowledge is power and successful action is based on understanding a situation, it would be counter-productive to the values embodied in the project. But I do want to suggest that action researchers must be particularly careful about the way their results are presented.

Action Research and Informed Consent

So far I have focused on the ethical issues associated with the explicitly value-laden approach of action research. Another set of issues centre around the dual nature of the project, as both action and research, and the question of informed consent by participants.

Most of the GIST intervention strategies were implemented by teachers in the schools. The research team worked with the teachers as colleagues. The nature and aims of the project were explained to the teachers in a series of preliminary meetings, both before and after they agreed to participate. Discussions continued throughout the life of the project. However ethical considerations demand not just information and consent, but 'informed consent', i.e. consent in the light of a full understanding of what is involved. I am not sure that this was obtained, or indeed could have been obtained.

The problems here were two-fold. One concerned the wider aims of the project, to change women's position in society. GIST was explicitly feminist in its conception. Yet most of the, mainly male, teachers with whom we worked led very traditional family lives, and their image of feminists centred around bra-burning and disrupting beauty contests. They felt threatened by and hostile towards many of the ideas of feminism. At the same time they were sympathetic to the idea of equal opportunities for all children, and were genuinely horrified at the idea that they might be discriminating against some of the pupils in their classes. We therefore took a tactical decision to concentrate on these 'professional' aspects of the project, and to de-emphasize the wider, more personal ramifications, in our dealings with teachers.

Whether this was the correct decision, from a tactical viewpoint, is debatable (Kelly, 1985b; Whyte, 1986). What is certain is that it did not conform to the high ideals of informed consent. We did not attempt to disguise the wider intent of the project, but neither did we go to great lengths to explain it. That would have demanded an intensive period of 'consciousness-raising' with teachers, and would have constituted an action research project in its own right. I think our decision to concentrate on the aims which we held in common is defensible, that in this case the ends justify the means. The greater ethical good of attempting to broaden opportunities for children outweighs the lesser ethical dubiousness of playing down the overall aim of the project. I am not arguing that the principle of informed consent should be abandoned: only that it should be viewed in combination with other ethical considerations, rather than as an over-riding principle.

The other problem with informed consent concerns our interest in teachers' own behaviour. We were not only collaborating with teachers to reduce sex-stereotyping in children, we were also researching the teachers' role in the reproduction of gender divisions. The dual nature of the study, as both action and research, was certainly made plain in the initial negotiations with schools. But it was much easier to explain to the teachers that we were researching children's attitudes and behaviour than to stress our interest in teachers' behaviour and attitudes. It is difficult to say to someone that you want to co-operate with them in reducing sex stereotyped option choices – but incidentally you think that they might be part of the problem! Although this was implicit in the workshops that we ran for teachers at the beginning of the project, and in the classroom observation sessions, it was probably not stressed as much as it should have been for truly 'informed consent'.

These problems were compounded by the evolving nature of the project. At no point in the research did we negotiate a formal contract with the teachers, setting out what we would be doing. Both the action and the research were always intended to be fluid, changing in response to changing conditions in the schools. In order to achieve fully informed consent we would have had to keep going back to the teachers for further negotiation over what we were going to do. This would certainly have been possible, but I do not think it would have been welcomed by the teachers. They (like us) were busy people, and meetings were frequently difficult to arrange. We got the impression that the research side of the project was seen as our business. We were fairly unsuccessful in persuading teachers to take on a research role, and they did not seem particularly interested in the data we were collecting.

None of this absolves us from the responsibility to look after teachers' interests if we have a clearer idea than they do of how the research might damage them. After most of our visits to schools we wrote notes about the teachers' behaviour and attitudes as manifested in our conversations. These later formed part of the project evaluation. Because we were visiting the schools as activists, collaborating with the teachers to implement some intervention strategy, they may well have temporarily forgotten that we were also researchers. This may have led the teachers to be less guarded in their comments to us than they would have been if they had been constantly aware that anything they said might be 'taken down and used in evidence' against them. This problem is not unique to action researchers – Burgess (in this volume) reports that well-established and accepted ethnographers face similar situations. But it may be more acute for action researchers because the research role is less visible — we did not formally interview teachers, and we could not duck out of sensitive discussions by stressing our research role.

We actually became aware of this problem about halfway through the project when the schools liaison officers in particular expressed their disquiet about writing post-visit reports. Both the schools liaison officers were former school teachers and neither had any experience of ethnographic research. Part of their disquiet was due to a feeling that note-writing was unproductive. But it was also related to the uncomfortable feeling that they were 'spying' on the teachers and pretending to be something that they were not when they went into schools as activists and came away as researchers. Although the GIST project could by no stretch of the imagination be considered as covert research, this personal strain is similar in some respects to that experienced by covert researchers. In a comment on William Caudill's covert study of a psychiatric hospital George de Vos (quoted in Bulmer, 1982) says that

> the strain on Bill between his role as an objective observer and his human sensitivity to people who were deceived by his dissembling developed into a very severe personal and career crisis.

I do not want to overstate the similarities; merely to point out that the dual role of researcher and activist can be difficult to maintain.

One way of overcoming this difficulty might have been to adopt a policy of feeding back our notes to the teachers concerned. The problems here are obvious. There is the extra labour involved in preparing presentable versions, which takes time away from other aspects of the project. Apart from this we would necessarily have had to be more circumspect (and less honest) in what we said if the notes were to be seen by the teachers. It is difficult to tell someone that you think they are a male chauvinist pig one day, and continue to work with them to eliminate sex-stereotypes the next day. We certainly gave teachers some feedback, in the form of vigorous argument, if we felt their behaviour was suspect; but this was part of the action component of the project. The only research notes which were fed back were those on classroom observation, and even then some of the file copies contained additional comments for our eyes only.

All researchers face similar dilemmas over giving subjects access to their own data. The additional problems for action research are that the subjects are also colleagues; and that there is a definite right and wrong attitude in the eyes of the project, which the teachers, by agreeing to participate, implicitly share. As Barnes (1979) points out, in social science people are more likely to be harmed by the process of social enquiry itself than by the application of the knowledge gained. As in all research we promised confidentiality and anonymity — but as in much research this was difficult to provide. Payne *et al* (1984) carried out an independent evaluation of the teachers' attitudes to GIST. Although this was anonymous, we on the research team found it easy to identify many of the teachers they had talked to. It would be equally easy for teachers in the schools to identify their colleagues from our notes on visits to schools.

In the end we made very little direct use of this material in our reports of the project, for fear of damaging the interests of teachers. But this solution raises its own ethical problems. If you believe, as I do, that researchers have a duty to the truth, and that knowledge can help to solve social problems, then suppressing knowledge is unethical. If future projects encounter similar problems to GIST in working with teachers on sex-stereotyping, and we have not written about our experiences in a way that is helpful, then we have failed in our job of finding out about the world and making that knowledge available. We have attempted to do this by writing of teachers' reactions in general terms, with little direct quotation either from teachers or from our fieldnotes (for example, Kelly, 1985b; Whyte, 1986). But this is only a compromise. Barnes (1979) argues that both knowledge and privacy are good, and that the fundamental ethical issue in social science is 'how much does research in social science threaten to destroy privacy, and how much does the protection of privacy threaten to block research?' This question is just as pertinent in action research as in more conventional methods.

Conclusion

I have argued in this chapter that action research raises ethical problems in two distinct areas — the transmission of values and gaining the informed consent of teachers. These problems are by no means unique to action research, but they take on a somewhat different form in this type of project. Action research is explicitly value laden, and our right to change the schools in accordance with our values rests on our ability to negotiate with teachers and convince them that our position is ethically sound and to the benefit of the children. But teachers may not completely understand or share the researchers' values, and to this extent their participation may not amount to fully informed consent. In addition the dual nature of the project as both action and research may lull teachers into a false sense of security, so that they become less guarded than in a traditional project about what they reveal of themselves to the researcher.

Ethical considerations like these did not feature very prominently in our thinking when we undertook the GIST project. Having now spent some time considering possible pitfalls and dilemmas, I have to say that I'm glad I did not delve too deeply into this subject earlier on. If I had I might never have had the courage to do anything. To quote Barnes (1979) again in trying to give full attention to the rights and interests of all parties to the process of inquiry, there is a danger that empirical research becomes restricted to innocuous topics that challenge nobody.

This phenomenon is frequently observed among postgraduate students, where too much consideration of ethics causes (or excuses) complete paralysis of the research. Of course I am not arguing that ethical issues should be ignored. Only that it is important to couple a consideration of the ethics of research, which inevitably concentrates on the possible harm that research can do, to a restatement of the importance of free enquiry into a wide range of issues. Knowledge is, albeit in a limited sense, power, and researchers have an ethical duty to make knowledge more widely available. If someone wants to declare an area off-limits for researchers then we have to ask very probing questions about whose interests are really being protected by the suppression of this knowledge.

Notes

1. My colleagues on the GIST project were Judith Whyte (co-director), Barbara Smail and John Catton (schools liaison officers) and Vera Ferguson and Dolores Donegan (secretarial). The project was funded by the joint panel of the Social Science Research Council and the Equal Opportunities Commission, the Schools Council, the Department of Industry Education Unit and Shell UK Ltd. This chapter was prepared for publication while I was supported by a Nuffield Social Science Research Fellowship. I am grateful to both colleagues and sponsors for the parts they played in bringing the project to fruition. This chapter owes much to discussions with Barbara Smail in particular, but its final form, including any errors or inconsistencies, is my responsibility.
2. The masculine pronoun is used here intentionally as most of the science and technology teachers involved in the GIST project were male.

References

ADELMAN, C. (Ed) (1984) *The Politics and Ethics of Evaluation*, London, Croom Helm.
ARNOT, M. (Ed) (1985) *Race and Gender: Equal Opportunities Policies in Education*, Oxford, Pergamon.
BARNES, J. A. (1979) *Who Should Know What? Social Science, Privacy and Ethics*, Harmondsworth, Penguin.
BULMER, M. (Ed) (1982) *Social Research Ethics*, London, Macmillan.
EBBUTT, D. (1985) 'Educational action research: Some general concerns and

specific quibbles' in BURGESS, R. G. (Ed), *Issues in Educational Research: Qualitative Methods,* Lewes, Falmer Press.

ERAUT, M. (1984) 'Handling value issues', in ADELMAN, C. (Ed) *The Politics and Ethics of Evaluation,* London, Croom Helm.

GUTTENTAG, M. and BRAY, H. (1976) *Undoing Sex Sterotypes,* London, McGraw Hill.

JEFFCOATE, R. (1981) 'Evaluating the multicultural curriculum: Pupils' perspectives' in JAMES, A. and JEFFCOATE, R. (Eds) *The School in the Multicultural Society,* London, Harper and Row.

KELLY, A., WHYTE, J. and SMAIL, B. (1984) *Girls Into Science and Technology: Final Report,* Department of Sociology, University of Manchester.

KELLY, A. (1985a) 'Action research: What is it and what can it do?' in BURGESS, R. G. (Ed) *Issues in Educational Research: Qualitative Methods,* Lewes, Falmer Press.

KELLY, A. (1985b) 'Changing schools and changing society' in ARNOT, M. (Ed) *Race and Gender: Equal Opportunities Policies in Education,* Oxford, Pergamon.

KELLY, A. (1989) *Getting the GIST: A Quantitative Study of the Effects of the Girls Into Science and Technology Project,* Manchester Sociology Occasional Papers No. 22.

PAYNE, G., HUSTLER, D. and CUFF, T. (1984) *GIST or PIST: Teachers' Perceptions of the Project Girls Into Science and Technology,* Manchester, Manchester Polytechnic.

STANLEY, L. and WISE, S. (1983) *Breaking Out: Feminist Consciousness and Feminist Research,* London, Routledge and Kegan Paul.

WHYTE, J. (1986) *Girls Into Science and Technology,* London, Routledge and Kegan Paul, 1986.

WILCE, H. (1984) 'No role change for science girls', *Times Educational Supplement,* 2 March.

6
Ethics of Case Study in Educational Research and Evaluation

Helen Simons

All human research has ethical dimensions, decision-oriented human research most of all. In case study, which features social life in all its particularity, ethical issues are inescapable. During the past twenty years, a period of growth in the popularity of this approach to the investigation of educational activity, these issues have assumed increasing importance, both for investigators and investigated. The reasons for this are not hard to find. The context of use has changed. Whereas the seminal publications of the modern period (Hargreaves 1967 and Lacey 1970) were sociological studies contributing to general knowledge of schooling, with no intended and certainly no direct consequences for their anonymized subjects, the main area of case study practice since that time has been contextualized by evaluative intent. At the present time the bulk of funded social research is sponsored by government agencies which are engaged in planned and purposeful intervention in the conduct of the social services, and which look to such research to provide a database for more effective intervention. Much of this research is called project, programme or policy evaluation — research that is linked to ongoing policy enactment. But even research that is not specifically linked to action is likely to be scrutinized for its relevance to and implications for policy. Our subjects know that, and are sensitive to any possibility of advantage or disadvantage that may ensue as a consequence of their collaboration. Although I shall be concerned in this chapter with the ethics of case study as this dimension has evolved in educational evaluation, it is as well to remember that the parallel renaissance of ethnographic research in sociology swims in the same political waters.

This chapter has four themes. First, by way of introduction to the ethical procedures I wish to discuss, I briefly outline how case study came to have a central role in educational evaluation within the framework of evaluation as a process of informing decision-making.

Secondly, I examine the rationale for the kind of ethical guidelines that have developed in external independent evaluations over the past fifteen years, adaptions of which are now widely in use in research and evaluation projects (see, for example James *et al*, 1985: Adelman, 1979, Kemmis and Robottom, 1981). These focus on establishing justifiable ways of maintaining respect for persons involved in research while meeting the responsibility to publicly report.

Thirdly, I explore whether these ethical guidelines or variations of them are useful in in-school studies where the research is conducted by the participants themselves.

Finally, I take a brief look at the current political context to see what modifications or adaptions might be necessary to the ethical guidelines in the different political context of the late 1980s and 1990s.

Evaluation and Case Study

In the mid–1960s when evaluators came to examine the effects of major curriculum reforms, many of the existing models of evaluation proved inadequate for this purpose. Focusing as they did on aims-achievement and utilizing experimental design approaches to research they failed to provide evidence of the multi-faceted achievements and pitfalls of curriculum reforms.

As a basis for understanding how and why curriculum reforms succeed or fail, therefore, they were limited in scope. To broaden the basis of understanding, a number of alternative approaches to evaluation soon developed. 'These included illuminative evaluation (Parlett and Hamilton, 1972), responsive evaluation (Stake, 1975), transactional evaluation (Rippey, 1973). The reasons for their emergence have been well documented elsewhere (see, for instance, Adelman, Kemmis and Jenkins, 1980; Hamilton 1978) and I feel no need to reproduce them here. One of these alternatives was the case study (MacDonald and Walker, 1975; Stake, 1985).

Case study, whether described as 'a bounded system' (Smith in Stake, 1981) or an 'instance in action' (MacDonald and Walker, 1975), recognizes the particular contexts in which innovations are embedded and aspires to describe and analyze the processes by which and the conditions in which innovations are implemented. In the context of informing decision-making, case studies have several virtues over input–output models. They allow judgments to be made in relation to particular circumstances and clienteles, they allow more of the complexity of educational processes to be portrayed and they permit documentation of change over time.

Case study is not a method as is sometimes assumed, but a focus of study, whether that focus be a single classroom, institution or system. The essential feature is the case. This is usually an entity of intrinsic interest, as Stake (1985) points out, not merely a sample from which to learn about the population. Choice of methods is related to the purpose of the study and the nature of the case. A wide range of methods (both quantitative and qualitative) may be utilized if they facilitate an understanding of the case. This point is well demonstrated by Stake (1985) in drawing attention to another commonly held misconception about case study — that all case studies are naturalistic.

> In some discussions, case study has been presumed identical to naturalistic enquiry. Naturalistic research is the study of objects in their own environment, with a design relatively free of intervention or control. This work is often organized around issues of interest to lay people (as opposed to specialists) and perhaps reported in ordinary (rather than technical) language. Some case studies are naturalistic, others are not. A researcher's report of observations of a school board, covering what has been important to the board, is usually naturalistic, whereas the school psychologists's report of special tests undertaken by a child is a case study, formal (abstract, discipline-based) rather than naturalistic. Other case studies not usually naturalistic are medical case histories, so-called 'n = 1 studies', biographies, many policy studies and some institutional research. Many educational case studies are naturalistic, but not all; many naturalistic studies are not case studies because they do not concentrate on a particular case.

In practice in the evaluation of change efforts, case studies are often naturalistic and case studies of change have tended (though not exclusively) to use qualitative methods such as interviewing, observation and documentary analysis.

One of the reasons for this is related to other aspirations of the evaluation process. Not only are findings from these methods frequently reported in language accessible to audiences the evaluation seeks to inform but, through interviewing particularly, they offer opportunities for participation in the process. Such methods, furthermore, can be tailored to the short time-scales within which evaluation often has to work.

New approaches resolve certain problems but create others. I will mention just two of the most obvious. The study of individual cases often means close-up portrayals of individuals as key generators or implementers of the innovation. This can be threatening unless the person(s) concerned have some control over the information they offer, or how they are represented in a report. Anonymity, one of the codes of convention typically adopted in social research, is rarely applicable. In a closely documented case describing the complexity and the idiosyncrasy of the case, key individuals will always be identifiable at least to those within the case. This may be just as threatening or more, some have argued, (Simons, 1987; Sherwood 1986) than being identifiable to those outside the case to whom the case study may be disseminated.

Secondly, in case study evaluation which has as one of its main aspirations informing judgments decision-makers may take, the knowledge generated by case study becomes a political resource. Individuals and institutions stand to gain or lose by the transmission and utilization of knowledge acquired in an evaluation.

For both these reasons individuals should have some control over how, in what form, and to whom information about them should become public, and the evaluator needs to operate with guidelines that ensure proper use of this resource. MacDonald and Stake (1974) state the obligation this way:

> ... all evaluators are engaged in the business of providing information which enables some people to know about, and to judge, the work of others ... In the field of education, these various actors may be defined as subjects or recipients of evaluation information, and sometimes as both. All have roles in education, as well as personal concerns, and the performance of those roles, as well as the opportunity to defend or alter them, depends partly on the amount and the nature of the information they possess relative to other educational actors. The evaluator is therefore engaged in the acquisition and transmission of a significant resource and this fact poses serious questions about how his handling of this resource should be regulated. (p. 1).

The rest of this chapter examines the procedures that came to be formulated to govern the flow of information between different groups in an evaluation context. I leave it to the reader to discern whether the procedures generated within this context have utility for other forms of research.

It was in exploring a 'democratic' approach to evaluation of innovatory programmes that the principles and procedures outlined below for the conduct and dissemination of evaluation were first conceived. The origin of this development in evaluation theory and practice has been recently documented (see Simons, 1987), but a summary of the essential position may be helpful here.

The model has as its central aspiration how to find the appropriate balance in the conduct of research between the public 'right to know' and the individual 'right to privacy'. This problem is translated into a set of procedures for the conduct and management of evaluation, procedures which safeguard participants' rights, which give them control of data they can be said to own, and which offers them negotiation about what is to become public knowledge. Individuals have opportunities throughout the evaluation to comment upon how they are represented, both separately and in the contexts of reports, and at different stages in the process of production and dissemination.

The concept of democratic evaluation (MacDonald, 1974) derives from the rhetoric of liberal democracy, a rhetoric that is morally and politically undeniable by those exercising delegated power. The rhetoric of political aspiration is held to justify a set of power-equalizing procedures that cut into the customary power relationships embedded in organizations by holding actors accountable to criteria endorsed by them. Such procedures cannot, of course, change the power relationships but what they can do is:

— accord equal treatment to individuals and ideas;
— establish a flow of information that is independent of hierarchical or powerful interests;
— maintain that no-one has the right to exclude particular interests or perspectives;

In such a context all relevant perspectives can be represented, information fairly equitably exchanged and participative deliberation encouraged.

The procedures were a response to the following questions identified as critical to the aspiration for a more democratic relationship between the researcher and the researched, and audiences the research seeks to inform.

— to whose needs and interests does the research respond?
— who owns the data (the researcher, the subject, the sponsor)?
— who has access to the data? (Who is excluded or denied?)
— what is the status of the researcher's interpretation of events, *vis-à-vis* the interpetations made by others? (Who decides who tells the truth?)

— what obligations does the researcher owe to his subjects, his sponsors, his fellow professionals, others?

— who is the research for? (MacDonald and Walker, 1975, p. 6).

These questions came to be embodied in principles of procedure for the conduct of school case studies in the experimental phase of the SAFARI Project[1] (MacDonald and Walker, 1974). They were stated as follows:

— interviews would be conducted on the principle of confidentiality:
— use of data would be negotiated with participants;
— interview data would only be used with individuals' consent;
— participants would have ultimate control over how far they allowed the whole study to become public;
— reports would aspire to reflect participants' judgments and perceptions of reality;
— reports would be progressively negotiated for clearance, first with individuals, secondly with departments, thirdly with the school as a whole or representatives of the school.
— participants would be invited to improve their accounts by additions, deletions or amendments, on the criteria of fairness, accuracy and relevance.

SAFARI was primarily concerned with establishing participants' rights within a collaborative framework. In this formation of the procedures the 'right to know' justification was therefore somewhat subsidiary to the 'right to privacy' principle in order to experiment with the procedures as a mechanism for engaging participants more fully and productively in the research process. In other cases as an external independent evaluator I have argued a stronger role for the 'right to know' principle in terms of the public interest (see Simons, 1984, 1986). But in SAFARI our main concern was to facilitate the school 'telling its own story, in this case of curriculum development within the school. It was also to give priority to involving participants in *formulating the conditions of the inquiry* rather than simply asking them to conform to research conventions.

Lest the reader think this ethical position of giving control to participants is unduly restrictive on the researcher in terms of the public interest s/he need look no further than the *Ethical Guidelines for the Institutional Review Committees for Research with Human Subjects* (Social Sciences and Humanities Research Council of Canada, 1981). Here are two excerpts from a most extensive list of ethical guidelines:

Risk/Benefit

In balancing the risks and benefits to human subjects involved in any research in the humanities and social sciences to be supported by the Council, greater consideration must be given to the risks to physical, psychological, humane, proprietary and cultural values than to the potential contribution of the research to knowledge, although the latter should always be borne in mind (p. 4).

Privacy

For the purpose of these guidelines, the right to privacy extends to all information relating to a person's physical and mental condition, personal circumstances and social relationships which is not already in the public domain. It gives to the individual or collectivity the freedom to decide for themselves when and where, in what circumstances and to what extent their personal attitudes, opinions, habits, eccentricities, doubts and fears are to be communicated to or withheld from others.

The following guidelines have been adopted in respect of privacy:

27. If there is to be a probing of private personality or private affairs the intention to do so should be made explicit, and where there is an implication or promise of protection of privacy, the protection should be more generous than the promise.
28. Informed consent should be obtained from those to be observed or studied in private settings.
29. Since concepts of privacy vary from culture to culture, the question of invasion of privacy should be looked at from the ᴨoint of view of those being studied rather than from that of the researcher (p. 5).

It is clear from these two excerpts that the right to privacy accorded to the individual in these guidelines takes precedence over the right of the researcher to generate public knowledge using 'human subjects'. It is also clear that such guidelines, or aspects of them, would not be appropriate in an evaluation context. For two particular reasons.

In the first place they do not take account of the fact that evaluation is a 'public decision procedure' (House, 1980) with an obligation to 'serve those who are discussing or regulating social actions' (Cronbach *et al*, 1980). Evaluation information is a political resource and enters the political process. There are consequences for the individual, that is true, hence the 'right to privacy' principle in the Safari guidelines, but the counter value that is subordinate in the Canadian guidelines, the 'contribution of the research to knowledge,' is not the only consequence of taking such a stance. In evaluation there are consequences for other professionals in the system and indeed other audiences that have a legitimate interest in what professionals do. Take the evaluation of a school, for instance, in which it was revealed that several teachers were racist in their classroom practices. In terms of the Canadian guidelines, those individuals would have the 'freedom to decide for themseslves when and where, in what circumstances and to what extent their personal attitudes, opinions, habits, eccentricities, doubts and fears are to be communicated to or withheld from others'. But the consequences of making that information public are not only consequences for those individuals. There are clearly consequences for the pupils. Many would also want to argue that parents of those pupils should be informed about such practices. It should not be possible for an evaluation to suppress that information. This points up the danger of drawing the case study boundary too narrowly. It is essential that the boundary includes the full political constituency. The boundary in this sense may be a consequence rather than a preordinate constraint upon the case definition.

Secondly, the Canadian guidelines are written from the point of view only of the researcher engaged in the pursuit of knowledge. The language of the guidelines makes it clear it is a one way process. The definition of the 'human subject' for instance 'signifies any person who is used as a source of raw or unformulated data in the conduct of research and who is not acting in the capacity of principal investigator or assisting such an individual'.

In the context of the Safari procedures, as one of the case study experimenters, my aspiration was not only to engage the participants in the research process, but to shift part of the responsibility to them for investigating and documenting their own situation. In this sense, my aspiration was closer to that espoused by MacDonald and Norris (1981):

> It is not enough just to give the people we study their final report or control over the data they constitute. By casting those we study as a non-political audience, as an audience with no access to the information creating machinery of evaluation; as an audience whose interests are adequately represented by their political organizations, we help reproduce the belief and the objective conditions for its persistence, that the powerless are politically docile and uninterested (p. 16).

Shared Assumptions

Variations of these ethical guidelines, as I have said, are now widely in use in research and evaluation studies. Whatever form the precise procedures take, the guidelines share a number of points in common.

First, all recognize the balance that needs to be maintained between the public right to know and the individual's right to privacy. How precisely this is achieved in any one context will be governed not only by the procedures devised for the particular study (taking account of the context) but also by how these are interpreted within that context.

It is important to underline, I think, that it is the balance between these two claims that is being sought. In some cases, for instance, it means that data which seems important to the researcher but carries a high risk for the individual must remain in the files. On the other hand it means that no one person has the right to declare as confidential, information that is already public knowledge or to veto information that has already been cleared by others for release in a public report. Nor does it mean that information can necessarily remain confidential for a time, as MacDonald and Stake (1974) point out:

> The continuous restriction of information that long ago should have been declassified helps to discredit the rules that protect justifiable confidentiality. The proper handling of confidential materials in an educational programme should not involve indiscriminate labels such as 'confidential' or 'secret' but should identify to whom it should be released, who is responsible for further release, and the period for which it should remain confidential (p. 5).

The aspiration behind the balance of principles is to 'protect people from inappropriate exposure and to increase the likelihood of proper use of information', not to prevent information becoming accessible at all.

The second feature of these guidelines common to all is the necessity for a set of specific procedures to guide the conduct of the study. Those writing about ethics often refer to the 'trust' that is important in research, the 'integrity of the researcher', or the 'respect' to be shown for individuals as though these virtues were separable from research practice.

Even if this were true, it would be insufficient, I suggest, as a basis for action. It may be the case that in the end the integrity of the research and the researcher depends upon the fulfilment of expectations generated by interpersonal perceptions. But that trust has to be won, not assumed. It is fragile and provisional, especially between those entering a research relationship for the first time. Even if trust can be claimed on the basis of a previous track record it still has to be demonstrated in a new case. And for that formal procedures are necessary.

This point has been most convincingly argued by Nias (1981) in her essay on trust where she claims that two necessary conditions for trust are predictability and perceived agreement over ends. Behaviours can only become predictable and agreement over ends affirmed as one gains knowledge of them.

> Trust, I have argued, depends upon the predictability of personal and institutional behaviour and of technical competence, and upon an awareness of shared goals. Yet in the educational system of a pluralist society there is bound to be conflict over the aims of education, and thus over the conduct of the schools (especially secondary comprehensive ones). To claim that this conflict can be resolved by mutual trust rather than by 'formal procedures' is to be guilty of circularity. It is also to ignore the part played in the establishment of trust by forms of organization . . .
>
> In other words, formal procedures and the interpersonal knowledge which they promote are not the antithesis of 'trust' but the necessary conditions for it. Moreover, they act upon each other. Formal procedures facilitate the growth of trust and help to ensure its survival (p. 222).

The third point the guidelines have in common is that they apply to all participants. This takes into account the fact that not only are all treated equally in the conduct of the study (there is no privileged access or treatment) but that it is difficult to tell who may be most at risk. Risk is not always hierarchically ordered. It is usually assumed that those most at risk are those in more junior positions, say in the school hierarchy, or in a temporary project role in an LEA. But this is not necessarily the case. It may be the chief education officer or the headteacher who has most to lose from a public account of the LEA or school's work.

Contextual Differences

There are certain features of these ethical guidelines that are familiar to all researchers and which are applicable whatever the context. Statements such as:

—no documents, files, correspondence will be examined without

explicit authorization nor will they be copied without permission;
— permission will be sought for publication of interview data that is attributable or identifiable to individuals;
— information that is not identifiable or summarizes general issues will not require specific clearance;
— data will be stored in locked files and destroyed after (a specified time)

There are other procedures that differ according to the context of application, the purpose of the study, the timescale of reporting and the resources available. Take the use of interview material for instance. Some researchers advocate the tape-recording and transcription of interviews, copies of which are sent to individuals to amend or elaborate as they wish. This then becomes a database for subsequent reporting. In the case of the PRAISE (1985) guidelines, a period of fourteen days is stipulated for return of transcripts. This is presumably to facilitate management of the project and the generation of report(s).

Other guidelines (see for example, Simons, 1984) do not engage this procedure of clearing the whole transcript but rather opt for clearance of the data in the context in which it is to be reported. There are two particular reasons for this. First, it is more practical when time and resources are short. But secondly, and more importantly, it gives participants the opportunity to comment on their testimony in the context in which it is to be publicly reported.

A second difference in the guidelines refers to the specificity of clearance procedures. Sometimes clearance is simply sought for the report to be made public. Sometimes an invitation is extended to participants to add a statement if they disagree with the interpretation. Other procedures specify that the report will be negotiated with those who are identifiable in it or those who represent different interests in the programme. Specific criteria for the negotiation are often, but not always indicated.

It is this procedure of negotiation that is crucial for maintaining the balance I referred to earlier between the right to know and the right to privacy. The UNCAL[2] guidelines are interesting on this point. Criteria for negotiation noted there are fairness, relevance and validity. Opportunities are invited for improving the reports on these grounds. But the procedures also add:

Of course, in some instances the UNCAL team will be unwilling to change the report, but will not circulate the report without consulting the NDPCAL (programme) Director and then, only with whatever additional commentary the project staff want to attach to it (MacDonald and Stake 1974, p. 3).

The point of indicating that the evaluation team may be unwilling to change the report acknowledges the fact that the evaluation has a responsibility to report publicly, and that negotiation does not mean, cannot mean, total acceptance of whatever individuals or groups wish to exclude. This procedure establishes the boundaries of the negotiation process. It is one that allows all individuals, evaluators included, to contribute to the fairness, accuracy and validity of the report. If judgments on these criteria are in dispute, individuals still have the right to report disagreements and to make additions. Such a procedure also ensures that negotiation does not lead to a false consensus on issues or emasculated reports.

A third difference lies in the extent to which interview or other material is 'on the record' or 'off the record' from the start. In the Safari guidelines for instance the starting point was confidentiality and data was progressively negotiated on to the public record. This was, as I have said, for the deliberate purpose of engaging participants in the research in a significant way. The price, in my case, was high in terms of a public record (see Simons, 1987) but not in terms of helping the school to become its own documenter of that public record. In other circumstances where I have had the responsibility to inform audiences outside the particular programme I have interpreted the principle of confidentiality somewhat differently, starting from the position that all interviews, for example, were on the record, unless individuals requested otherwise.

A similar position with regard to on and off the record was adopted in the PRAISE (1985) and Nottinghamshire TRIST (1985) Guidelines;

> The evaluators will treat all relevant interviews, meetings, oral and written exchanges with participants (including DES sponsors) as 'on the record', unless specifically asked to treat them as confidential.

This move from an 'off the record' position to an 'on the record' position with confidentiality available rather than laid down at the outset, was a response, at least in the way I have used the procedure, to the need to produce reports more quickly to facilitate the process of dissemination. In an even later set of guidelines (Simons, 1986) I have refined the procedure yet again to try and more appropriately meet both the right to privacy of individuals and the right to information by others. The statement reads:

> The principle of confidentiality will operate to protect private
> and personal data from unnegotiated dissemination.

This statement accepts the point that some data offered in confidence
may need to go on the public record if relevant for the study but that
such data has to be negotiated with the individual on criteria known to
them from the outset.

A fourth difference in statements of guidelines is the degree to which
audiences are specified and who has the responsibility for circulating
reports. It is here perhaps that the biggest difference occurs. This difference
is invariably related to three factors:

— the degree to which sponsors assume control over reporting;
— the degree to which the researcher wishes to maintain an
  independent reporting stance;
— the structure of relationships within the case itself.

These factors are often in conflict and agreement on the principles of
dissemination if not the actual audiences for the report(s) needs to be
determined at the outset. Increasingly sponsors are becoming more explicit
about claiming the right to decide whether or not a research or evaluation
report is published. There is a strong and weak version of this contractual
claim. The weak version is represented by the phrase 'publication will
not unreasonably be withheld,' though it leaves open to question of course
what is reasonable in any one case, and who decides what is reasonable.
The strongest version is represented by the following statement from
an LEA's guidelines for a TRIST evaluation.

> These reports (i.e. the evaluation reports) will be presented to the
> Project Director for transmission to such audiences as he judges
> to be appropriate.

Such control in the hands of one person cannot be said to serve the 'right
to know' even of those within the project. It also provides the opportunity
for a report that is critical of the project to be suppressed by one person.

My own view is that relevant audiences for reports should be
negotiated and declared at the outset, but with the proviso that these
may need to be re-negotiated throughout the process of the evaluation
itself. In an independent external evaluation, the aspiration should be to
disseminate as widely as possible to those who can be claimed to have
a legitimate interest in the study. It should also be clear in these
negotiations whose responsibility it is to see that the reports are

disseminated and that there are appropriate resources to meet this obligation.

In the light of the experience of several studies the guidelines outlined in the appendix are those I now find most useful in conducting an independent evaluation that has to operate within a time-line of one to two years, that allows some data to be utilized for formative feedback to audiences within the programme without detriment to the individual, and that respects the need to report to audiences outside the immediate programme. The context in which they were developed was a TVEI programme, the location an LEA, the audiences, several groups within the LEA plus audiences outside the LEA. These audiences which were negotiated with the LEA included the MSC, other local TVEI evaluations and the evaluation community.

These guidelines are similar to earlier statements of such guidelines (MacDonald and Stake, 1974; Simons, 1984) and rest on the same justification but they contain four crucial additions that seemed necessary given the particular context of the innovation.

In TVEI the LEA is not only the sponsor of the evaluation but is also responsible for the innovation. Unlike the innovatory projects of the late sixties and seventies which in most cases had a period of development followed by an evaluation, here the evaluation took place alongside the development. TVEI furthermore was introduced in haste. There was little time for pre-planning and training. Guidelines were open and curriculum development strategies left to the creativity of LEA personnel. To have to engage in public evaluation before one has time to experiment leaves little scope for risk-taking and creates a lot of anxiety. The temptation to lean on the evaluation for support was as great as the temptation for the evaluators to be helpful by avoiding criticism of the programme. In such a context four additional procedures seemed crucial to maintain the evaluation as a credible public service, both within and outside the authority.

The first was to set strict deadlines for comment on reports to accelerate interim feedback and inform decision-making. The second was to introduce the notion of a collective responsibility on the part of participants for accurate and fair reporting, i.e. participants should not assume that only the evaluator has that responsibility; they too have a role to play in the process of accurately and fairly documenting development of the programme. The third was to suggest that an external consultant be appointed to provide a check, if invoked, on the impartiality of the evaluation. The fourth was to acknowledge that in a situation new to all where misunderstandings may occur, all parties should be open to apology, correction and, if necessary to renegotiation of procedures. (See Appendix to this chapter.)

Internal Case Study

When in the late 1970s there was a major shift in curriculum evaluation from external to internal case study of schools I began to examine whether the principles and procedures developed in external case study designed to secure access and win trust for a 'stranger' in the school with an evaluative mission were applicable in in-school case study. I took the view, then, contrary to those who assumed that such procedures were either too cumbersome or could be discarded in the context of collegial relationships, that such a structure was essential to deal with the even more problematic circumstance where the evaluators are residents of the institution.

Institutions have clearly established norms and roles which may need to be transcended to establish working boundaries for an evaluation process. The particular argument I advanced to support and justify this view has been outlined elsewhere (Simons, 1985). What I did not explore in the 1985 paper were precisely how the procedures may need to be altered to take account of the fact that the evaluators were internal to the school. In this section I take that discussion a little further by examining the relevance of some common procedures for protection of privacy and access to information for insider studies.

A school self-evaluation case study exhibits many of the intimate features of case study of schools conducted by external researchers, such as the conflict between the individual's right to privacy and the professional's public accountability; the conflicts that arise when hitherto undeclared values become part of a public agenda; and the difficulty of disentangling performance from design issues.

In school self-evaluation however there are particular difficulties associated with the fact that case workers are an inevitable, continuing part of the functioning of the institution. Their every decision, for example, is public. They cannot be protected by the case worker's procedure governing right to privacy in a one-to-one negotiation with an external researcher. They are accountable furthermore to their colleagues. Where the case worker is external to the school, participants can always blame the researcher if things go wrong or disturb the politics of the school. That can happen in an internal study too of course but in the external case, blaming the researcher can be functional to maintaining the stability of the institution, in the internal case it may be dysfunctional.

Within school studies, too, there is less opportunity to dismiss the interpretations of the case worker, something that is frequently helpful in coping with the dissonance a researcher's interpretation may create in the school. The external researcher can always take flight with his/her interpretations intact which may in the end be forgotten by the school anyway. Internal evaluators have to face public discussion of their interpretations and accept that colleagues may not share their views. It is in facing these difficulties and conflicts however that the potential for change within the institution lies. Procedures for conducting the study are needed to enable discussion of conflicts and disagreements to take place without detriment to the development of the institution.

In exploring the limits of evaluation case study where the case worker is internal to the institution, I will first examine which of the conventions adopted by external researchers to offer individuals some protection in the research act are appropriate and which are not. I shall concentrate on four: confidentiality; informed consent; anonymity and pre-publication access.

It may be necessary to restate the problem for which these conventions are a resolution. Smith (1980) has stated it thus:

> The core ethical problem in any social science research is acting in the context of two conflicting values — the pursuit of truth through scientific procedures and the maintenance of respect for the individuals whose lives are being lived, focally or peripherally, in the context of one's research project (p. 192).

The principle of informed consent, 'people willingly agreeing in full view of aims and purposes, problems and procedures and relevant information' (*ibid*, p. 193) is equally applicable in participant evaluation, providing certain pre-conditions exist such as an open management structure, participant identification of problems and procedures, opportunities for negotiation and exchange of information. Of course there may be differences over what would constitute 'relevant information' and 'full view of aims and purposes'. These would need to be discussed. If the aims and purposes change during the study, consent should be sought again in full knowledge of the reasons and conditions for the change. Adelman (1979) has proposed the notion of a 'rolling' contract to cope with this eventuality.

Two sub-procedures of informed consent adopted by external researchers are less applicable: the suggestion that potential participants in the study read a previous report or study of the researcher to see what they may be getting into; and the suggestion that a written contract spell out and embody the agreements made. The first assumes a product is an outcome of the study which may not be the case within a school self evaluation. The second, more a procedure to ensure 'informal consent' has been given and aims and procedures agreed, may be too formal. While the procedures must be clear to all in an internal study, their embodiment in a written contract may detract from the kind of structure and relationships it is necessary to build up to allow effective school self-study to take place. The aspiration in an internal study should rather be to gradually formalize informal structures and processes to facilitate greater openness and exchange of information. Written procedures may facilitate this process. Reiteration and demonstration of procedures in action is most likely to secure it.

The principle of confidentiality invoked to afford individuals some protection over the use of data offered by them in research, poses two particular problems in an internal evaluation. While it is quite possible to utilize this principle in a one-to-one negotiation, it may not be particularly meaningful when the structures are open and the issues under discussion are more or less already public knowledge or should be public knowledge as they concern the interests of children collectively. It may even create mistrust. For example, one teacher may say to another 'This is in confidence' and this indeed be respected only to find that the comment or issue forms part of a report, not because the person to whom it was said breached the confidence but because its content was obtainable from other sources.

The second issue concerns confidentiality agreements with pupils. Can such agreements mean anything to pupils? Is it reasonable and fair to offer them confidentiality? Is it necessary? I think it is although there are three particular difficulties in using the procedure with pupils. The first is their lack of real choice. The second is the same as that above, the unwitting breach or perception of breach of confidence, despite a commitment to confidentiality. The third is the fact that a teacher, not an external researcher is the evaluator. Given the authority structure of most schools, it may not be easy for pupils to believe that teacher/evaluators are operating with a set of conventions separate from their authority role as teachers.

Anonymity is often linked with confidentiality, a promise that goes with it. But here I wish to keep them separate. The concept of confidentiality has an important function in the social process of building up the appropriate relationships for open, honest discussion. The concept of anonymity offers individuals some privacy in the research process or protection from identification while allowing more explicit discussion or reporting of contentious issues. Anonymization however is almost impossible to achieve, certainly in an internal study. While it still may be an important principle to maintain when reports are disseminated, decreasing the likelihood of identification over time and distance, it is questionable whether it is appropriate at all in an internal study especially when the aspiration is to facilitate open dialogue between participants.

The reasons for suggesting its inappropriateness in internal studies are three. First, the sub-procedures adopted by external researchers of changing the names of places, persons and organizations is simply not possible. Secondly, an important function of self-evaluation is the move towards openness and towards providing a credible account that can be checked by independent observers. Thirdly, part of the function of school self-evaluation is to promote intraprofessional accountability and this can more appropriately be established where individuals are 'on the record'.

There remains the problem of how to offer individuals some protection over their privacy for that is an equally important principle in internal as well as external evaluation, more so, some might argue, as participants are more vulnerable where they cannot escape from the researcher's presentation through anonymized coding. Smith (1980) reminds us of the delicacy of the issue:

> Obviously all of us must 'face the truth' around us at various times and in various ways. However, being a part of making a semi-permanent record of a particular individual has a humbling and disquieting aspect to it (p. 202).

This is written from the point of view of the external researcher but the sentiment is one that should also be respected in internal studies.

The fourth convention, prepublication access, at first appears to have little relevance in the sense that publication is not generally an outcome of internal evaluations. Increasingly however, under the Grant-Related In-Service Training (GRIST) arrangements school self-evaluation may be part of an LEA's overall evaluation processes. To this extent they are public. It is also the case of course that moving from a private to a public agenda within a school is itself a public process, one that is often perceived to more threatening that public reporting beyond the school. It is for this reason that the practice of forewarning participants of the issues that will be reported publicly is also relevant in internal studies. In the context of school self-evaluation, Eraut (1984) has called this 'controlled leakage'. The function of this procedure is to alert the individual to issues that will become public so that he or she is prepared and more able to face them publicly.

The changes that would be required to the procedures for an internal study are implicit in the above discussion. It would be repetitive to reproduce them here. It may be important to add however in conclusion that certain pre-conditions may be necessary within an institution to secure their acceptance. The reasons for having a set of guidelines in internal studies are often not perceived at the outset. Only when difficulties are encountered does the need arise. This is particularly an issue in internal studies where participants assume that collegiality exists independent of structures that underpin and support the development of cooperation and intraprofessional accountability.

The Future?

The ethical guidelines referred to in this chapter for the access to and release of data were generated in the mid-1970s out of concern to pay more allegiance to, and give participants more of a say in the representation of themselves in public reporting.

In the late 1980s, and as far as we can foresee into the 1990s as well, the context is one of increasing centralism and managerialism, increased categorical funding of curriculum, in-service and evaluation initiatives and increased control over what questions it is legitimate to pursue in evaluation and research.

Maintaining a balance between the principles discussed in this chapter was difficult enough when the centralizing tendency was merely gathering force. Now that we are witnessing quite unprecedented control over schools, local education authorities and universities accompanied by more and more requests for accountability of institutions and individuals, what response can we make that balances risk for individuals with due regard for proper accounting and yet keeps the system open to deliberation and critique?

The situation is exacerbated by the fact that higher education institutions are increasingly reliant on funding agencies, whether these be government departments, LEAs or quasi-government agencies like the Manpower Services Commission (MSC) most of whom are seeking to legitimate decisions rather than inform or challenge policy. The notion of the pilot experiment is long gone. Evaluations are increasingly used for legitimation and advocacy rather than critique and enrichment in the system.

The context has changed in another important respect. There has been a major shift in responsibility for curriculum and inservice development. LEAs are both the sponsors of curriculum and inservice development programmes within their authorities *and* responsible for their evaluation. This could lead to cooptation as evaluators respond sympathetically to the anxieties and concerns of local education officials, advisers and project officers who themselves, of course, are subject to increasing controls, financial constraints and political demands. But it could also provide an opportunity for professionals at the local level to work together to determine the conditions in which and the procedures by which they would wish to be evaluated thereby strengthening the professional response of the whole community.

It is difficult to be optimistic and there are plenty of examples to quote of national and local evaluations which have given up on independence either by subscribing to sponsor's controls on publication or compromising on the issues to be addressed or the depth to which they are pursued. There are other examples of siding with the professionals (for good reasons in many cases) at the expense of public reporting. Such practices are understandable in the fight for survival but they actually serve little purpose in the end if the aspiration so often quoted for evaluation of improving the operation of the social system is still an aim.

To retreat to a 'publish and be damned' response seems a retrograde step though there may be occasions when such a course of action is necessary in the public interest. Yet the process I have described of gradually negotiating with individuals may seem to have little purchase given the pressures of time and pressures for more and more public accounting.

Such a mediating role, however, may be even more important to sustain in a climate that threatens the availability of research findings. We need to keep the lines of communication open if we aspire to have any influence at all, through evaluation and research reporting, on what happens in schools.

There are two lines of action it seems crucial to pursue. The first is to continue to utilize procedures that offer all individuals the opportunity to become self-critical, to objectify their own experience, to gain the confidence to open up their work to public critique. The extension of professional self-evaluation procedures beyond schools to other parts of the education service is part of this aspiration. In terms of improving schools and systems as MacDonald and Walker (1975) have written ' a specialist research profession will always be a poor substitute for a self-monitoring educational community' (p. 11).

The second line of action for the professional community is to strengthen its public skills in relation to parents, governors and the lay community generally, to widen its deliberative constituency. Both external and internal case workers have a role to play in this process, the internal by documenting the work of schools in ways that reflect its educational achievements without risk to its staff; the external by negotiating justifiable access to and dissemination of school case studies with a proper concern for accountablity and protection of risks to individuals.

In the heady days of the 1960s when resources were more freely available and optimism about education at its height, education professionals, I think it is fair to say, paid too little attention to the school as an institution in the wider community. Schools suffering from exclusive practices in the past have left themselves vulnerable to state control. The resolution in the current climate is not to retreat to a protectionist stance or to insulate the school against external agents but to build an alliance with those who have been neglected in the past — the wider constituency of parents, governors and the lay community — to extend knowledge about the work of schools. The ethical procedures discussed in this chapter provide a framework within which this aspiration can be pursued.

Appendix

PRINCIPLES AND PROCEDURES FOR AN INDEPENDENT EXTERNAL EVALUATION

The purpose of evaluation is to document the experience of the programme in action for the guidance of educational decision-making. This means making the work of the programme accessible to a range of relevant audiences both within and beyond the programme. The following procedures for the access to and negotiation of information are proposed as guidelines for the gathering and transmission of information in the evaluation.

— the evaluation seeks reasonable access to documents and people. Evaluators assume they can approach administrators, teachers, students and other persons directly or indirectly concerned with the programme in order to obtain a fair, balanced and accurate report of the programme.
— the evaluation will not examine documents, files, correspondence without explicit authorization of project personnel and will not copy from these sources without permission.

— the principle of confidentiality will operate to protect private and personal data from unnegotiated dissemination. Such data will require clearance on the criteria of relevance, accuracy and fairness. The same procedure will apply to attributed comment which will require clearance in a reporting context.

— evaluators will make clear the purpose of interviews and the anticipated audiences for the information gained. Interviewees should feel free to discuss their work, including any difficulties, as they see fit, exercising whatever discretion they would normally adopt in discussing the work of the programme with colleagues. In this way they share with the evaluation some responsibility for fair, accurate and relevant reporting.

— direct quotation and attributed judgments in reports require the explicit permission of the respondent. Non-attributable information used in summarizing findings across projects or in raising general issues about the programme does not require specific clearance.

— external evaluation reports will be negotiated with the groups they concern on the criteria of accuracy, relevance and fairness. Where differences of view prevail the evaluation may not wish to change the report but agrees not to circulate it without consultation and only then with whatever additional commentary the group concerned want to attach to it within the management deadlines of the evaluation.

— negotiation of reports will take place within strict deadlines. This is necessary to ensure evaluation serves its function of informing decision-making. The evaluation cannot be held accountable for comments received after the deadlines have passed.

— every care will be taken to protect the sensitivities of people within the programme but no one person or group will have the right to veto the external evaluation reports.

— the evaluation will engage the services of an external consultant to provide a check, if invoked, on the impartiality of the evaluation and to act as an independent arbiter in the event of a disagreement arising between the evaluation and the authority over the public reporting of the evaluation.

— a negotiated evaluation can only proceed on a basis of trust and mutual respect for all the parties concerned. When misunderstandings occur, all parties should be open to apology, to correction and, if necessary, to further negotiation of the negotiation procedures themselves (Simons 1986).

Helen Simons

Notes

1 SAFARI (Success and Failure and Recent Innovation) was funded by the Ford Foundation in 1973 to explore the medium-term effects of centrally-developed curriculum projects. For further details see MacDonald and Walker, (1976).
2 UNCAL (Understanding Computer Assisted Learning) was the independent educational evaluation of the National Development Programme in Computer Assisted Learning, funded, again, in 1973, by the Department of Education and Science (DES). (See MacDonald *et al*, 1975). Both SAFARI and UNCAL were multi-site case-study projects exploring, with different emphases, a democratic approach to evaluation.

References

ADELMAN, C. (1979) 'Some dilemmas of institutional evaluation and their relationship to preconditions and procedures'. Paper presented to the Annual Meeting of the American Educational Research Association, San Francisco, *Studies in Educational Evaluation* (1980) **6**, 2, Oxford, Pergamon Press, pp. 165–83.
ADELMAN, C. (Ed) (1984) *The Politics and Ethics of Evaluation*, London, Croom Helm.
ADELMAN, C., KEMMIS, S. and JENKINS, D. (1980) 'Rethinking case study: Notes from the second Cambridge Conference' in SIMONS, H. (Ed) *Towards a Science of the Singular*, Norwich, CARE.
CRONBACH, L. J. and ASSOCIATES (1980) *Toward Reform of Program Evaluation: Aims, Methods and Institutional Arrangements*, San Francisco, CA, Jossey Bass.
ELLIOT, J. *et al* (1981) *School Accountability*, London, Grant McIntyre.
ERAUT, M. (1984) 'Institution-based curriculum evaluation' in SKILBECK, M. (Ed) *Evaluating the Curriculum in the Eighties*, London, Hodder and Stoughton, pp. 54–63.
GLASS, G. (Ed) (1976) *Evaluation Studies Review Annual*, 1, Beverly Hills, CA, Sage Publications.
HAMILTON, D. (1978) 'Making sense of curriculum evaluation: Continuities and discontinuities in an educational idea', in SHULMAN, L. (Ed) (1978) *Review of Research in Education*, 5. Itasca, IL., Peacock Press, pp. 318–47.
HAMILTON, D. *et al* (Eds) (1977) *Beyond the numbers game: A reader in Educational Evaluation*, London, Macmillan.
HARGREAVES, D. H. (1967) *Social Relations in a Secondary School*, London, Routledge and Kegan Paul.
HOUSE, E. R. (1980) *Evaluating with Validity*, Beverly Hills, CA, Sage Publications.
JAMES, M. *et al* (1985) 'Ethical guidelines', PRAISE (Pilot Records of Achievement in Schools Evaluation), Milton Keynes, The Open University.
KEMMIS, S. and ROBOTTOM, I. (1981) 'Principles of procedure in curriculum evaluation', *Journal of Curriculum Studies*, **13**, 2, pp. 151–5.
LACEY, C. (1970) *Hightown Grammar*, Manchester, Manchester University Press.

MACDONALD, B. (1974) 'Evaluation and the control of education', in MACDONALD, B. and WALKER, R. (Eds) *SAFARI I: Innovation, Evaluation, Research and the Problem of Control,* Norwich, Centre for Applied Research in Education, University of East Anglia, pp. 9–22. Also in TAWNEY, D. (Ed) (1976) *Curriculum Evaluation Today: Trend and Implications,* Schools Council Research Studies, London, Macmillan Educational.

MACDONALD, B. *et al* (1975) 'The Programme at two', an evaluation report on The National Development Programme in Computer Assisted Learning', Norwich, Centre for Applied Research, University of East Anglia.

MACDONALD, B. and NORRIS, N. (1981) 'Looking up for a change — Political horizons in policy evaluation', Norwich, Centre for Applied Research in Education, University of East Anglia, mimeo. An earlier version of this paper is published in POPKEWITZ, T. S. and TABACHNIK, B. R. (Eds) (1981) *The Study of Schooling: Field Based Methodologies in Educational Research and Evaluation,* New York, Praeger, pp. 276–88, under the title 'Twin political horizons in evaluation fieldwork'.

MACDONALD, B. and STAKE, R. E. (1974) 'Confidentiality: Procedures and principles of the UNCAL evaluation with respect to information about projects in the National Development Programme in Computer Assisted Learning', Norwich, Centre for Applied Research in Education, University of East Anglia, mimeo.

MACDONALD, B. and WALKER, R. (Eds) (1974) *SAFARI I: Innovation, Evaluation, Research and the Problem of Control,* Norwich, Centre for Applied Research in Education, University of East Anglia.

MACDONALD, B. and WALKER, R. (1975) 'Case study and the social philosophy of educational research'. *Cambridge Journal of Education,* 5, 1, pp. 2–11.

MACDONALD, B. and WALKER, R. (1976) *Changing the Curriculum,* London, Open Books.

NIAS, J. (1981) 'The nature of trust', in ELLIOTT, J. *et al, School Accountability,* London, Grant McIntyre, pp. 211–23.

NISBET, J. and NISBET, S. (Eds) (1985) *World Yearbook of Education 1985, Research, Policy and Practice,* London, Kogan Page; New York Nichols Publishing Company.

NOTTINGHAMSHIRE TRIST GUIDELINES (1985) 'Evaluation of the Nottinghamshire TRIST programme. Ethical Guidelines', Nottingham, Trent Polytechnic.

PARLETT, M. and HAMILTON, D. (1972) 'Evaluation as illumination: A new approach to the study of innovatory programmes', Occasional Paper 9, Centre for Research in the Educational Sciences, University of Edinburgh. Reprinted in HAMILTON, D. *et al* (Eds) (1977) *Beyond the Numbers game: A Reader in Educational Evaluation,* London, Macmillan, p. 6–22, and GLASS, G. (Ed) (1976) *Evaluation Studies Review Annual,* 1, Beverly Hills, CA, Sage Publications, pp. 140–57.

PRAISE (1985) (Pilot Records of Achievement in Schools Evaluation) 'Ethical guidelines', Milton Keynes: The Open University.

RIPPEY, R. M. (Ed) (1973) *Studies in Transactional Evaluation,* Berkeley, CA, McCutchan.

SHERWOOD, L. (1986) 'Teachers' Perceptions of Educational Change: A Case Study of Teacher Learning. Unpublished MA dissertation, London Institute of Education, University of London.

SHULMAN, L. (Ed) (1978) *Review of Research in Education,* 5, Itasca, IL., Peacock Press.

SIMONS, H. (1978) 'School-based evaluation on democratic principles', *Curriculum Action Research Network,* Bulletin No. 2, January, Cambridge Institute of Education.

SIMONS, H. (1984) 'Guidelines for the conduct of an independent evaluation' in ADELMAN, C. (Ed), *The Politics and Ethics of Evaluation,* London, Croom Helm.

SIMONS, H. (Ed) (1980) *Towards a Science of the Singular: Essays about Case Study in Educational Research and Evaluation,* CARE Occasional publications, No. 10, Norwich, Centre for Applied Research in Education, University of East Anglia.

SIMONS, H. (1985) 'Against the rules: Procedural problems in school self-evaluation', *Curriculum Perspectives,* 5, 2, pp. 1–6.

SIMONS, H. (1986) 'Principles and Procedures for an Independent External Evaluation' Mimeo.

SIMONS, H. (1987) *Getting to Know Schools in a Democracy,* Lewes, Falmer Press.

SKILBECK, M. (Ed) (1984) *Evaluating the Curriculum in the Eighties,* London, Hodder and Stoughton.

SMITH, L. M. (1980) 'Some not so random thoughts on doing fieldwork: The interplay of values', in SIMONS, H. (Ed) *Towards a Science of the Singular: Essays about Case Study in Educational Research and Evaluation,* CARE Occasional Publications No. 10, Norwich, Centre for Applied Research in Education, University of East Anglia.

SOCIAL SCIENCES AND HUMANITIES RESEARCH COUNCIL OF CANADA (1981) *Ethical Guidelines for the Institutional Review Committees for Research with Human Subjects.*

STAKE, R. E. (Ed) (1975) *Evaluating the Arts in Education: A Responsive Approach,* Columbus, OH, Charles E. Merrill Publishing Company.

STAKE, R. E. (1981) 'Seeking sweet water': Case study methods in educational research'. Audio-tape published by the American Educational Research Association.

STAKE, R. E. (1985) 'Case study', in NISBET, J. and NISBET, S. (Eds), *World Yearbook of Education 1985, Research, Policy and Practice,* London, Kogan Page New York Nichols Publishing Company.

TAWNEY, D. (Ed) (1976) *Curriculum Evaluation Today: Trend and Implications,* Schools Council Research Studies, London, Macmillan Educational.

Part Two
Ethical Issues in Empirical Research

7
Ethics and The Law : Conducting Case Studies of Policing

David Bridges

Preface

> Maybe the right to know ... will lead to undesirable results.
> Maybe it will clash with other principles ... The main thing
> however is that, as in most moral matters, whether the right
> should be given and over what area it should be extended need
> to be argued in the context of particular cases. (Pring, 1984)

There are probably still some researchers in some fields who imagine
themselves to be engaged in the disinterested pursuit of what, once
discovered, will be an unambivalent truth. They may further anticipate
that having discovered that truth, its publication or communication will
be a moral right or duty which presents only minor technical problems
in its execution.

However, for many of us engaged in research into social situations
such as those provided by educational and training institutions, few if
any of these characterizations of research apply. Researchers will recognize
that they may well have interests at stake in the research and perhaps
even in the events or institution under investigation; truth will be
inescapably ambivalent; and its communication will almost inevitably
raise both epistemological problems rooted in the gap between what is
said and what is heard (Elliott, 1984) and moral questions about
researchers' rights and obligations to publish the truth as they see it. Truth
and honesty continue to be aspirations or criteria against which the
research is conducted, but what they demand of research and the
researcher will rarely be unambiguous. Researchers know too that these
will not be the only practical or moral imperatives bearing upon their
research enterprise.

As Pring (1984) argues, therefore, our rights to know and to publish what we find out have to be assessed in relation to the circumstances and the context of particular cases.

This chapter attempts to describe and explore the way in which imperatives to honesty and openness presented themselves and were responded to in one such set of circumstances in which I was invited to do three case studies of policing for a Home Office project on police training. I should stress that my own previous experience of case study research was all in the context of schools and classrooms (for example, Bridges, 1981 and 1983). In the context of researching policing I was a complete beginner, so this chapter is offered from the perspective not of a criminologist but of an educational researcher in the unfamiliar setting of policing.

The Nature of the Research

The Home Office project on police training, which represents a radically new approach to the initial training of police officers, is the responsibility of a team based at the Centre for Applied Research in Education at the University of East Anglia. An initial and highly critical review of police training was conducted under the direction of Professor Barry MacDonald for the Home Office and in response to, among other things, the Scarman Report. Out of the review arose the curriculum development project directed by Professor John Elliott and with a team which included educational researchers as well as seconded police officers. The curriculum development project required, among other things, a range of case studies of some of the most common forms of ordinary policing as a resource for new teaching and learning strategies.

The studies which I was asked to produce were: (i) of the work of two police officers on night duty in an area patrol car and focusing on a road traffic accident which involved a drink and driving offence; (ii) of a police officer's handling of a case of shoplifting; and (iii) most routinely, of traffic stops involving minor road traffic offences.

The case studies were intended to provide not an evaluation of the policing but a resource which police officers in initial training could use the better to understand the business of policing. As such they were intended to present as far as possible honest and realistic accounts of day to day policing rather than the carefully rehearsed models of an idealized procedure which were currently employed in police training. Senior police officers did of course tend to pick out what they regarded as pretty sound officers to participate in the studies where they had the option — though events tended quickly to defy careful control. The officers directly involved sometimes joked about being on their best behaviour, but they also frequently pointed out ways in which in practice their procedures departed from 'what they will teach you at college'. The case studies all contained examples of practice which fell short of or offended against text book expectations. The merits and demerits of putting such examples before new recruits in training was the subject of interesting debate between the project team and officers attached to traditional training methods.

Along with this first demand for *a reasonable measure of normality or realism* in the case studies were four others which will have a ring of familiarity to those involved with illuminative research in educational settings.

The second requirement was that a particular element of policing should be *well contextualized* by reference to, for example, local policing policy, the local community setting, current public concerns and the kind of parade-room briefing that had set the tone and priorities for the day. The thesis of the curriculum developers was that to understand what police officers actually do one must understand the context in which their actions and decisions are taken.

A third requirement was for a *multiplicity of perspectives*. The case studies were intended to portray the variety of perspectives upon a particular episode to be found among, for example, arrested persons, witnesses and senior station officers as well as the beat officers most directly involved. An important part of the pedagogy to be employed in conjunction with the case studies would be to explore with officers the different ways in which the same events might be seen by people standing in different relations to them.

The fourth requirement of the studies was that they would wherever appropriate *document the decision making*, discretion and judgment that police officers were called upon to exercise in their work. They had often been taught routines and routine procedures in their training and they sometimes used them. But in practice police officers are called upon to exercise considerable discretion and judgment of which they are themselves only partly aware. We sought quite deliberately, by questioning and by asking officers to describe and explain what they were doing and why, to document this 'intelligent' dimension of policing.

A fifth requirement of the case studies was that in their final form they should *include cross references to relevant regulations, laws and procedures* with which officers handling the kind of episode studied would need to be familiar. Some of these the researchers collected as they went along; others would be added subsequently by officers on the curriculum development team.

The kind of case study indicated here invited a research approach based upon participant observation and interviews. In each case I was attached to an officer or officers for a period of time (three or five days) and I accompanied them about their routine business. All of them worked under the same police authority and in the same town so it was possible to get to know senior police officers and the local setting reasonably well. The studies did not however set out to describe all that the relevant officers did over the period in which I accompanied them but focused on key exemplars of the aspect of policing we were concerned to illustrate. Interviews with those party to the chosen episodes were recorded and transcribed and selections from the transcriptions included in the final study. In the case of the routine traffic stops we also used a video camera. This was helpful in being able to show the kind of vehicle faults to which officers were drawing people's attention and was, we felt, not too intimidating in the context of minor and low key offences. We chose not to use a video for a drink and driving offence (it would have been technically difficult at night anyway) or in connection with the shoplifting, where we felt it would simply be too obtrusive.

Apart from the notes taken from participant observation, the interview data and the video recording, the case studies were based upon and included selections from relevant documents (each case involved masses of form filling) background reports and the odd poster relating to the drink and driving campaign in progress at the time. In the drink and driving case I also took photographs at the scene of the accident.

The products of this research were low on analysis and high on data. They represented as much as anything a kind of montage of the data collected in the ways described above. The studies were intended to act as a resource to support a variety of pedagogic styles but especially group discussion and role play activity. From this point of view the selection and editing of materials was governed by the five principles previously referred to plus a conscious attempt to leave a significant measure of interpretation and evaluation in the hands of future students. In this sense the product more closely resembled a case record than a case study. ·

This then is an outline of both the aspirations and the eventual outcomes of the research and the context of the technical and ethical problems which we had to address.

Some Ethical Principles

The kind of study I was engaged on called for honesty and openness on behalf of those who were giving account of their own situation and responses. How else could we secure 'realism', 'multiple perspectives' or any understanding of the kind of decision making which lay behind practice? But how do you create the conditions in which honesty and openness may flourish? As MacDonald (1982) puts it:

> Creating the conditions in which the interviewee says what he means, means what he says, says what he thinks and thinks about what he says, are the major tasks of the interviewer.

The answer is partly technical. You can for example provide a physical or social setting in which people will be free from interruption, secure from eavesdroppers or simply physically comfortable. You can avoid using an over-intrusive tape-recorder. You can adopt an interviewing approach which will allow or encourage your interviewee to explore questions rather than to answer in monosyllables. You can offer procedural conditions, for example, anonymity or control over the release of data, which will reduce initial self-censorship even if it is at the cost of some later limitation on what is published. (*cf.* discussion of interviewing styles in Powney and Watts, 1987 — especially perhaps Ebbutt's contribution.)

But honesty and openness in any relationship are supported by and demand reciprocal obligations. As Simons (1977) argues, 'In case study research the inter-personal dimension is an integral part of the research ... Trust is the basis for the exchange of information.' In particular, I propose:

(i) if the researcher is inviting the subject to enter into a relationship which is honest and open the researcher owes his or her subject too a similar level of honesty and openness;

(ii) if the researcher is encouraging honesty and openness of a kind which exposes the subject to risk of hurt or injury then the researcher has some obligation to protect the subject from that hurt or injury.

In offering these principles I have asserted what is undoubtedly open to debate. There may be circumstances in which, for example, the perceived corruptness or oppressiveness of the research subject or the unequal power relationship between subject and researcher disallows the relationship described here or justifies a different, a more antagonistic or subversive approach. But as MacDonald and Norris (1981) argue, this kind of 'partisan' evaluation offers an attack on the realities of power which may be honourable but is also likely to be short-lived. 'The partisan will find the gates of the power-house of policy generation firmly closed to his definitionally hostile enquiry . . . it is difficult to change what we have no opportunity to understand.'

I was not in any case seeking in this context to change policing — unless very indirectly by contributing to the development of a more intelligent form of training. Nor was I to experience any closed doors except those temporarily closed to me by the security officer of a national supermarket chain. In these circumstances I was given little reason to abandon the two principles which I have proposed. The honesty and openness of the research appeared to be compatible with what Simons (1987) refers to as 'a respect for the legitimacy of authorized activities.'

Applying these Principles in Researching Policing

In practice I felt that I was received with less suspicion and more openness in police stations than I would have been had I been making a similar approach to a school — and this came as something of a surprise to me. Indeed if this comparison is more widely supported it should perhaps be a source of concern to schools — it adds a further dimension of meaning to Holt's (1969) description of school as 'a dishonest as well as a nervous place'.

There are a number of possible explanations for this contrast. Certainly I was introduced to the local force chief superintendent by one of his old friends and colleagues who gave me a personal stamp of approval sealed immediately over several rounds of drinks. The chief superintendent too seemed to have a remarkable capacity to require or command not merely surface cooperation but a ready sense of collegiality between his officers and myself. My work was in any case intended for an in-house readership of police officers, and experienced officers welcomed the intention to describe policing 'as it really is' to officers in training.

Perhaps it is significant that the fact of fallibility and the arrangements for dealing with it among police officers are professionally institutionalized. (In this respect they are unlike teachers.) In a short period in one station an officer was arrested for drink and driving by colleagues; another was pulled off patrol car duty because he had twice damaged the car in chases; the station was subject to outside investigation because some money appeared not properly to be accounted for; and an officer was under review because three complaints had been laid against him for roughness with prisoners. My own judgment is that this group of officers was at least as decent, caring and responsible as an average school staff. They simply worked in an environment which lived in constant alertness to their every failing, which provided every opportunity for those failings to be formally scrutinized and in which the human fallibility of police officers as well as their clients was very visible. Somehow, and perhaps surprisingly, this seems to be compatible with an atmosphere remarkable for both its openness and its collegiality.

Whatever the explanation, I found police officers positively eager to volunteer opinions, anecdotes and experiences and to talk with almost disingenuous frankness about their work. In these circumstances I felt more strongly the moral obligations I owed to them than the need to probe ruthlessly behind any curtain of concealment.

However the task presented or threatened other complications to a researcher seeking both to establish a reciprocal commitment to honesty and openness and to protect his subjects from hurtful consequences of that commitment. Some of these loomed larger as hypothetical possibilities than they did in my actual, though I have again to emphasize limited, experience.

The Researcher as Mole

All the written documents to be found in a police station are covered by the 1911 and 1920 Official Secrets Acts and researchers working on this Home Office project are deemed to be 'non-civil servants . . . given access to government information' for the purpose of this research. We automatically became subject to the conditions of the Act [see Appendix A to this chapter] and had to sign a declaration to the effect that we understood this. In practice this did not significantly inhibit my research viewed as a product for a client (the Home Office). It added a special force to what might have been a more freely negotiated contract over control or ownership of the final product. The obligations imposed by the Act reinforced what might in any case have been a reasonable professional constraint upon the researcher not to gossip carelessly about or to leak irresponsibly information which he or she came by in the course of the research. At the time following the bombing of Libya by United States planes for example, many police stations would have contained information about security precautions to which anyone moving freely within the station might have access. The legal obligation of secrecy in respect of such matters was not without significance.

The scope of the Official Secrets Act was however sufficiently comprehensive to place considerable inhibitions on the way I could talk about my work outside the police community. The case studies will not be available for scrutiny by the wider research community — and this must indeed undermine their claim even to be research. Even in writing this chapter I have felt a need to be cautious about the specificity of the examples I have given.

But then, there are an increasing number of contexts in which part of the contract for research and evaluation work gives the body commissioning the research the right of control over, including the right to prohibit, its publication. As Simons (1980) has pointed out, 'there is a growing trend in this country for evaluations to be subject to restrictive contractual controls.' In a context in which they were already fighting massive political battles with elements of the police establishment the project team saw the inhibition provided by the Official Secrets Act as unobstructive to their central pedagogic purposes, helpful in providing some reassurance to senior officers and in any case inescapable without a change in the law which applies with equal force whether or not one actually signs the Act.

The Researcher as Witness

The researcher was deliberately seeking to be with a police officer at the scene of an accident or crime as soon as possible after it happened. He might even in the course of a patrol be a direct witness. Certainly he would expect to observe the scene and to be present when statements were made. He would be observing the police procedure directly — and indeed using a cassette-recorder to record as much of it as possible. Thus potentially the researcher was witness to: (i) significant circumstances of an accident or crime; and (ii) significant features of police procedure which could itself become the object of challenge in the courts or of complaint by an arrested person. Further, should either a person charged with an offence or the police decide to call the researcher as a witness in court, the researcher could not refuse without committing contempt of court, which is an imprisonable offence.

The features of the situation seemed to me to raise certain problems in relation to the ethical principles previously enunciated i.e. a reciprocal obligation of honesty and openness linked with the concern of the researcher not to do hurt or injury to his subjects. Prisoners could be lulled into false security by the knowledge that I was not a police officer and confide in me information which, were it brought out, would damage their interests. For example, one man arrested after colliding with a parked car confessed to me during an interview that this was in fact the second car he had hit that evening and that he had had 'a bellyful' — though in the event both pieces of information emerged through independent witnesses. Equally, however, if police officers failed in any detail of the very specific and detailed (and in January 1986 newly introduced) procedure they were to follow or exhibited any loss of self control in a tense situation, the arrested person could use my corroboration against the officer. I could not pretend in this situation that I was not there — nor did I have complete personal or professional discretion as to whether I would allow my privileged observation to be used against the interests of my subjects, whether they were police officers or the general public.

In practice we came to a number of procedural arrangements and understandings which gave me some reassurance in this situation — though in the event none of them were really tested.

(i) The Chief Superintendent of the station to which I was attached agreed that he would not call me as a witness in proceedings against any prisoner.

(ii) The Chief Superintendent took the view that his officers had to be accountable for their actions and that if they were 'daft enough to do anything stupid' while in my company they would have to take the consequences.

(iii) The project agreed on a code of conduct [see Appendix B to this chapter] which included the principle (item 20) that 'Where giving witness is discretionary on the part of the case study worker he/she will avoid giving evidence as a witness for either prosecution or defence.'

(iv) Any person who was to be given a formal police caution would in advance of that be asked formally whether he or she agreed to my presence and asked to sign accordingly [see Appendix C to this chapter]. This statement included the explicit reassurances that 'in the event of proceedings (the researcher) will not be called as a witness' and that 'any record made will not be available to the police'.

(v) My recordings were not in fact made in a way which would satisfy legal requirements for their use as evidence. In practice I deliberately broke those requirements (for example, by not using tape from a sealed packet, not showing the tape to defendants, etc.) to ensure their ineligibility.

Undoubtedly these safeguards left considerable practical gaps. We do not know how well they would stand up under pressure because, fortunately or unfortunately, they were not in the event put to the test of court action.

I also felt unconvinced that the conditions under which a member of the public was approached for permission for me to observe the proceedings — immediately after being arrested on a charge of shoplifting or within minutes of a midnight collision — were hardly conducive to cool and measured deliberation. It is perhaps revealing that all those who refused were involved in relatively minor traffic offences. However it is difficult to see the alternative — and in each case they had an opportunity towards the end of the proceedings and several hours after the crisis to change their minds.

Our own attempts to address the issue of the special status of the confidence between subject and researcher raise fundamental questions about the entitlement of *bona fide* researchers (*cf.* doctors, priests and journalists) to protect sources and evidence gathered in the course of their professional work from the demand of the courts that they should give public testimony. We did not ourselves of course secure any change in the legal position, but we did secure moral commitments from the law enforcers which gave the evidence which we gathered a certain protected status.

The Researcher as Police Officer

The final issue is only marginally to do with honesty and openness, but I experienced it partly in these terms. It was quite clear that while I wished to keep as close as possible as an observer to police officers' experience of their work, I was *not* a police officer, I should not attempt to do their work nor must I ever present myself as someone with police powers. Our eighth ground-rule read: 'In no circumstance will police authority be claimed or cited in approaching non-police personnel.'

In the event however it was not so easy to distance oneself from the role. When a police car is called to an incident in the middle of the night and three men get out, most members of the public imagine them to be three police officers — even if one of them is wearing a sports jacket. If you are standing in the road among a stack of battered cars at 11.30 pm on a wet Saturday you need a yellow reflecting jacket — even if you turn it inside out to conceal the word POLICE. If you are standing outside a house at 1.00 am with the burglar alarm ringing beside a shattered window (standing *still* so as not to create confusing trails for that rather excited Alsatian that has just arrived) you can hardly shut your eyes to avoid seeing an escaping burglar even if you thereby risk contaminating your study! Explaining that you are working for a Home Office project on police training hardly distinguishes you in most people's minds from the police force proper. And it is not necessarily the most urgent concern for officers arriving at the scene of an accident or crime to explain to the fearful and the distraught that one of their number is not really, as it were, one of their number.

This is of course not a new problem in participant observation. I introduce it here because it illustrates two other dimensions of the ethics of honesty and openness in case study research. First, that the version of the truth which we communicate is partly communicated for us by a situation or setting which may speak in terms other than those which we might choose — and we cannot always control this. Secondly, that the truth which we are able to tell is partly constrained by what our audience is able to hear or to understand.

Conclusion

All of this experience indicates that the bringing of case study research into conformity with declared ethical principles is unlikely to be a simple matter. It will continue to involve that same dialogue between simple moral principle and practical, living ambiguity and compromise as the rest of our lives.

The kind of interplay of moral and legal constraints on research which I have tried to describe here may appear unfamiliar to some researchers whose work has so far been restricted to the educational context. However there are many indications that we shall all very soon have to learn to handle both kinds of constraint. The view of educators as a professional community bound by academic and professional obligations was perhaps always something of a romantic ideal, but, such as it was, it is rapidly being replaced by a market structure in which the bonds are cash and contracts. In such a setting it seems likely that the force of civil and in some relevant respects (for example, libel) of criminal law will be brought much more closely to bear upon the educational researcher (see Simons, 1980), and another dimension of moral complexity will be added to an already complex area of principled behaviour.

Appendix A

Official Secrets Acts

Declaration **To be signed by members of Government Departments on appointment and, where desirable, by non-civil servants on first being given access to Government information.**

My attention has been drawn to the provisions of the Official Secrets Acts set out on the back of this document and I am fully aware of the serious consequences which may follow any breach of those provisions.

I understand that the sections of the Official Secrets Acts set out on the back of this document cover material published in a speech, lecture, or radio or television broadcast, or in the Press or in book form. I am aware that I should not divulge any information gained by me as a result of my appointment to any unauthorised person, either orally or in writing, without the previous official sanction in writing of the Department appointing me, to which written application should be made and two copies of the proposed publication to be forwarded. I understand also that I am liable to be prosecuted if I publish without official sanction any information I may acquire in the course of my tenure of an official appointment (unless it has already officially been made public) or retain without official sanction any sketch, plan, model, article, note or official documents which are no longer needed for my official duties, and that these provisions apply not only during the period of my appointment but also after my appointment has ceased. I also understand that I must surrender any documents, etc., referred to in section 2 (1) of the Act if I am transferred from one post to another, save such as have been issued to me for my personal retention.

Signed

Surname *(Block letters)*

Forename(s)

Date

E 74 (5-74-0)

Extracts from the Official Secrets Acts, 1911 and 1920

Section 2 of the Official Secrets Act, 1911, as amended by the Official Secrets Act, 1920, provides as follows:

"2   (1) If any person having in his possession or control any secret official code word, or pass word, or any sketch, plan, model, article, note, document, or information which relates to or is used in a prohibited place or anything in such a place, or which has been made or obtained in contravention of this Act, or which has been entrusted in confidence to him by any person holding office under Her Majesty, or which he has obtained or to which he has had access owing to his position as a person who holds or has held office under Her Majesty, or as a person who holds or has held a contract made on behalf of Her Majesty, or as a person who is or has been employed under a person who holds or has held such an office or contract, —

(a) communicates the code word, pass word, sketch, plan, model, article, note, document, or information to any person, other than a person to whom he is authorised to communicate it, or a person to whom it is in the interests of the State his duty to communicate it, or,

(aa) uses the information in his possession for the benefit of any foreign power or in any other manner prejudicial to the safety or interests of the State:

(b) retains the sketch, plan, model, article, note, or document in his possession or control when he has no right to retain it or when it is contrary to his duty to retain it or fails to comply with all directions issued by lawful authority with regard to the return or disposal thereof; or

(c) fails to take reasonable care of, or so conducts himself as to endanger the safety of the sketch, plan, model, article, note, document, secret official code or pass word or information:

that person shall be guilty of a misdemeanour.

(1A) If a person having in his possession or control any sketch, plan, model, article, note, document, or information which relates to munitions of war, communicates it directly or indirectly to any foreign power, or in any other manner prejudicial to the safety or interests of the State, that person shall be guilty of a misdemeanour.

(2) If any person receives any secret official code word, or pass word, or sketch, plan, model, article, note, document, or information,

knowing, or having reasonable ground to believe, at the time when he receives it, that the code word, pass word, sketch, plan, model, article, note, document or information is communicated to him in contravention of this Act, he shall be guilty of a misdemeanour, unless he proves that the communication to him of the code word, pass word, sketch, plan, model, article, note, document, or information was contrary to his desire."

Section 1 (2) of the Official Secrets Act, 1920, provides as follows:

"(2) if any person —

(a) retains for any purpose prejudicial to the safety or interests of the State any official document, whether or not completed or issued for use, when he has no right to retain it, or when it is contrary to his duty to retain it, or fails to comply with any directions issued by any Government Department or any person authorised by such department with regard to the return or disposal thereof: or

(b) allows any other person to have possession of any official document issued for his use alone, or communicate any secret official code word or pass word so issued, or, without lawful authority or excuse, has in his possession any official document or secret official code word or pass word issued for the use of some person other than himself, or on obtaining possession of any official document by finding or otherwise, neglects or fails to restore it to the person or authority by whom or for whose use it was issued, or to a police constable: or

(c) without lawful authority or excuse, manufacturers or sells, or has in his possession for sale any such die, seal or stamp as aforesaid

he shall be guilty of a misdemeanour."

(2523) 3 604896/834286 1/74 300 m NCS 821

Appendix B

Provisional Ground-rules for the Research and Production of Case Studies and Case Materials for Police Probationer Training

Preamble: The following ground-rules apply to work and workers whose involvement is entirely dependent on the authority of the Stage II Review Team. Where work conducted under different authorization will contribute to the Stage II case study programme some ground-rules will need to be modified on a case by case basis.

1 Case study foci will be selected and commissioned by the Stage II Review Team. (To ensure curriculum coverage.)

2 Case study workers will be commissioned by the Stage II Review Team. Only individuals so commissioned will be authorized to be engaged in the field research. Each such individual will bear a letter to this effect.

3 The Stage II Review Team will exercise exclusive control over publication and will have the right to edit, correct, destroy, use, etc. any materials submitted by case study workers. (To ensure coherence with the curricular principles.)

4 Case study workers will be required to sign a document which states that they understand the Official Secrets Act. (A standard requirement of personnel working on research contracted by the Home Office.)

5 Initial access to field sites will be negotiated by the Stage II Review Team. (To ensure the normal sampling considerations and to facilitate the gaining of access to field sites.)

6 Access to field sites will be sought for and restricted to the purpose of producing teaching and learning materials for police training, at the discretion of the Stage II Review Team. (To reassure actors against possible fears of 'covert' research.)

7 Police authorization will be sought as far as involvement with police personnel is concerned. (To adopt the standard procedure for research in a police setting.)

155

8   In no circumstance will police authority be claimed or cited in approaching non–police personnel. (To adopt the standard procedure for research outside the police.)

9   The basic principle governing the process and product of case study fieldwork is that of anonymity. In addition to the anonymization of persons, Forces, places, dates and times will be anonymized and will only be made known on a 'need to know' principle. (To protect persons both within the police and the community.)

10 Knowledge of the real location of field sites will be kept confidential between the Stage II Review Team and the individual case study worker. (See 9 above)

11 Given the promise of anonymity there will be no general commitment to providing feedback to actors in the field sites. Any selective feedback will be at the discretion of the case study worker.

12 In any situations where anonymity is not secure and where its breach would have serious repercussions for persons whose actions etc. feature in the study, but where the case study is valuable, the case will be negotiated to ensure its accuracy and fairness.

13 There will be no 'authorship' of case studies. Contributions will be acknowledged wherever it is appropriate but fieldworkers will not be identified in relation to the particular case studies they produce. (See 9 above)

14 Only information relevant to the case will be collected by case study workers. In the event that a change of focus becomes necessary this will be negotiated by the case study worker after consultation with the Stage II Review Team. (Prescribed foci may prove difficult to pursue – the events may not occur – but the need to maintain curricular coverage will require the Stage II Team's coordinating involvement.)

15 Case study workers will state at the outset of their fieldwork what their information needs are. Should changes need to be made in light of the fieldwork, these changes will be negotiated. (Since circumstances change during research studies, initial research designs must be seen as provisional.)

16 No confidential documents to which case study workers may be given ad hoc access will be copied without specific authorization.

17 If a case study worker is asked to withdraw from a scene by the relevant operational commander, case study workers will withdraw.

18 If a case study worker is asked to withdraw permanently from a particular case or its construction, the case study worker will withdraw and the case will be abandoned.

19 In the event of a request for the withdrawal of a case study worker from a case or its construction, the Stage II Review Team will have the obligation to decide whether to attempt to reopen the case through negotiation.

20 Where giving witness is discretionary on the part of the case study worker he/she will avoid giving evidence as a witness for either prosecution or defence.

21 All complaints against case study workers from whatever source will be investigated by the Stage II Review Team.

22 Once the teaching and learning materials have been created in finished form, the source files will be kept secure for two years to allow further improvement in the light of pilot use. At the end of two years the source files will be destroyed.

23 Copyright in the materials will be with the Home Office.

Appendix C

DEFENDANT'S NAME _____

I wish to talk to you about an alleged offence of _____

The person accompanying me is Dr David BRIDGES who has been engaged by the Home Office to gather information to assist in future police training. In the furtherance of this study it is necessary for him to observe how Police Officers work. He will take no part in the interview whatsoever and in the event of proceedings will not be called as a witness. Dr Bridges will need to take notes/record the conversation and any record made will not be available to the Police and will not be identified to you at any stage.

Under the conditions I have read to you are you willing for Dr Bridges to remain during the course of the interview?

Read to Defendant _____ Time

_____ Date

_____ Agreed

_____ Signed

Bibliography

ADELMAN, C. (Ed) (1984) *The Politics and Ethics of Evaluation,* London, Croom Helm.

BRIDGES, D. (1983) *Case Studies in School Accountability Vol. II: Robert Peel,* Cambridge, Cambridge Institute of Education.

BRIDGES, D. and EYNON, D. (1983) *Issues in School Centred In-service Education,* Cambridge, Cambridge Institute of Education.

EBBUTT, D. (1987) 'Interviewing groups of students' in POWNEY, J. and WATTS, M. (Eds) *Interviewing in Educational Research,* London, Routledge and Kegan Paul, pp. 100–5.

ELLIOTT, J. (1984) 'Methodology and ethics' in ADELMAN, C. (Ed) *The Politics and Ethics of Education,* Beckenham, Croom Helm, pp. 19–25.

HOLT, J. (1969) *How Children Fail,* Harmondsworth, Penguin.

MACDONALD, B. and NORRIS, N. (1982) 'Looking up for a change — political horizons in policy evaluation'. Norwich, Centre for Applied Research, University of East Anglia (Mimeo).

MACDONALD, B. and SANGER, J. (1982) 'Just for the record? Notes towards a theory of interviewing in evaluation'. Paper presented to American Educational Research Association Conference, New York (Mimeo).

NORRIS, N. (Ed) (1977) *SAFARI: Theory in Practice,* University of East Anglia, Centre for Applied Research.

POWNEY, J. and WATTS, M. (Eds) (1987) *Interviewing in Educational Research,* London, Routledge and Kegan Paul.

PRING, R. (1984) 'Confidentiality and the right to know', in ADELMAN, C. (Ed) *The Politics and Ethics of Education,* London, Croom Helm, pp. 8–18.

SIMONS, H. (1977) 'Building a social contract: Negotiation, participation and portrayal in condensed field research', in NORRIS, N. (Ed) *SAFARI: Theory in Practice,* University of East Anglia, CARE.

SIMONS, H. (1980) 'Negotiating conditions for independent evaluations'. Paper presented at the British Educational Research Associations Annual Conference in Cardiff — recently reissued in ADELMAN, C. (Ed) (1984) *The Politics and Ethics of Evaluation,* London, Croom Helm, pp. 56–68.

SIMONS, H. (1987) *Getting To Know Schools In A Democracy: The Politics and Process of Evaluation,* Lewes, Falmer Press.

8
What is Evaluation After the MSC?[1]

Jon Nixon

This chapter is an attempt to think through some of the problems and dilemmas I faced as the local evaluator of the Sheffield Technical and Vocational Education Initiative (TVEI)[2] scheme that commenced as a fourth-round project in September 1986. The 'Sheffield experience', as documented elsewhere (see Nixon, 1987), is wide and varied; TVEI in Sheffield represents only one strand of a complex programme of Authority-wide curriculum change that is highly distinctive. Nevertheless, the Sheffield TVEI scheme is, in certain respects, typical of the way in which the later TVEI schemes have developed nationally, and, as such, raises issues that are common to other regional schemes and indeed to the evaluation of categorical funding programmes generally. Those issues, for the purposes of this chapter, focus on the emphasis within the regional TVEI schemes on the *formative* aspects of local evaluation; an emphasis which, given the political context within which local evaluators are obliged to operate, is highly problematic.

TVEI in Context

The role of curriculum evaluation is currently being modified by a number of contextual factors, not least of which is the increasingly centralized control of the education service. This control — consolidated through the imposition of a 'national curriculum' — has for some time been exerted through categorical funding programmes that specify priority areas, impose a strict system of accountability, and have government approval if not backing. Chief among such programmes is the TVEI, which was first announced in the House of Commons on 12 November 1982, and has subsequently been funded through the Manpower Services Commission (MSC).

There is now considerable variety of aims and approaches among the many regional TVEI schemes. As yet no definitive categorization of these schemes has emerged, although Murray Saunders has made a useful start in distinguishing between a 'weak version of TVEI', whereby its effects are 'confined and absorbed by existing school practices' and 'strong interpretation of TVEI', whereby an attempt is made 'to revamp the whole curricular map of the 14–18 age range'. The former, he argues, is characterized by 'accommodation', the latter by 'adaptive extension' (Saunders, 1986, pp. 5–6).

It would seem that, as TVEI has developed, the 'strong interpretation' model has gained dominance. Moreover the national extension of TVEI, announced in the White Paper, *Working Together — Education and Training* (DES, 1986), seems likely to tilt the balance still further in this direction; £900 million injected into the education service over the next ten years cannot fail to have a considerable impact nationally on the whole 14–18 curriculum. Increasingly, therefore, TVEI is becoming associated with curriculum structures, such as modularization, which facilitate cross-curriculum planning, and with styles of teaching which highlight the practical application of learning rather than its discrete subject domains.

A major component of the developing TVEI scenario is what Hopkins has referred to as a 'plethora of enquiry'. The DES and HMI, most funding agencies, many independent research workers, as well as university and college departments are involved in the evaluation of TVEI. The MSC, moreover, also mounted its own complex programme of evaluation, including demographic and financial data bases, the national evaluations carried out by the NFER and the University of Leeds, individual contracts with independent researchers to investigate specific aspects of TVEI, and the local evaluations of each project. The latter, to which a minimum of 1 per cent of each regional scheme's annual budget was devoted, constituted (according to Hopkins) the most significant strand in the complex pattern of research and evaluation currently being woven around TVEI (Hopkins, 1985, p. 1).

The local evaluations varied considerably across the regions. At one end of the continuum was the single seconded teacher with little or no experience of evaluation and, at the other, the arguably more experienced university-based evaluator for whom the local evaluation of TVEI was only one of several research commitments. Between these extremes were to be found advisers, advisory teachers and higher degree students, all fulfilling the role of evaluator. Within some regions, such as Sheffield, the local evaluation included a combination of several of these elements. Add to these varied arrangements the almost complete lack of any coordination between local evaluators in different regions, and a picture begins to emerge of isolated pockets of research activity within which each evaluator was obliged to negotiate her or his working brief with the LEA concerned.

Given the varied pattern of local evaluation nationally, it is at first glance surprising that across the many local evaluations a common methodological concern can be clearly discerned. The Sheffield scheme was not alone in having a local evaluation brief which justified its expenditure in terms of continuing feedback to the project managers regarding the progress of the project. Indeed, central to almost all the local evaluations of TVEI is a stress on the formative aspects of evaluation: its potential for informing decision-making and for conceptualizing the development of the project in action.

Viewed historically this emphasis within the regions on formative evaluation might be seen as a natural progression from the distinct style of evaluation developed within Britain throughout the late 1960s and 1970s. A key characteristic of that style was its focus on the *process* of curriculum development and the changing *perceptions* of those teachers responsible for such development. Whether approached through the 'insider' movement of teacher research (see May 1981) or by way of the ethnographic tradition of 'outsider' research (see Burgess, 1985), this style of evaluation has been of lasting significance and its legacy is clearly discernible within TVEI local evaluation projects.

From a more practical perspective, the emphasis on formative evaluation can be viewed as a response to the changing pattern of curriculum development within TVEI. The increasing dominance of what Saunders (1986) referred to as the 'adaptive extension' model of TVEI has, in the more recent schemes, resulted in the permeation of TVEI philosophy and practices both across the curriculum and beyond a discrete cohort of students. Thus, the notion of TVEI as a carefully 'controlled' experiment has—at least among those responsible for implementing it—given way to a more developmental perspective which allows for the wide-ranging and varied impact of the schemes nationally. Viewed from this perspective evaluation is seen as having an important part to play in shaping the innovation as it develops.

This shift towards the 'adaptive extension' model should not, however, be viewed simply as an unproblematic progression. It is also, in part, a political adaptation, designed to ensure the full commitment of participating LEA's. For, as Fulton (1986) has observed.

> financial mechanisms needed to be supplanted by political sensitivity and a determined effort to encourage local authorities

to volunteer, by buying off some of the critics and giving them a chance to use TVEI to achieve their own ambitions for innovation (p. 8).

The implications of this perspective for those involved in the regional TVEI schemes are far-reaching and require a serious reconsideration of the nature and purpose of formative evaluation.

Formative Evaluation Reconsidered

In 1967 Michael Scriven drew his now classic distinction between summative and formative evaluation. In retrospect that distinction can be seen to represent something of a watershed, though it is by no means as simple and straightforward as popular usage would sometimes seem to suggest. Primarily, it served as a pointer to an emergent redefinition of the role of evaluation and the interests served by those who are involved in this process.

The distinction rested as much upon differing views of curriculum as upon conflicting notions of evaluation. Summative evaluation, as conceived by Scriven, is underpinned by the idea of a curriculum as a programme designed and implemented to meet certain prespecified goals: the role of evaluation in this context was to assess the extent to which those goals had been achieved. Formative evaluation, on the other hand, arose as a response to a more general urge within curriculum studies to look critically at the kinds of educational goals being set and at their function within curriculum development. Thus, in part, Scriven wanted to reclaim for evaluation the authority to question the value—or 'worthwhileness'—of these goals, rather than just to accept them as taken-for-granted yardsticks.

He wanted also, however, to draw attention to the *unintended* outcomes of curriculum programmes and saw evaluation as having a key role to play in this respect; through, for example, a process of progressive focusing on emergent goals and changing emphases within the programme. Thus, while the notion of formative evaluation implies regular though intermittent feedback, its stress intially was as much on the focus of the inquiry as on styles and frequency of reporting.

The 'new wave' evaluators who followed Scriven were to a large extent exploring the implications of this stance. 'Illuminative' (Parlett and Hamilton, 1977), 'holistic' (Macdonald, 1971) and 'responsive' (Stake,

1972) evaluation were three clearly articulated approaches which pushed forward the frontiers of thinking in this area. Though less judgmental and with a greater stress on audience, the advocates of these closely related approaches shared with Scriven a common purpose. They saw the role of evaluation as being to problematize process; to question the assumptions which underpin the curriculum in action, rather than to view it as an unproblematic expression of its own stated aims. Theirs was a reasoned refusal to take at face value the rhetorics that justify and seek to explain curriculum practice.

An interesting parallel to this shift in emphasis can be found in the field of literary criticism, where the notion of 'intentionalist fallacy' paved the way for a spate of theorizing whereby the text was no longer conceived as a direct expression of authorial intent, but as the product of a grid of socially constructed codes and conventions. The text, in other words, could no more be judged solely as a product of the author's meaning, than the curriculum could be judged solely in terms of the curriculum planners' stated objectives. The evaluator, like the interpreter of a text, was obliged to recognize unintended meanings as well as acknowledge consciously implied intentions.

This perspective, which informed the development of evaluation throughout the 1970s, is in certain crucial respects singularly inappropriate to TVEI, where outcomes are not only prespecified, but where that prespecification is reified into a formal contract between the LEA and the MSC. Under the terms of the funding agreement, an LEA is contractually bound to 'deliver' the curriculum package as specified in its TVEI submission. The critical reflective function that formative evaluation might otherwise be expected to fulfil is, therefore, seriously limited; it can help tease out the practical implications of the original statement of intent, but is rarely expected to question its basic assumptions.

Two examples may help to clarify the argument at this point. The first can be found in the emphasis within the Sheffield TVEI submission on course development through the modularization of the whole curriculum. As the scheme has moved into its implementation phase, the weaknesses of this strategy have become increasingly apparent: its stress on *course* development at the expense of *staff* development; its emphasis on curriculum *structures* at the expense of classroom *practice*; its imposition *across* schools of a *single* schedule of GCSE mode 3 course submission and validation. The important point here is not that a regional scheme requires modification and revision (which scheme wouldn't?), but that, given the contractual agreement between Sheffield LEA and the MSC to 'deliver' a modularized curriculum, any attempt to question seriously the fundamental assumptions underlying modularization would be fraught with difficulties.

The second example relates to the more general emphasis within TVEI on the supposed self-evident benefits to be derived from off-site learning experiences, such as residential and work experience placements. The largely unexplored assumption is that students will necessarily receive a more 'relevant' education, if the environment of learning is extended to include off-site experience of this kind. While this assumption may be justified, it remains to a large extent unquestioned given the premium that is placed upon it within a wide range of regional TVEI submissions. Again, any attempt to challenge that assumption is likely to be either met with incomprehension or viewed as crudely obstructionist.

Thus, although the latter TVEI schemes have adopted a more ambitious, and arguably more sophisticated, approach to curriculum development the bureaucratic framework by means of which the revised curriculum is to be 'delivered' remains largely unchanged. This means that the role of local evaluators within TVEI is highly problematic. Either they adopt a weak interpretation of the notion of formative evaluation, and thereby risk becoming the mere tools of management conveniently bracketing any serious exploration of the values implicit in the schemes they are evaluating; or they hold out for a strong interpretation and, at best, find some elbow room within their cramped surroundings for limited forays into the field of critical reflection.

The Role of the Local Evaluator

Before considering some of the ways in which evaluation is being redefined in order to resolve this dilemma, it may be worth exploring in a little more detail how the contradictions inherent in the evaluator's role manifest themselves 'in the field'. The definition of that role is, in practice, far from straightforward and in certain crucial respects is highly contested. Given the politically sensitive cross-institutional contexts within which evaluators operate, they are likely to raise different sets of expectations in different situations and among different groups of participants. This may lead to some confusion—or even sense of betrayal—among these various groupings. Under these circumstances, there is a temptation for evaluators to try to simplify their role by identifying uncritically with the espoused values and viewpoint of a particular faction.

Moreover, the participants themselves become adept at setting up blocks against the evaluator adopting a more critical and distanced stance. A common ploy, for example, is to ensure that the evaluator is privy to information which, because of its confidentiality, cannot be divulged. The evaluator's developing insights and analyses are thus constructed around evidence which is ethically inadmissible. In a situation such as this evaluators can disclose very little, precisely because they have so much to tell. It is the very richness of their data which renders it invisible.

Clearly, this is a common problem for any evaluator who relies heavily on interview data and fieldnotes. It is, however, a particularly acute problem in the local evaluation of TVEI, where the evaluator is obliged to develop a close working relationship with participants in a wide variety of formal and informal settings. As the social interactions between the participants and the evaluator become more varied and complex, the problem becomes increasingly pressing. It is exacerbated, moreover, by the fact that, in the role of confidante, local evaluators may feel themselves to be fulfilling a genuinely useful function in providing a safety valve for tensions and resentments within the project. They may also derive considerable satisfaction from servicing the project in this way. That sense of satisfaction is achieved, however, at considerable cost to their critical and independent judgment.

Earlier attempts to resolve this and related problems have relied heavily on a legal–rationalist approach, which attempted to make explicit the kinds of ethical procedures an evaluator might adopt in aspiring to operate according to democratic principles. These principles were first explored in practice in the Success and Failure and Recent Innovations (SAFARI) project, which began in 1973 under the direction of Barry McDonald. As a case study worker attached to that project, Helen Simons developed a set of ethical procedures which stemmed from the notion of 'participant control'. The key principles which underpinned these procedures she defined as 'negotiation', 'confidentiality' and 'impartiality' (Simons, 1977, 1978 and 1981).

Such an approach, it should be noted, assumes a degree of moral consensus which in no way characterizes the ideologically divided context within which TVEI is currently being implemented and evaluated at the local level. Indeed, the principles cited by Simons now seem less like the resolution to an ethical problem, and more like a restatement in ethical terms of a problem which, increasingly, is political in its import and implications.

The political nature of that problem is apparent in the increasing demand within TVEI for hard evidence regarding the progress and impact of specific schemes. In what has since become a seminal paper, Simons

(1977) has defined negotiation as 'a two-way process' involving the evaluator in 'discussing with participants throughout the study whether or not they will allow their data to become public' (p. 28). This process is clearly time-consuming and time is in short supply for evaluators committed to the rapid turnabout of data that the term 'formative' has come to imply. The problem is particularly pressing in the later schemes, where LEAs are anxious to present evidence of the early impact of their projects in order to back-up their bids for 'national extension' money (see DES, 1986). There is, therefore, considerable tension between the kinds of procedures advocated by Simons and the time-scale within which local TVEI evaluators are constrained to operate.

The problem cannot, however, be reduced simply to one of time management. It is essentially a political problem in that it involves a consideration of the power relations pertaining between the various stake-holders in the local evaluation. The premium placed on negotiation as a 'two-way process' can all too easily serve to mask the complexity of these relations, whereby the project is accountable to the LEA which is in turn accountable to the MSC. Invariably the pressure for hard evidence comes from above, often before there is any discernible impact at the classroom level. The evaluation thus becomes a key site on which the tensions between the various institutional groupings are played out.

Clearly stated procedures regarding the release of evaluation reports can only go so far towards easing these tensions. Such procedures vary from project to project. However, the procedure adopted in Sheffield is that all local evaluation reports are released to the Chief Education Officer (CEO) through the Project Director. In effect this means that each report is negotiated with the project management team prior to being formally released to the CEO. The further release of the report to the MSC is, therefore, by implication the responsibility of the LEA, though the evaluator in writing the report is well aware that there is an obligation on the LEA to make the report available to the funding body. Thus, the procedures, while to some extent safeguarding the interests of the project and the LEA, can at best ameliorate the effects of operating within a hierarchical and heavily centralized bureaucratic framework.

Partial Resolutions

Stated in these terms the argument places considerable emphasis on the determinist aspects of TVEI. It should be stressed, however, that in practice few of the more mechanistic assumptions of TVEI go unchallenged. In particular, within the local evaluations of the various regional schemes, there are two significant points of emphasis which ill-accord with the centrally controlled framework within which TVEI operates.

The first of these is the stress within the local evaluations on the change process itself. Traditionally, within the formative evaluation of education programmes there has been a serious lack of attention to what Fullan (1982) has referred to as 'the "black box" of implementation':

> Testing data provide information on the achievement of desired educational objectives. Implementation involves questions of which *instructional activities* would best address objectives. Unfortunately, much of the conflict and debate in education focuses on objectives and outcomes without attending to the critical intervening activities (i.e. instruction and learning activities) which link them together (p. 248).

Within the local evaluation of TVEI, however, there has been a clear emphasis on *processes* as well as *outcomes*. The focus, in other words, has been less on variables such as student outcomes or attitudes and more on the elements of the change process itself; on, that is, the use of new materials, new teaching styles, new learning experiences, and on the values implicit in these new practices. Change has, increasingly, been conceived, not as a linear progression, but as a complex and multidimensional process involving shifts in perception and belief as well as alterations in structure and design.

The second point of emphasis relates to the increased participation by teachers on the evaluation of the change process (see Nixon, 1986). Given the focus on implementation, teachers clearly have a vital role to play in the local evaluation of the TVEI schemes. For it is they who have access to the relevant data; they who are responsible for the implementation of the programme at the classroom level; and they, finally, whose changing perceptions are a key factor determining the effectiveness of the curriculum programme being undertaken.

It would be a mistake, however, to think of the need for change only in terms of what *teachers* do and think. Equally important is what those around them — within the institutional contexts of school, LEA and MSC — do. In this respect there is a considerable onus of responsibility on senior management teams in schools, LEA advisory services and MSC regional TVEI advisers to support the idea that formative evaluation should be concerned primarily with understanding the change process rather than measuring outcomes and attitudes. The currently fashionable recourse to the notion of formative evaluation can in fact serve to mask some serious differences among the various interested parties regarding the nature and purpose of the evaluation task at the local level.

In practice the notion of formative evaluation remains unproblematic until such time as evidence of effective implementation is deemed to be required. At that point, the focus of the evaluation – process or outcome? the experience of learning or the formulation of quantifiable results? – becomes an issue. Clearly, those reponsible for drawing up and agreeing the evaluation brief have a responsibility here to define what they mean by formative evaluation, but equally those anxious for evidence ought to resist the temptation to redefine that slippery term to suit their own ends. Evaluators who see their task as being, in part at least, to gain access to that '"black box" of implementation' cannot be expected to switch focus and provide immediate data on outcomes.

The resource implications of the kind of formative evaluation being attempted at the local level also require clear recognition both by the funding agency and by the LEAs who administer the funds. If, as is the case in the more recent TVEI schemes, teachers are to be given a more central role in the evaluation process, the funding levels need to be higher than is usually the case at the moment. Similarly, the time-scale ought to be rethought, so as to allow teachers ample opportunity to reflect systematically on their own and their colleagues' practice. The emphasis within TVEI on the 'delivery' of change, makes it difficult for practitioners to 'own' it at the conceptual level. Yet, it is precisely that ideal of the common 'ownership' of change to which many local evaluations aspire.

Many of the procedural problems associated with the local evaluation of TVEI are, as we have seen, a direct result of the complex political context within which the local schemes have to operate. While the notion of formative evaluation has been adopted as a relatively unthreatening response at the local level to the increased call for accountability, it can be seen, in the long-term, merely to heighten the key ethical problem with which local evaluators have to live. Contracted, as they are, to facilitate the development of increasingly complex programmes of work which require constant modification and adaptation, they are nevertheless operating within a bureaucratic framework whose implicit model of change remains crudely mechanistic. The problem is not just that the notion of formative evaluation is being marginalized, but that it is being changed fundamentally. In spite of the increased emphasis on teacher participation and on the processes of learning and teaching, evaluation, under MSC funding, has run the very real risk of becoming the mere tool of management.

Jon Nixon

Thus, although the current emphasis on the formative aspects of local evaluation is generally taken as a mark of TVEI's increasing progressivism, it should be treated with some considerable scepticism. In particular local evaluators need to make clear at the outset the values that—for them—are implicit in, and inform, this particular evaluation stance. Insofar as these entail a commitment to genuinely democratic and participatory principles, the extent to which such a stance is appropriate to TVEI might then be seriously, and openly, questioned.

Notes

1 Since this paper was written the Manpower Services Commission has changed its name several times and is now known as the Training Agency.
2 The term TVEI should, throughout this chapter, be understood to refer to the Pilot scheme. At the time of writing the Extension had only just been announced.
3 A version of this chapter appears in the *British Journal of Education Studies*, **37**, 2, 1989.

References

ADELMAN, C. (1981) *Uttering, Muttering*, London, Grant McIntyre.
BURGESS, R. G. (Ed) (1985) *Field Methods in the Study of Education*, Lewes, Falmer Press.
DEPARTMENT OF EDUCATION AND SCIENCE (1986) *Working Together—Education and Training*, (White Paper), London, HMSO.
FIDDY, R. and STRONACH, I. (Eds) *TVEI Working Papers*, CARE, University of East Anglia.
FULLAN, M. (1982) *The Meaning of Educational Change*, Ontario, OISE Press/The Ontario Institute of Studies in Education.
FULTON, O. (1986) 'Bonjour tristesse?' Paper presented to The British Educational Management and Administration Society (BEMAS), University of Birmingham, 24–25 April.
HAMILTON, D. *et al* (Eds) (1977) *Beyond the Numbers Game*, London, Macmillan Education.
HOPKINS, D. (1985) 'Evaluating TVEI: Some methodological issues', in HOPKINS, D. (Ed) *Evaluating TVEI*, Cambridge, Cambridge Institute of Education.
MAY, N. (1981) 'The Teacher as researcher movement in Britain'. Paper delivered at the annual meeting of the American Educational Research Association, Los Angeles, April, in SCHUBERT, W. and SCHUBERT, A. (Eds) (1982) *Conceptions of Curriculum Knowledge: Focus on Students and Teachers*, College of Education, Pennsylvania State University pp. 23–30.

MacDonald, B. (1971) 'The evaluation of the Humanities Curriculum Project: A holistic approach'. Paper delivered at the annual meeting of the American Educational Research Association, New York.

Nixon, J. (1986) 'Feeling the change: Thoughts on the evaluation task for Sheffield', *Sheffield Educational Research, Current Highlights*, (SERCH), **8** pp. 1–4.

Nixon, J. (Ed) (1987) *Curriculum Change; The Sheffield Experience*, USDE Papers in Education, Division of Education, University of Sheffield.

Norris, N. (Ed) (1977) *SAFARI 2: Theory in Practice*, CARE, Occasional Publications No. 4, University of East Anglia.

Parlett, M. and Hamilton, D. (1977) 'Evaluation as illumination: A new approach to the study of innovatory programmes', in Hamilton, D. *et al* (Eds), *Beyond the Numbers Game*, London, Macmillan Education, pp. 6–22.

Saunders, M. (1986) 'The innovation enclave: Unintended effects of TVEI implementation', in Fiddy, R. and Stronach, I. (Eds) *TVEI Working Papers* CARE, University of East Anglia, Norwich, pp. 1–10.

Schubert, W. and Schubert, A. (Eds) (1982) *Conceptions of Curriculum Knowledge: Focus on Students and Teachers*, College of Education, Pennsylvania State University.

Simons, H. (1977) 'Building a social contract: Negotiation and participation in condensed field research', in Norris, N. (Ed) *SAFARI 2: Theory in Practice*, CARE, Occasional Publications No. 4, Norwich, Centre for Applied Research in Education, University of East Anglia, pp. 24–46.

Simons, H. (1978) 'School-based evaluation on democratic principles', *Classroom Action Research Network Bulletin*, 2, Cambridge, Cambridge Institute of Education, pp. 11–17.

Simons, H. (1981) 'Conversation piece: The practice of interviewing in case study research', in Adelman, C. (Ed) *Uttering, Muttering*, London, Grant McIntyre, pp. 27–50.

Stake, R. (1972) 'Responsive evaluation'. Mimeographed Urbana–Champaign, Centre for Instructional Research and Curriculum Evaluation, University of Illinois.

9
Ethics and Politics in the Study of Assessment

Harry Torrance

Introduction

Within education assessment practices and their consequences have been a crucially important and contentious area for many years. Their importance is even more manifest now as the current government attempts to engage in a massive programme of curricular and pedagogic change through the control of assessment and certification procedures. Given that the potentially negative educational consequences of assessment have long been identified, for example the narrowing 'backwash' effect of the 11 + on the primary school curriculum highlighted almost as soon as the 11 + was instigated after the Second World War, and given that sociologists such as Michael Young began asking questions about the determination of examination syllabuses and methods almost twenty years ago (Young, 1971), it is strangely paradoxical that such a vitally important field of inquiry remains largely unexplored. This is not to suggest that assessment and examinations research has not taken place, it has, and indeed for perhaps thirty years from the 1920s to the 1950s research on assessment was virtually synonymous with educational research, boosted as it was by the developing administrative imperative of selecting children for grammar school. But this research took place in the context of a concern to identify and measure individual differences and its substance and methodology were primarily technical rather than educational. Assessment was taken as both a topic of enquiry and a research tool with investigations centring on the validity and reliability of a particular test or tests. Even work which questioned the consequences of testing (for example, Floud and Halsey, 1957; Yates and Pidgeon 1957) largely took the methods for granted.

More recently authors such as Broadfoot (1979, 1984) and Whitty (1985) have delineated a broader range of concerns but an interest in technique and technology continues to dominate research into assessment. In considerable degree this is due to most research into assessment being undertaken by examination boards and thus still being concerned with monitoring the validity and reliability of examinations, rather than investigating their social role or impact on teaching. That is, research on assessment can in large part be construed as in-house quality control and market analysis by commercial organizations. Of course, monitoring the validity and reliability of examinations is neither an easy nor an unimportant task (*cf.* Torrance, 1986a) and one can accept that the examination boards are working in good faith to protect the interests of candidates, the fairness of examinations. Yet fairness clearly depends on much more than technical appraisals such as analyzing the spread of marks across particular questions.

In such a situation it is perhaps not surprising that the ethics and politics of assessment, and of the study of assessment, rarely get an airing. Given this context this chapter will attempt to review a range of ethical issues in the study of assessment and not simply restrict itself to the particular problems of conducting fieldwork. These will feature however, and indeed will to a considerable extent pervade the whole chapter, grounded as it is in the experience of studying assessment procedures and practices over some years. The review will be organized around three main sets of ethical and political issues; those arising from: changing assessment procedures; qualitatively investigating assessment practices; and government sponsorship of development and evaluation in the field of assessment.

Some Consequences of Changes in Assessment

Most research on assessment which has taken place outside the confines of the examination boards has been concerned to monitor changes in assessment practices and procedures. It has rarely preceded, far less informed, such changes (an issue which will be returned to below when current government initiatives are considered). An exception to this rather broad generalization might be the work of Cyril Burt (and to a lesser extent, in terms of overt impact on policy, Godfrey Thomson). Burt's work on intelligence testing in the 1920s and 1930s provided the intellectual underpinning for the practice of selection and in one form or another still pervades many seemingly intuitive conceptions of 'ability'. Yet even his work tended to follow in the wake of and hence legitimate developing policy options and pressing administrative needs (Sutherland, 1984; Torrance, 1981). In the 1950s and 1960s the main institution concerned with assessment research was the National Foundation for Educational Research (NFER). Its two major programmes of work were concerned with post-hoc studies of policy decisions — monitoring the conduct and effectiveness of the 11 + (for example, Yates and Pidgeon, 1957) and investigating the comparability of CSE and GCE grades (Nuttall, 1971; Wilmott and Nuttall, 1975). This pattern of work has continued and indeed developed at an even quicker pace in the 1980s with major changes in assessment and certification being announced with little attention being paid to either technical or pedagogic issues although considerable previous research evidence could now be called on (Gipps, 1986; Nuttall and Goldstein, 1986).

The justificatory rhetoric of educational change is always that of improvement. New assessment procedures are claimed to be reflecting and rationalizing that which is best in the system at the present time as well as looking to the future. The Department of Education and Science (DES) wishes the new General Certificate of Secondary Education (GCSE) to test what children 'know, understand and can do' (DES, 1985, p. 2). Coursework and oral work have come to the fore in recent years and many GCSE National Criteria suggest these are appropriate assessment tools as does the government's Secondary Examinations Council (SEC, 1985) and the Task Group on Assessment and Testing (TGAT 1987). Thus the government is apparently encouraging wider use of practical, oral and coursework assessment to test understanding and application in tandem with final papers which have traditionally been used to test the recall of knowledge. All well and good perhaps, but changing assessment procedures and practices implies changing the criteria by which success and failure are measured. Children will now be expected to be proficient at oral work as well as written work, at sustained work as well as short one-off tests. Changing the 'ground rules' in this way will have an impact on individual performance and may well change the number and nature of pupils who succeed and fail. Are some sorts of pupils 'better' at oral or practical work than academic work? If so, for what reasons? Such questions are obviously difficult to answer. Empirically, in given situations, some children clearly do perform better at practical rather than academic tasks and increasing the weighting of practical work in examinations ought to benefit them. However, these children are often called 'less able' particularly by teachers, many of whom persist in interpreting coursework, practical work and so forth in terms of 'giving the less able a chance', to accumulate marks, than in terms of providing all children with a broader educational programme (*cf*. Macintosh, 1986; Torrance, 1982; 1985). Whether with changing teaching and assessment practices the 'less able' come to be seen as 'more able' is a moot point and a very difficult one to investigate given the problem of defining ability and treating it as independent of both particular performances and teacher expectations. It is an issue which might emerge more overtly in the context of a specific development like the Technical and Vocational Educational Initiative (TVEI) rather than the general context of GCSE. Of course developing different definitions of ability is unlikely to be the intention of the present government and it is a possibility that would have to be seen in the light of what we know about gender and race in education as well as social class. The very reverse of what I have outlined may happen with implicit cultural competences — rather than explicit skills and attributes — becoming even more important to the process of assessment than at present is the case. Some of the evidence I will cite below is certainly not encouraging on this issue. However the main point I wish to note here is the extent to which changes in the technology of assessment involve changes in the value system in which the technology is located.

Another facet of this issue, but one which is probably of more immediate concern, certainly to teachers, is the changes in teaching methods which changes in assessment can bring about. Many teachers and pupils still have little or no experience with new methods of assessment and will be deskilled by the changes wrought by GCSE and the new programme of national assessment. One head of history who had recently introduced the Schools Council History Project (SCHP) to his department (the philosophy of which has considerably influenced the GCSE history criteria) put it thus:

> ... on the AEB course ... you're looking for specific points really, factual points ... with the Schools Council history ... you've got an evidence paper which is (to do with) using skills and interpeting and evaluating evidence; how does one mark that? ... then of course there's the coursework ... although you are given specific objectives and you have to fit your work to that, you still have to work out ... how you are going to award your marks ... this is the first opportunity I've had to introduce it on a full scale ... (you learn by) experience, trial and error ... (Tape-recorded interview, 1 February 1983).[1]

Furthermore this 'trial and error' was being undertaken in a context of falling rolls and the publication of examination results:

> ... we're in a middle class catchment area and at the end of the day the average parent ... will say that they want their child

> to get 'X' O-levels . . . on the traditional history course . . . we get good results. Now whether or not we're going to achieve the same with the Schools Council history, I don't know . . . (Tape-recorded interview, 1 February 1983).

This particular teacher was attracted by the approach of SCHP and adopted the project voluntarily and gradually. To 'reskill' himself he phased in the project over a number of years starting with his 'top' history groups which he believed would be easiest to work with in the first instance. This option of gradual development does not exist when change is imposed. Thus GCSE will be likely to advantage some teachers and pupils — in this example those who already have some experience of SCHP — and disadvantage others. Of course it might be argued that GCSE is just a special case in the continual process of curriculum development. But changes in curriculum, especially if restricted to individual subject areas as has been the case in the past, can take place slowly and do not necessarily involve examination work in the first instance. Changes in curriculum can be 'experimental' without carrying too many consequences, changes in assessment cannot. At stake are the examination results and life-chances of individual pupils and the reputations and career development of individual teachers, indeed of whole schools.

If we penetrate the process and conduct of changes in assessment a little more we can uncover further unintended consequences which can spill over into teaching and teacher-pupil relations. 'Discussion', for example, is a regularly cited example of a new approach to teaching and assessing pupils, particularly where controversial issues are being explored. But discussion, perhaps conceived of as detached, liberal debate and operationalized by teachers as an assessment 'technique' because the 'exam asks for it', can be interpreted by pupils as more akin to counselling than testing. And of course this is all the more possible when teachers try to integrate their assessment with their teaching and formality dissolves. Thus pupils may come to reveal considerably more of themselves than they ought, or than teachers can cope with. As a head of parentcraft put it:

> . . . what we try to do is get them to see both points of view . . . be able to carry an argument and be prepared to argue both sides . . . we get them in groups . . . it is quite tricky here. We have quite a lot of sort of social problems. Dad'd gone off and someone else has moved in and we don't know who dad is . . . it's really sad, terribly sad, some of the things they come out with . . . (Tape-recorded interview, 25 February 1983).

Such problems are all the more likely to arise as schools develop profiles or records of achievement and more explicitly attempt to discern, assess and record 'motivation and personal development' (DES, 1984, p. 3).

Qualitative Methods in the Study of Assessment

Implicit in the highlighting of these sorts of problems, particularly in the words of teachers themselves, is a method for identifying and investigating them in the first place. Asking broader questions of assessment and examinations and trying to penetrate the complex interrelation of assessment, curriculum and pedagogy demands the conduct of detailed qualitative fieldwork in schools and indeed in examiners' meetings: interviewing and observing teachers, pupils and examiners in situ, in action. There is not the space here to rehearse all the arguments for and against qualitative methods. Clearly many issues of validity, reliability and not least ethics are raised by qualitative work (*cf.* Burgess 1985a, 1985b and other chapters in this volume). But two features of qualitative fieldwork are particularly worthy of note in the context of assessment — that of researcher influence on the conduct and outcome of the process under study and that of exposing routine (and by teachers' own admissions sometimes unsound) practice to potentially unfair criticism.

Researcher influence on events is a common enough issue of concern in discussions of research methods. Barnes (1979) makes the point that in social research researcher influence on the process of events is as important as researcher activity with regard to any subsequent dissemination of findings — the 'use and abuse' of 'results'. Also of course, with regard to ethics, one's potential impact on the lives of the subjects of one's research is as important a consideration as the perhaps more technical concern of monitoring one's impact on the data collected. This is particularly the case when studying assessment. There have been many times when I have attended marking and moderating meetings and been asked my opinion of pieces of work. Given that one is often perceived as an 'expert' in assessment, or even 'from the board', it is sometimes difficult, though not impossible, to avoid being drawn into discussion. More acute still however, are the occasions when one may actually have an impact on the performance and subsequent grade awarded to candidates — vulnerable minors placed in an already threatening and stressful situation. As I recorded in my fieldnotes during one period of observing oral testing in parentcraft:

... The experience looked as though it affected different girls in different ways (only girls were involved in this test). Some were clearly very nervous ... Most of the girls seemed to come out as (the teacher) expected. She didn't think that the visiting moderators or indeed my own visit made any great difference, although it's always possible, particularly since for the first question they were asked to talk about the onset of labour which may have been embarrassing for them in my presence ... (Fieldnotes 10 March 1983).

In this case a female researcher might have been more appropriate than myself — though that option did not exist. The issue is one of striking a balance between gaining some access to events while remaining sensitive to the problems caused by access. I attended this particular oral examination because I knew that two strangers — external moderators — would be present in any case and therefore I hoped my presence would not be seen as completely out of the ordinary, and because I had developed a reasonably open relationship with the teacher whose pupils were involved and who assured me that my presence would not be a problem.

Interestingly enough however it is not my presence at events which has concerned me most when reflecting on the ethics of such research. Perhaps because one simply cannot know how well candidates would have performed, perhaps because I am very careful (or all too insensitive!), perhaps because what impact one has is thinly spread when oral tests, for example, are but one part of an overall examination of a candidate's work (20 per cent in the case of the parentcraft examination referred to above), my concern, instead, tends to focus on the second of Barnes' (1979) categories — the dissemination of research findings. In a period of intense interest and acrimonious debate about the purpose and conduct of assessment, especially related to issues of 'standards' and teacher accountability, investigating teacher involvement in assessment in order to better understand and perhaps improve it, could lead instead to providing sceptics with easy ammunition. The fieldwork referred to in this chapter took place before the go-ahead for GCSE was announced and before the role that school-based assessment might play in it was finalized. Even now ideological opposition to government policy on GCSE is still very vociferous from within the Conservative Party's own ranks and recent announcements concerning the national curriculum and national testing may yet reopen the whole debate.

In order to generate a fuller understanding of teacher involvement in assessment the researcher needs to gain access to and report in detail on the conduct of that involvement — 'warts and all' — yet such evidence could prove highly damaging in a different context. This is all the more possible because in many cases teachers are their own harshest critics, unwilling to condone bad practice or ignore the resource implications of doing a job such as moderating coursework properly:

> ... (at) moderation meetings I was appalled by what I would call the lack of professionalism ... the fellow ... who would say 'look, I've promised this lad a grade 1, he's been ever such a good lad' ... (Deputy Head, tape-recorded interview, 6 July 1983).

> ... I would say the standards of assessment are nothing short of abysmal ... two or three hours to look through 200, 300, 400, folders, and moderate examination scripts ... I know for a fact that some of my borderlines are never even looked at ... (Head of Department, tape-recorded interview, 26 January 1983).

Likewise, to continue with the example of oral examining, selective extracts from observations could generate a very one-sided account of practice:

> ... I arrived at the school to be taken to 'room 40' ... It eventually transpired to be the careers room ... The room itself was fairly bare with two desks pushed together in one half of the room, a couple of filing cabinets, a wall-length notice board with odd posters from colleges and universities stuck up ... an uninteresting and really rather dingy room but not one, presumably which candidates would be totally unused to ... It was, I suppose, twelve foot by six foot in length and width. The sun was shining strongly in through a very large window at the end of the room and the room really got quite hot after a while ... The careers room was next to the music room, apparently, and until the bell went at ... ten past ten there was loud noise coming from the next door room — drums, trumpets, pianos ... the first two pupils observed, I thought, were under great pressure ... At other times ... loud traffic noise penetrated, also pupil noise as the bells went between lessons and people scurried past outside the building and down the corridor outside the door ... (Fieldnotes from an English oral examination, 1 March 1983).

Obviously such evidence is important to note but coming to understand the intentions and the problems of oral examining also means coming to understand its variety. Oral examining is not a uniform technique readily applicable to any situation. Its conduct varies across subjects and across schools and attention must be paid to contrasts and comparisons to generate a 'fair' account.

Thus for example the parentcraft examination referred to earlier involved the chief examiner and subject panel of the examining board producing written questions for candidates and specimen answers for their teachers (who acted as examiners in the school for the purposes of the test). It was quite literally an examination conducted through the medium of the spoken word:

> ... The oral exam consists of a number of questions which the board sets, and by the board I mean a sub-committee of the parentcraft panel ... this sub-committee writes the questions and writes a range of acceptable answers which the teacher has in front of her ... the girls came in one at a time. They had the printed question cards in front of them ... The teacher read the cards and the girls had to respond. If they did so well and fully, then they were heading for a 1 or a 2, if they did so hesitantly and had to be prompted, which happened in most cases, then they would be a 3, 4, possibly even 5 ... (prompting) was not actually stopped by the moderators though they certainly took it into account when the grades were decided ... It's a very restricted time limit and some quite detailed answers are required in order to get into the higher grades ... (Fieldnotes from a Parentcraft oral examination, 10 March 1983).

In history however the 'oral' was in effect a viva-voce on a candidate's project work, with course objectives being used to structure marking (marking, this time, not grading) but without the provision of a marking scheme as such:

> ... (One teacher had) offered her CSE group the option of doing a project to replace one of the examination questions as allowed in the regulations. It seems only three pupils chose to do this. (The head of department) did the interviewing — an attempt at objectivity ... Each interview lasted ten-fifteen minutes with the head of department explaining to me (and seeking support for) his assessments, for two-three minutes in between. Eight marks could be awarded for four objectives. The tendency was to allocate them 2:2:2:2 though most of each interview was spent on the first objective — knowledge — and least time, if any, on

the second — historical terminology ... The others were causation and the ability to make value judgments. The objectives (especially the last two) were used as a helpful guide ... Overall, marks were awarded on knowledge plus 'the rest'; holistic rather than fragmentary; and comparisons, even between three candidates, were made ... thus rank ordering did feature. Where the objectives were used was in (the head of department's) questioning. He asked 'leading questions' to try to elicit knowledge, causation, value judgments ... (Fieldnotes from a history oral examination, 8 March 1983).

The English oral, by further contrast, involved reading aloud from a familiar text and then speaking on a prepared topic such as a hobby:

... they all read for perhaps a minute, ninety seconds, roughly two paragraphs from a book. Then they spoke on a topic of their choice which (the teachers) interviewed them about. One girl spoke about amateur dramatics ... another of her involvement in the Duke of Edinburgh's Award Scheme, another of a trip to see 'Duran, Duran' ... but most spoke about their work experience ... The responses were also very varied. The girl talking about amateur dramatics was, 'gushy', really, is the word. She brought in an album of photographs of herself in plays and musicals. She talked non-stop for about five minutes. I'm not sure what she 'communicated' though, except that she wanted to do well in the examination ... At the other end of the scale one girl came in and hardly said a word ... two sentences about working in a record shop, said it was 'boring', and then literally replied 'yes', 'no' to a few questions. Ironically enough she 'communicated' superbly well. She thought the work experience was a 'boring' waste of time and indeed the exam ... (Fieldnotes from an English oral examination, 1 March 1983).

The dilemma here is clear enough and despite trying to offer a 'rounded picture' I am in danger of being hoist with my own petard — wrenching material out of context while recognizing the problems of wrenching material out of context! Obviously one has to acknowledge the interplay of observation and interpretation, and select, edit and balance material in accordance with data generated under different circumstances, and findings emerging in different contexts. The general issue of exposing contentious practices to potentially unfair scrutiny remains however. Obviously individuals can to a considerable degree be protected by anonymity (though not necessarily from their colleagues or from, say, local authority advisory staff who happen to recognize a setting or a situation). But teachers in general and the 'idea' of school-based examining not only cannot be protected by giving schools and/or teachers anonymity but should not be. This is the thinnest of all lines to tread since it involves offering critical accounts, but critical accounts which are fair and reasonable; which should identify how certain practices — good or bad — have come about, what it is reasonable to expect teachers to accomplish in given circumstances, and also, if possible, how those circumstances might be improved (*cf.* MacDonald, 1974 and 1977 for a fuller discussion of 'fairness' and 'reasonableness'). Fair and reasonable accounts of one aspect of examining must also attend to other aspects. Thus, for example, in focusing on the problems of school-based examining, one should not lose sight of the fact that traditional timed papers also have many problems and drawbacks, in terms of both their validity and their impact on children's educational experiences. Such drawbacks, as articulated by examiners, teachers, and pupils, need to be reported. Likewise issues such as differing subject regulations and assessment criteria — assessing 'communication' for example — obviously take us beyond the practice of individual teachers, competent or otherwise. Thus accounts need to be placed in as full a context as possible, with comparisons and contrasts drawn across subjects, teachers, schools and even regions if possible, and with examiners as well as teachers being involved in the study. Accounts also need to be shown to participants in the research process before they are made more widely available.

This need to move beyond descriptive critique to fair and reasonable evaluation, to combine understanding with the generation of options for improvement, situates my work within the developing practice of multisite condensed fieldwork case study (MacDonald, 1974, 1977; Walker, 1974; Stenhouse, 1982; Simons, 1987) rather than more traditional ethnographic work. Of course case study is not without its problems or its critics (Atkinson and Delamont, 1985). One of its major problems, given my emphasis on full reporting, is that the longer a report is, the less likely it is to be read. This obviously puts pressure on researchers who aspire to influence policy and practice to produce short, accessible reports — in direct contradiction of the need to locate accounts in context. The first draft of the report I wrote drawing on the interviews and observations referred to in this chapter ran to 292 pages. The final version came out at 115 pages. I also produced a summary report at thirty-seven pages and a number of journal articles at around ten-twelve pages. Clearly there are no easy solutions to this sort of problem. One makes one's judgments about what to report and how to report it in the light of the sorts of issues raised here, along with more general considerations such as what the purpose of the report is, its intended and likely audience(s) and so forth. However the problem of studying a particularly sensitive topic and attempting to work at the interface of research and policy leads me to the third and final concern of this chapter — whether work on assessment, given the increasingly overt politicization of assessment initiatives, comes to be seen as 'policing' rather than investigating the design and implementation of policy.

Evaluating Changes in Assessment

This issue of the role of evaluation in present circumstances returns us in part to some of the problems raised at the beginning of the chapter. It was suggested that changes in assessment are 'for real' and necessarily impact on the working practices and life chances of teachers and pupils. This general point is being compounded by two particular features of the current scene — the interest of educational professionals in school-based or school-focused in-service training and professional development; and the direct political investment of the government in general, individual ministers in particular, in initiatives now under way.

School-focused in-service training has been conceived over the last few years as the most effective means of generating and sustaining the commitment of teachers to new ideas and practices. But this conception has been developed in the context of what one might broadly call the 'teacher-as-researcher' movement: an approach to professional development which both assumes and celebrates teacher autonomy and teachers' capacity to engage in curriculum development. School-focused in-service is thus grounded in a particular (micro-level) theory of change and is essentially concerned with the process, rather than the substance, of change. Teachers themselves, perhaps in collaboration with the wider community of educational professionals, are assumed to supply the content. If this ever were a sound analysis and strategy it hardly remains so now, and with regard to changes in assessment like the introduction of GCSE or profiling it is fast becoming the case that the rhetoric of professionalism and school-based development is simply being used to co-opt teachers and secure change, the direction and content of which has already been decided (*cf.* also Harland, 1987). In such circumstances 'evaluation' may come to be perceived a wholly instrumental activity, offering at best perhaps, 'intelligence' about where in-service resources might be most effectively deployed, at worst, the appraisal of teachers with regard to their willingness and competence to 'deliver' change.

This is not to suggest that such a possibility is necessarily being pursued self-consciously by sponsors and users of evaluation, nor to question the good faith of the many project directors, advisory teachers, in-service co-ordinators, and so forth, to which new initiatives and in-service arrangements have given rise (particularly Educational Support Grant (ESG) funding and Grant-Related In-Service Training (GRIST)). But it is to highlight the problem of, for example, a school being forced to take on board GCSE and then being encouraged to focus in-service work on the detail of its implementation — the design and assessment of coursework assignments, the safe-keeping of records, the administration of examination board procedures — rather than engage in a fuller educational dialogue with regard to its nature and purpose. The irony of course is that teachers operating under current pressures will in any case want detailed help (instructions?) at the expense of wider discussion.

In many respects this issue is even more problematic when involvement with a new initiative is supposedly, in the 'pilot' stages, voluntaristic. As one coordinator of profiling recently put it to me:

> ... profiling ... was announced with the leaded glove of Keith Joseph: 'by 1990 you are all going to have to do this chums so you'd better get started now' ... (quoted in Torrance, 1986b, p. 8).

The imperative here is to 'get started' or get left behind, and resolve problems 'on the hoof' rather than explore them. Tutorial systems, reporting systems, teaching styles, all will slowly alter and there is no going back: once started the institution *will* change irrespective of whether or not the 1990 deadline for national implementation is retained. Of course many teachers, often ones who started reluctantly in circumstances similar to those described above, have become convinced of the efficacy of new approaches to teaching and learning, and to the promotion and recording of achievement. However it is looking increasingly unlikely that they will have either the curricular flexibility or the resources to carry through their ideas in the future.

So broader studies of the logic and consequence of proposed changes in assessment may well become increasingly hard to find, in part because the 'proposed change' is, in policy terms at least, already accomplished change, and in part because any institutional engagement with the proposed change will help to bring it about. This problem could be further compounded by the issue of tight financial control and political sponsorship — neither hard-pressed LEAs seeking more ESG funding, nor politicians whose direct involvement is obvious to all are going to welcome bad news, or even good news if it takes too long to arrive! As Kushner and MacDonald (1987) have recently argued:

> With the demise of mediating agencies such as the Schools Council in favour of more unilateral political origination of programmes, government ministers are now more closely associated with major programmes and have a correspondingly greater stake in their public success . . .
>
> These leaner, more linear structures of command and compliance . . . are bigger, less self-questioning, more single-minded in their search for vindicative data, quick to publicize success stories, quicker still to suppress or dismiss bad news from any quarter . . . These programmes, though they may well bear the official status of 'pilot' or 'experiment', and though they may be saturated with evaluation processes apparently designed to establish their worth, are expressions of political conviction rather than explorations of educational hypotheses (p. 155).

Kushner and MacDonald's prescription is to continue to engage in evaluation since it still offers, at least potentially, access to study the powerful — the programme designers — as well as the relatively powerless — the programme implementers. This may be so and certainly the aspiration must be to evaluate policy, not just its implementation. But perhaps now more than ever is the time for the sort of evaluation which Kushner and MacDonald advocate, and which I have acknowledged as influencing my work, to move beyond a concern for the ethics and politics of fieldwork — important though that is — and engage on the one hand with the broader concerns of the social sciences, particularly history and social structure, and on the other with the broader school community, particularly pupils and parents. To return to the case of assessment, the history of testing — its educational development and justification, and its social function — is crucial to an understanding of present practice and an analysis of current proposals. Likewise the audience for such analysis must include other interested parties in addition to teachers, administrators and politicians. Currently, parents in particular are not only a widely cited and legitimate audience for general information about schools, they are also, along with pupils, a highly appropriate and crucially important audience for informed discussion about GCSE, profiling, benchmark testing, etc. which will affect their children's life chances. Quite how such discussion could take place is another matter, taking us into the realms of journalism and pressure group politics rather than research. Yet if the ethical and political issues reviewed in this chapter are to be fully addressed, then ultimately they require researchers to seek legitimacy for their enquiries and recommendations from a wider constituency than is at present the case.

Note

1 All interviews and observations quoted in this section and the next section of the chapter derive from a study of teacher involvement in examining which I conducted between 1982 and 1984 and which was funded by the Southern Regional Examinations Board. The final report of the project — *Case Studies in School-based Examining* — is available from the Assessment and Evaluation Unit, Southampton University.

References

ATKINSON, P. and DELAMONT, S. (1985) 'Bread and dreams or bread and circuses? A critique of "case study" research in education', in SHIPMAN, M. (Ed) *Educational Research: Principles, Policies and Practices,* Lewes, Falmer Press.

BARNES, J. (1979) *Who Should Know What?*, Harmondsworth, Penguin.

BROADFOOT, P. (1979) *Assessment, Schools and Society*, London, Methuen.

BROADFOOT, P. (Ed) (1984) *Selection, Certification and Control*, Lewes, Falmer Press.

BROADFOOT, P. (Ed) (1986) *Profiles and Records of Achievement*, London, Holt, Rhinehart and Winston.

BURGESS, R. (Ed) (1985a) *Field Methods in the Study of Education*, Lewes, Falmer Press.

BURGESS, R. (Ed) (1985b) *Strategies of Educational Research: Qualitative Methods,* Lewes, Falmer Press.

DEPARTMENT OF EDUCATION AND SCIENCE (1984) *Records of Achievement: A Statement of Policy*, London, DES/Welsh Office.

DEPARTMENT OF EDUCATION AND SCIENCE (1985) *GCSE General Criteria*, London, HMSO.

FLOUD, J. and HALSEY, A. (1957) 'Intelligence tests, social class, and selection for secondary school', *British Journal of Sociology*, **8**, pp. 33–9.

GIPPS, C. (Ed) (1986) *The GCSE: An Uncommon Examination*, Bedford Way Papers No. 29, London, University of London, Institute of Education.

HARLAND, J. (1987) 'The new INSET: A transformation scene', in MURPHY, R. and TORRANCE, H. (Eds) *Evaluating Education: Issues and Methods,* London, Harper and Row.

KUSHNER, S. and MACDONALD, B. (1987) 'The limitations of programme evaluation' in MURPHY, R. and TORRANCE, H. *op. cit.*

MCCORMICK, R. (Ed) (1982) *Calling Education to Account*, London, Heinemann/Open University Press.

MACDONALD, B. (1974) 'Evaluation and the control of education', in MACDONALD, B. and WALKER, R. (Eds) *Innovation, Evaluation, Research and the Problem of Control*, Norwich, Centre for Applied Research in Education.

MACDONALD, B. (1977) 'An educational evaluation of the national development programme in computer assisted learning' *British Journal of Educational Technology*, **8**, 3, pp. 176–89.

MACDONALD, B. and WALKER, R. (Eds) (1974) *Innovation, Evaluation, Research and the Problem of Control*, Norwich, Centre for Applied Research in Education.

MACINTOSH, H. (1986) 'The sacred cows of coursework', in GIPPS, C. *op. cit.*

MURPHY, R. and TORRANCE, H. (Eds) (1987) *Evaluating Education: Issues and Methods*, London, Harper and Row.

NUTTALL, D. (1971) *The 1968 CSE Monitoring Experiment*, Schools Council Working Paper 34, London, Evans/Methuen Educational.

NUTTALL, D. and GOLDSTEIN, H. (1986) 'Profiles and graded tests: The technical issues' in BROADFOOT, P. (Ed) *Profiles and Records of Achievement*, London, Holt, Rinehart and Winston.

SECONDARY EXAMINATIONS COUNCIL (1985) *Coursework Assessment in GCSE*, London, Secondary Examinations Council.

SHIPMAN, M. (Ed) (1985) *Educational Research: Principles, Policies and Practices*, Lewes, Falmer Press.

SIMONS, H. (1987) *Getting to Know Schools in a Democracy*, Lewes, Falmer Press.

STENHOUSE, L. (1982) 'The conduct, analysis and reporting of case study in educational research and evaluation', in MCCORMICK, R. (Ed) *Calling Education to Account*, London, Heinemann/Open University Press.

SUTHERLAND, G. (1984) *Ability, Merit and Measurement*, Oxford University Press.

TASK GROUP ON ASSESSMENT AND TESTING (1987) *A Report*, London, HMSO.

TORRANCE, H. (1981) 'The origins and development of mental testing in England and the United States' *British Journal of Sociology of Education*, **2**, 1, pp. 45–59.

TORRANCE, H. (1982) *Mode III Examining: six case studies*, York, Longmans for the Schools Council.

TORRANCE, H. (1985) *Case Studies in School-based Examining*, University of Southampton, Department of Education.

TORRANCE, H. (1986a) 'What can examinations contribute to school evaluation?' *Educational Review*, **38**, 1, pp. 31–43.

TORRANCE, H. (1986b) 'Understanding profiling: Public theories and private discoveries'. Paper delivered to the St Hilda's Ethnography Conference on Education and Training 14–18, Oxford, September.

WALKER, R. (1974) 'The conduct of educational case study: Ethics, theory and procedure', in MACDONALD, B. and WALKER, R. *op. cit.*

WHITTY, G. (1985) *Sociology and School Knowledge*, London, Methuen.

WILMOTT, A. and NUTTALL, D. (1975) *The Reliability of Examinations at 16 +*, London, Macmillan Education.

YATES, A. and PIDGEON, D. (1957) *Admission to Grammar Schools*, London, Newnes.

YOUNG, M. (1971) 'An approach to the study of curricula as socially organized knowledge', in YOUNG, M. (Ed) *Knowledge and Control*, London, Collier-MacMillan.

10
Change and Adjustment in a Further Education College

Pauline Foster

Conversation overheard in the corridor:

Tom: Hello Harry. You look as if you've got problems.

Harry: Not me. It's the system that's got problems — it's got it all wrong!

Introduction

In this chapter I set out some of the ethical issues that concerned me during the course of my research in a college of further education. The work within the college was part of a wider project that looked at adult retraining in private industry, further education, agriculture and the service sector within a defined geographical area in the north east of the United Kingdom.

My research within further education involved an in-depth study of five adult retraining courses within building construction and electrical engineering departments. On average a dozen male students aged between 21 and 45 were enrolled on each course; and course tutors, also male, were appointed to be responsible for the setting up of courses and their day-to-day running.

I interviewed each course tutor and student twice, once at the beginning and once at the end of the course using a semi-structured interviewing technique. Wherever possible I took advantage of what Jenkins refers to as a 'normal talk strategy' (Jenkins, 1986) to allow respondents to speak freely about the issues which most concerned them, and used a form of participant observation in classrooms, taking part in class activities where it was appropriate, but being careful not to disrupt the normal course of events. This, I felt, would enable me to get closer to individuals and immerse myself in the daily life of the college. It also meant that I could make comparisons between my own first hand observations and those of the students and staff whom I interviewed. These methods also added an element of flexibility to the research, so that if unanticipated developments occurred, they could be taken into account and accommodated within the overall research plan. Using these methods I hoped to discover the experiences and perceptions of tutors and students and gain some understanding of the retraining process.

Towards the latter part of my time at the college the local education authority (LEA) took a decision to reorganize the college structure. Initially this issue seemed peripheral to my research but gradually it came to impinge, not so much upon the data I was collecting, as upon the data collection process itself. At the same time the Manpower Services Commission (MSC) withdrew funding from three of the adult training courses I was studying. This further development served to increase the pressure on the staff who taught the adults on these courses; and had implications for my research in that staff were forced to devote time and energy to devising and setting up new courses to replace those lost. They therefore had less time to talk to a researcher. Their own careers were threatened and retrieving what had been lost took priority.

It was a psychological blow too, their status within their department was less secure. When I broached the issue of the loss of funding they were reluctant to discuss it. They could be almost fatalistic about what was happening to them; and most looked for individual solutions and began applying for jobs in other institutions. All treated the matter casually in conversation with me, which belied the serious intent obvious in their demeanour and action.

There is the ever present danger that circumstances and events may overtake the research — that the original focus of the research alters form in some way or becomes part of a wider issue. The temptation to readjust the focus to cover the wider issue can be strong but the wider issue may prove tangential to the central theme of the research. However, there is an equal danger in adopting a blinkered approach thus failing to explore what is really happening. Much depends on getting the focus right; on having access to data; and on a flexible research design. Over and above this the researcher herself needs to maintain an openness and flexibility of mind as far as this is possible.

Controversy was not an issue in the initial stages of the research. As stated before, the reorganization and loss of funding were later developments. Consequently I tended to deal with the changes these events imposed on a day-to-day basis at the level of personal interaction, and the overall structure of the research design remained unchanged. This is not intended as a contradiction of the point I have made earlier but rather to illustrate that this line of approach was most appropriate to my research.

Researching a Controversial Issue

A situation is said to be controversial when what is occurring in the particular social setting is the subject of debate or dispute; when there is opposition or disagreement amongst contending parties. Because of a lack of consensus and unpredictability individuals may be said to experience uncertainty, bewilderment and general insecurity. The balance is upset and any change is frequently met with suspicion.

This is how I saw the situation at the college, and given the sensitive nature of some of the circumstances in which I found myself, I had to remain non-threatening in an already threatening situation when my very *raison d'être* as a researcher is to probe — itself a threatening act.

Both training and education are controversial issues in the widest sense. They are political concerns and it is changes in government policy in both these areas and their subsequent translation into the more parochial concerns of college life that served to create the conditions that made the last two terms of my time in the institution a stressful period for all who worked there.

For the respondents in my research the situation of controversy was created more immediately by two events. Firstly there was the policy of the local authority to reorganize the college, moving from a traditional hierarchical model towards a functional matrix within a short time span allowing for minimal consultation and lead in. Secondly, a decision made by the Manpower Services Commission to withdraw funding from some of the adult retraining courses at the college. To understand why these events should have occurred when they did, and almost simultaneously, it is necessary to examine the wider context of change within further education.

Traditionally further education has been marketed as a provider of quality training. This rested upon a belief in the professionalism of the staff and the perceived superior level of facilities and resourcing. For some time, however, this assumption has been challenged due to a contraction in the traditional areas of FE work funded via the Rate Support Grant

(RSG), for example craft apprenticeships. The RSG income has failed to keep pace with inflation. Consequently, if the college did not wish to enter a phase of decline, it needed to look beyond the local education authority for funding. Currently approximately 38 per cent of college income is provided by the MSC, whereas ten years ago 99 per cent of the income for the college was RSG.

The focus on prevocational education has shifted away from craft skills towards more short-term labour market requirements. The loss of funding for three adult retraining courses was seen by staff within the building department as indicative of this shift and part of MSC policy to divert funds into the New Job Training Scheme. It was suggested by an informant outside the department that, given the current economic and political situation, further education must 'either respond in an entrepreneurial way and become geared up to the capitalist ethos or find itself . . . becoming increasingly peripheral and marginal'. He was highly critical of the college's ability to respond immediately at middle management level to 'changing reality' and complained of 'institutional inertia'. He was referring specifically to failure to submit alternative bids to MSC in order to retain the funding for these adult courses.

The reorganization was seen by the local education authority as a rationalization exercise and part of an attempt to respond in a more efficient and flexible manner to the changing character of the workload and greater emphasis on prevocational education as well as demographic changes. But this is within the context of declining resources in public sector further education. The LEA made it clear that they were not prepared to inject additional monies to resource the new college structure and new appointments were to be made within these restrictions and in particular the necessity of keeping protected posts within the new structure to a minimum. This is in line with the National Joint Council conditions of service and in agreement with the local branch of the college lecturers' union.

The college reorganization resulted in the legal closure of two institutions and the creation of a single multisite college. All jobs were to be reapplied for, and many were redesignated within an assimilation procedure. The 'ringed fence system', which was imposed to protect hierarchical distinctions within the context of no increase in resources, effectively blocked the possibility of accelerated promotion. Individuals complained bitterly that the natural career trajectory of staff was thus distorted and those who initially saw the reorganization as a way of advancing their career in a static job market, felt demoralized.

More significantly, several of the managerial appointments were 'unpopular' because, in the perceptions of many of the teaching, administrative and technical staff, they failed to meet the real needs of the organization. Few staff believed they had benefited from the reorganization, and one respondent suggested about three people out of a total of 300 staff were pleased with the outcome. However, even the beneficiaries sought to distance themselves from decisions made by the appointing panels in order to maintain credibility within the organization.

The particular features of the controversy which increasingly impinged upon my research were the uncertainty and insecurity of the situation. Furthermore, institutional reorganization lays bare the mechanics of an institution − it shows up the rust and broken cogs. This may be intentional, but equally, it may reveal matters which are best kept from public scrutiny. As a researcher one faces the ethical dilemma of how much to reveal and how valid is information given off the record. Accuracy is important, yet it is a cold inflexible word; and the scenario which I present is only one of many possible scenarios when seen through the eyes and minds of other individuals. There is much more I would have liked to have said about the institution and the individuals who worked within it, but my fear is that such information may be misinterpreted by others to produce a distorted picture and thus reflect badly upon the institution. Balance is essential as is anonymity, but maintaining anonymity can sometimes conflict with accuracy. Here the researcher must reach a compromise (Platt, 1976, p. 202).

The remainder of this chapter discusses some of the compromises I reached in attempting to maintain that balance between collecting and recording the most accurate and useful data whilst maintaining the cooperation and goodwill of the sources of that data. It also focuses on many of the methodological and ethical issues with which I wrestled during the course of the research, and which were heightened and magnified by virtue of the prevailing conditions within the institution.

Making Entries

A great deal hinges on making a successful entry into an organization. Although it is possible to renegotiate conditions of entry once the researcher has gained the confidence of respondents and gatekeepers, to have the parameters of one's research clearly and acceptably defined from the beginning renders medium and long term planning more practicable.

For this and other reasons ease of entry influenced my choice of research topic. I had taught in another further education college for six years full-time and in this particular college for one year part-time; and a friendship of some years' standing with a full-time employee of the college helped cushion my approach to the Principal when first seeking access. He was able to approach the Principal on an informal basis on my behalf, whilst our known close association provided the Principal with a sort of collateral that might ensure I did not step beyond the limitations he was keen to set. This person subsequently took on the guise of a 'key informant' rather in the style of Whyte's 'Doc' (Whyte, 1955).

This situation was not without its ambiguities. My close association on a personal level with the college and some of its staff for the previous three years rendered my situation as a researcher complex in terms of the relationships I was able to initiate and develop with tutors and students. It was a situation I felt unable to alter significantly. The seeds of association had been sown and had germinated in the months and years prior to the commencement of the research. Instead my intention was to be circumspect, watchful, and constantly aware of the manner in which individual informants acknowledged and took account of my relationship with my 'key informant', who had access to background information that would normally have been inaccessible to a researcher. In attempting to be circumspect I never intended to behave in any way that did not come naturally to me; only to the extent that when you are a guest in another's home you don't 'dunk' your ginger biscuits in the tea — at least not when the host is watching. Untypically my relationship with the teaching staff had a past and a future, and as suggested by Platt (1981, p. 77), in such situations:

> One is anxious that the interviews should not be socially unpleasant occasions and that one should appear well in the eyes of people who constitute a significant reference group and with whom one will continue to live when the research is over.

Despite my close association with the college and the advantage this gave me in entering 'into the matrix of meanings of the researched' (Wax, 1980, pp. 272–3), I could never feel, nor be, fully integrated. I was not a member of staff, I was a researcher, and I was a woman researching men. I was also identified with the 'ivory tower', I was the academic and they the practitioners. Although I had been a further education teacher, I was not *au fait* with 'working the system', or the specific copying strategies developed within those particular departments. Nevertheless, I had been initiated into further education teaching and had run the gauntlet of students and administrative staff some years previously. There was considerable common ground for small talk over coffee and I was familiar with the personalities and general geography of this multisite college. I was thus able to achieve some of those conditions outlined by Wax whilst still conscious of the ambiguity of my role.

A researcher entering the field must face many of the same dilemmas as anyone entering a particular social situation for the first time — for example, starting a new job or joining a course at college or university — all those social skills that are used to weigh up people and organizational patterns, as well as to interact at the appropriate level, are the essential accoutrements of the researcher.

However, for the new employee there is a desk or bench specially allocated to her. Not so for the researcher. Without the protection of a 'niche' within the system the researcher can feel vulnerable, helpless and dependent upon certain key individuals in the organization who may be keen to act as guide and advisor at some times but not at others. Without a geographical base she shifts around occupying other people's space, sitting on other people's chairs and desk edges, trying not to occupy the same space for too long for fear the intrusive element of research becomes too much for those who are being researched.

The staffroom situation was familiar to me, but even as a teacher myself I had always felt an intruder in staffrooms that were not my own, especially all-male staffrooms which were usually occupied by craft or science tutors. The calendars invariably broadcast the message that here 'no woman has gone before' but also the smells were different: dusty, woody and oily smells. White coats hung on doors and infrequently used hard yellow hats rested on windowsills collecting dust. Strange volumes and instruction manuals perched precariously atop piles of unmarked work and 'banda' handouts, whilst wooden set squares and drawing boards lay propped against desk sides.

My first entry into a staffroom at the college was the occasion of some shuffling and shifting of books and chairs so that I could be given a comfortable seat whilst the tutor talked to me from a standing position. As time progressed my presence was almost taken for granted and later, when events threatened the security of the tutors, I was ignored. No one enquired as to whether they could assist me and my own enquiries were met with cursory answers and confused looks, followed by the immediate disappearance of the individual concerned bearing a pile of papers. I learned not to make too many enquiries. Unfortunately, when individuals feel insecure, when their world is threatened with change that is beyond their control, they are likely to respond in an unpredictable manner to persons within their midst whose role is unclear, and the role of the researcher is rarely understood by those not engaged in research.

I would have preferred not to be in that college at this particular time. Tutors were concerned about their jobs and some of them looked positively unwell. The timetable of my research would have allowed a prolonged absence, yet I felt there were important data to be collected. It was a dilemma I faced by choosing not to arrange any more face to face interviews with tutors for a month or two. I delayed these until this trauma was all recent history. I decided to continue with the classroom observation and student interviews since the students were only marginally affected by the reorganization and withdrawal of funding. This way I could be present in the college without causing distress or inconvenience to those who were preoccupied with the announcement of impending change. In addition I did not want to be seen to be taking an unhealthy interest in their distress, and a lot of the information about events in the wider college came unsolicited and only too readily from friends and former colleagues. I contented myself with brief chats with tutors in corridors whilst making my way to various classrooms, and over coffee at breaktimes without the ubiquitous notebook to hand.

Collecting Data

My own personal experience and knowledge of the college was from somewhere near the bottom looking up, whereas my key informant viewed events from somewhat higher up the hierarchy from a functional management level. Friends and colleagues fitted in somewhere between the two. A rich picking ground for data it may have been, but it was fraught with problems. It is impossible to pursue issues with friends in a social situation on a systematic basis. Without the notebook handy much of the data which seemed sharp and pertinent at the time merged into general impressions by the time a notebook was to hand; and escaping to the bathroom too frequently for the purpose of scribbling down a few brief notes only serves to draw attention to oneself. Anecdotes and grievances were often aired over bottles of wine on a Friday evening and by Saturday morning they seemed less significant to both teller and listener.

As the reorganization got underway everyone had a grievance: injustice seemed rife within the college but attempts to relate those grievances were inevitably partial. We are always selective, often unconsciously, in such a way as to present ourselves in a favourable light. In relating a story we omit detail which seems irrelevant to us because it is taken for granted or because emotional concerns blind us to its relevance. Thus many of the stories I collected in this way presented an incomplete, distorted and often incomprehensible picture of reality. The problem for me was making sense of them as someone who was essentially an emotionally uninvolved outsider. I agonized over whether such data represented 'a usable coherent body of research data (or merely) a collection of non-comprehensible and unreliable individual statements' (Jenkins, 1986, p. 35).

We may try to be open and flexible as researchers but the way we perceive and interpret events or even our choice of subject is governed to an extent by our own biographies and the way we have come to see the world and our own position in it. So what counts as truth reflects the pressures that society imposes, and when people are unaware of such pressures a situation of false consciousness could be said to exist (Trigg, 1980). Much of my data has been sifted through the consciousness of two individuals, the informant and the researcher, each in turn selecting, reorganizing and analyzing events into a pattern that makes sense in terms of their own world views. Few of my respondents gained or even attempted to gain any real global understanding of what was happening to them. For this reason it was impossible for them to discuss the issues in any detail. I could merely acknowledge this as a fact and hope that through a sympathetic approach to data collection people would be willing to expose their sometimes confused thoughts to the notebook of the researcher.

Furthermore, those relating these stories were not doing so to help my research and I was not listening only as a researcher. For them it was a cathartic exercise, events were sometimes embellished and presented as amusing anecdotes. I pondered over whether it was ethical to use such data as research material, whether material presented in such a manner could be used for more serious purposes? This was indeed dangerous territory since 'the researcher who treats his friends as subjects will soon find that he (she) has neither' (Klockers, 1977, p. 218).

Davis referred to this as the sociologists' 'original sin', that is the doubt experienced by a researcher when she deliberately befriends someone or 'manipulates a preexisting friendship in order to get data' (Thorne, 1980, p. 291).

The prospect of imminent change concerned many within the organization. One of the reasons people fear change is because its outcome is sometimes an unknown quantity and such unease is enhanced when information is scarce. As stated earlier, the college reorganization was carried out within a short time span which allowed for only minimal consultation and it is under such circumstances that gossip increases; when people seek the information which is denied them (Bok, 1982). Gossip is also an opportunity for comparing oneself with others (*ibid*). When one feels insecure, engaging in less than complimentary gossip about a colleague leaves one feeling in a relatively advantageous position. Gossip can also serve to police 'ethical behaviour' (Appell, 1980, p. 352). But the researcher should remember that 'the disappointed, the incompetent, the malicious and the paranoid all too often make groundless accusations' (Bok, 1982, p. 213).

As gossip the stories were fascinating, often amusing, farcical and sometimes pathetic. But these outpourings were invariably marginal to my research topic. They led me off in diverse directions.

Gossip is about people and their relationships to other people. Sometimes it is designed deliberately to mislead, sometimes it is passed on because of some long harboured and deep-seated resentment, or merely for amusement. It lacks formal rules and cannot be relied upon for its accuracy and reliability (Bok, 1982). Nevertheless, I am not sure it ought to be dismissed as inaccurate and useless. There was the problem of selecting what was useful and also of not allowing another's assessment of an individual to cloud my own perceptions of that person, not only in terms of good research technique but also that I may do justice to that individual. I felt, however, that such gossip could be put to good use in informing discrete and tactful questioning. Here the difficulty was maintaining the pretence of an innocent, of pretending that my key informant had not already supplied detailed information about the issues I was raising with a tutor, or of posing potentially threatening questions as if they were bland and inconsequential. So much of my data on the reorganization and the reassessments that were being made consequent upon the withdrawal of funding were culled from casual observations and conversations. Even then people could be evasive and protective of their own corner.

As mentioned previously, initially all the tutors willingly talked to me or ferried me back and forth from various sites, one of which was thirty miles from the main college. They were perhaps flattered by my interest in them and their courses and there was perhaps an element of novelty and a certain status in having a woman companion. Tutors discussed the progress of individual students with me, but in time one or two of them became more reticent, and the time I demanded of them was given less generously. I believe that a number of different circumstances came together to produce this response and at the same time these circumstances fed off the uncertainty and insecurity that tutors were feeling at this particular time.

At regular intervals I was issued with invitations to attend social events. There were visits in the summer to local places of interest, competition darts and pool evenings in which I was expected to participate on the side of whichever course I was researching at that time. There were Christmas drinks and end of course dinners. I accepted almost every invitation enthusiastically and revelled in the attention I was given at such events. For the tutors however, these events were both ritual and duty, and such duties clearly became more onerous as they found themselves under increasing pressure from within the college. They participated less enthusiastically and took their leave of the company earlier in the evening. On one occasion the students pre-empted the staff and issued me with an invitation which caused me some embarrassment when I realized at a later date that the tutors were not party to this invitation. When the staff left early my own natural inclination was usually to stay on a little longer, although the legitimacy of my presence at such events seemed to me to be compromised with the departure of the tutors.

There was a sense in which I felt the tutors expected and wanted me to belong to their side of the divide but my demonstrated wish to experience both resulted in suspicion and unease on the part of one tutor in particular. His approach had been especially warm and accommodating up to the point where I attended the aforementioned function. I supposed that his control over my movements in relation to his course and his group of students had been wrested from his grip, and I had shown as great a willingness to associate with students as I did with staff. I learned later that he had cross-examined one of the students about my activities at this function and was keen to link my name with a particular student. This tutor stood to suffer more than most as a result of the withdrawal of funding. He gradually became more wary, less open and increasingly preoccupied whenever we met. I relate this series of events because it illustrates a number of ethical issues which concern the researcher in any research setting and suggests that changes in the attitudes and behaviour of the researched may have a significant effect on the ability of the researcher to access data. The course tutor was initially given responsibility as my principal contact within the department, and he was now effectively creating a protective distance between us. His world had already undergone unwelcome change due to reorganization and withdrawal of funding and now the person whom he had been feeding with information which he controlled was seen to be identifying with the other side. I had compounded an already uncomfortable situation.

The major ethical question is how far can a researcher identify with the researched and to what extent should research relationships be allowed to develop into friendships and be acknowledged as such. This is especially pertinent when such friendships can damage relationships with others in the field. In the search for data and also regrettably because of personal inclination, and despite being aware of the consequences, I had identified too closely with the students. I had first gained the confidence of the course tutor and then lost it. To openly acknowledge that I might have erred in some way would be tantamount to admitting guilt which was inappropriate. It was merely that the expectations of one party, the course tutor had not been met.

Although I subsequently chose to behave in the research setting as if nothing had changed and as if I was innocent of the consequences, I remained concerned on two counts. Firstly, a personal but minor point is that it does not auger well to make enemies within any organization unless one is in a position of power or influence. My previous experience of petty intrigues within the organization taught me the effectiveness of mild character assassination through gossip and I was concerned not to become a victim of such, given my personal connections with the institution. Secondly, the effect on my research might be devastating, but on balance the course of action I chose proved to be the most fruitful both in terms of data and research experience. In a final formal interview with the tutor several weeks after the course had disbanded he made oblique reference to many of the derogatory comments about the course which he suspected, quite accurately, that the students had made. I had deliberately delayed this interview until the immediate crisis situation caused by imminent change had subsided to a level where individuals could see their way clear, at least in the shorter term, and were aware of their new posts in the reorganized college.

At this meeting the tension of our more recent encounters was released and he was prepared to discuss in some detail his concerns of the past few months, but his still formal manner and the way in which he sandwiched the interview tightly between two other appointments, at a time of year when teaching commitments for all staff are minimal, indicated to me his wish to reassert his selective control over my data.

Spying

The college Principal had granted permission to study adult retraining within the college, but had specified particular departments and courses to which I would have access. During the course of our initial interview he appeared to modify this selection of courses in minor ways, which gave the impression that he had not previously thought through the implications fully. He then summoned the head of one department and the deputy head of another department to his office in turn, and the aims and practicalities of my research were explained to them. Although I felt I discerned some anxiety on the face of at least one of these individuals, it is impossible to link this directly with the prospect of being researched.

It was not until about twelve months later, when I heard that the MSC, who funded these courses under their Adult Training Strategy, had made a policy decision to withdraw funding from three of the five courses I was studying, that I suspected any real significance in the Principal's choice. Although the Principal asked to see a draft copy of my thesis he was aware that my research would not produce any written material for about three years and his own knowledge of sociological research might have told him that the final report may not be in a form that could be of any real use to him. So it is impossible to read into the Principal's choice any clear strategy, except to suggest that he was probably aware that some adult training courses were under threat.

Whether I was consciously being used as a 'spy' in any planned and organized way is unclear. However, for some of those individuals whose daily life within the college I observed, I was indeed a 'spy in the camp'. This response was sometimes a reflection of their misunderstanding of the purposes of my research. Several times they asked if information would be reported back to the MSC and one tutor, despite my protestations to the contrary, directed criticism of the MSC at me as if to suggest I was in a position to pass them on. Quite frequently I was teased by students and staff about hidden tape-recorders and notebooks secreted upon my person.

When I requested permission from course tutors to carry out classroom observation over a typical week, their interpretation as to what this should involve varied. Probably because I could not dismiss the sense of being an intruder, or not having a legitimate role, I preferred to make these requests rather casually. I implied to tutors that they should feel at liberty to set the parameters of my involvement. I thus hoped to convey the impression that I remained mindful of the inconvenience and difficulties inherent in the situation, whilst respectful of their own positions of responsibility in running their courses. I wanted to minimize the level of interference and resentment and for them to feel that the situation was under their control. I felt confident of being able to manoeuvre within the interstices of the conditions set by tutors, and furthermore the limits set on my movements were data in themselves.

One tutor regulated my access by bureaucratizing the arrangements by which I could enter other tutors' classrooms. Tutors were selected and compliance was requested by memo weeks before I was due to visit the college. I was then presented with a schedule giving details of tutors who had agreed to participate plus times and classroom numbers. The schedule was presented to me in a fashion that suggested it was non-negotiable and the course tutor had effectively excluded himself from participation with no explanation offered.

Another course tutor offered me free rein to come and go as I pleased. He did however, omit to inform other tutors teaching on the course of my planned absence in the classroom. As a result I was involved in renegotiating the conditions for my observation some five or six times during the course of that week.

No tutor ever refused me permission, nor did they attempt to lay down conditions under which I should have operated. I was, however, unhappy with the situation where I had to negotiate access with individual tutors two minutes before they were about to begin teaching the class. The opportunity this presented of getting realistic data rather than a special display put on to impress a visitor, was outweighed by the unfairness of the situation. Even the most stimulating of teachers cannot make every lesson their best. Certain topics are inevitably tedious and do not lend themselves to more imaginative teaching techniques. I also wanted tutors to understand that they were being given a fair chance, that I was sympathetic and would not take sides. I was not evaluating individual performances, which were, for the purposes of the research insignificant.

Nevertheless, I would have been naive not to expect a degree of suspicion, and the clearest example of this came from a tutor who was the subject of frequent student criticism. Even the course tutor accepted the validity of such criticism, but a shortage of teachers in the field made this particular tutor's services indispensable. The tutor was informed in advance that I would be observing in the classroom and he lodged no objection. He was adequately prepared and presented a tolerable but very dull and formal lesson. I reached saturation level, made my excuses, and left the classroom after one hour and a half, as the students had predicted I would. The next day at coffee two students pointed out to me that the tutor had given the best lesson of his teaching career the previous day, but on my departure had reverted to his characteristic style. He had also pointed out to the class that he had put on a special show for me since 'somebody will read her report'. He obviously saw me as a 'spy', although he was ignorant of my 'paymaster's' identity.

The word spying implies observation done covertly, in secret; and the ethics of covert social research have been extensively discussed in the literature. For example the Homan/Bulmer debate in the *British Journal of Sociology*, 1980 (Bulmer and Homan); Bok, 1982; Erikson/Denzin, 1982. In the case of my research, however, observation was done overtly to the extent that I could be plainly identified as a researcher.

My defence is that I have not knowingly been a 'spy'. I may have been 'opportunistic' and used a form of 'impression management' in establishing relationships with respondents. I may even have attempted to control the amount of information I revealed about myself and my research (Jacobs, 1980). Nevertheless, in order to make recompense for what I regard as minor sins, I tried to give respondents every opportunity to present themselves as they would have wished, and as they would in any social situation. We do not and cannot always tell the subject exactly what it is we are interested to research (Roth, 1970). Often we do not know what it is that we seek. The interests and priorities of the research may shift as the research situation itself changes, as happened in the case of this research. Wax (1977) has described this flexibility as a major strength of the field research method, although it can create problems when the researcher attempts to adhere to a 'tight notion of informed consent' (Thorne, 1980, p. 287).

Bulmer also suggests that, although we may regard ourselves as doing overt research we are not always 'open and frank about our purposes and interests' (Bulmer, 1982, p. 5). Or we choose to stress only the least threatening aspects of our research. Of this I must plead guilty, although the intention was never deliberately to deceive. I was concerned to keep my explanations simple so that students and staff understood the nature of my research thus minimizing suspicion and feelings of insecurity.

We obviously have limited control over how any published material will be used, the researcher can merely respect confidentiality when this is appropriate and ensure that individual remarks are non-attributable. Respondents frequently harrassed me about being allowed to read my report when it was completed obviously interested to know how they themselves were represented, even though I stressed that anonymity would be maintained. I agreed to allow them to read the parts that concerned them whilst knowing that they would be bitterly disappointed since,

> ... the sociological view of the world — abstract, relativistic, generalizing — necessarily deflates people's view of themselves and their organization ... something precious to them is treated as merely an instance of a class. (Becker, 1964, p. 273)

Conclusion

In writing about my research I have mainly concerned myself with the ethical problems of data collection and have outlined the peculiarities of my own situation, that of being a woman researching men and of being closely associated with the institution and yet being an outsider. The research took place against a background of crisis within the college which left individuals feeling vulnerable and uncertain about their future. The greatest challenge I faced in these circumstances was not so much understanding the plight of these individuals, but of communicating empathy and of knowing how much of the data I obtained could ethically be used for publication.

References

APPELL, G. N. (1980) 'Talking ethics: The uses of moral rhetoric and the function of ethical principles', *Social Problems*, **27**, 3, February, pp. 350–7.

BECKER, H. S. (1964) 'Problems in the publication of field studies', in VIDICH, A. J., BENSMAN, J. and STEIN, M. R. (Eds), *Reflections on Community Studies*, New York, Harper and Row.

BOK, S. (1982) *Secrets: On the Ethics of Concealment and Revelation*, New York, Pantheon Books.

BULMER, M. and HOMAN, R. (1980) 'The ethics of covert methods', *British Journal of Sociology*, **31**, 1, pp. 46–65.

BULMER, M. (Ed) (1982) *Social Research Ethics*, London and Basingstoke, MacMillan.

DENZIN, N. and ERIKSON, K. (1982) On the Ethics of disguised observation: An exchange between Norman Denzin and Kai Erikson, in BULMER, M. (Ed) *Social Research Ethics*, London and Basingstoke, MacMillan Press Ltd.

JACOBS, S. E. (1980) 'Where have we come?' *Social Problems*, **27**, 3, February, pp. 371–8.

JENKINS, R. (1986) *Racism and Recruitment*, Cambridge, Cambridge University Press.

KLOCKERS, C. B. (1977) 'Field ethics for the life history', in WEPPNER, R. S. (Ed) *Street Ethnography*, Beverley Hills, CA, Sage.

PLATT, J. (1976) *Realities of Social Research*, New York, Wiley.

PLATT, J. (1981) 'On interviewing one's peers', *British Journal of Sociology*, **32**, 1, March, pp. 75–91.

ROTH, J. A. (1970) 'Comments on "secret observation"', *Social Problems*, **9**, 3, pp. 283–4.

THORNE, B. (1980) '"You still takin' notes?" Fieldwork and problems of informed consent', *Social Problems*, **27**, 3, February, pp. 284–97.

TRIGG, R. (1980) *Realities at Risk: A Defence of Realism in Philosophy and Science*, Sussex, Harvester Press.

VIDICH, A. J., BENSMAN, J. and STEIN, M. R. (Eds) (1964) *Reflections on Community Studies*, New York, Harper and Row.

WAX, M. L. (1977) 'On fieldworkers and those exposed to fieldwork: Federal regulations and moral issues', *Human Organisation*, **36** (3) pp. 321-8.

WAX, M. L. (1980) 'Paradoxes of "consent" to the practice of fieldwork', *Social Problems*, **27**, 3, February, pp. 272-83.

WEPPNER, R. S. (Ed) (1977) *Street Ethnography*, Beverley Hills, CA., Sage.

WHYTE, W. F. (1955) *Street Corner Society*, Chicago, University of Chicago Press.

11
'Whose side are we on?' Ethical Dilemmas in Research on 'Race' and Education

Barry Troyna and Bruce Carrington

Introduction

In this chapter, we want to identify the principles upon which antiracist research in education might be founded. The ethical dilemmas facing researchers in this field will be examined and the tensions and contradictions which currently exist between antiracist theory and practice highlighted. To bridge this gulf, we draw particularly upon the sociological insights of Gouldner (1975) and the contributions of critical theorists such as Lather (1986). We argue that their respective conceptions of research not only provide the basis for a critical appraisal of available substantive work on 'race' and education in the UK, but also a framework within which the following, essentially ethical, questions might be addressed. First, how can antiracist researchers reconcile their partisanship with objectivity? Second, what role (if any) should white researchers play in antiracist research? Third, what role should research play in promoting racial equality in educational access, treatment and outcome? Fourth, to what extent ought the research act itself *actively* challenge commonsense (for example, stereotypical, racist, populist) beliefs and perceptions? Fifth, can antiracist principles be reconciled with the need for external sponsorship and funding? Finally, what steps can be taken to facilitate the development of greater reciprocity and collaboration between the antiracist researcher and those whom she/he researches? Let us begin, however, by clarifying how we conceive of antiracist education.

As we have attempted to show elsewhere (Carrington and Short, 1987; Short and Carrington, 1987; Troyna and Williams, 1986) educational policies and practices based on this ideology should be concerned primarily with the structural and institutional basis of racism and racial inequality, both in schools and society. Because of the fundamental links between 'race', power and privilege, we have argued that any curricular initiative in this sphere should form an integral part of a wider programme of political education informed by the principles of social justice, equality and participatory democracy. As well as calling for changes in the formal curriculum to include teaching about 'race' and ethnic relations, we have advocated a reappraisal of the hidden curriculum to redress racial inequalities and eliminate discriminatory practices. This draws attention *inter alia* to staffing, assessment, setting and banding. The operational concepts we have used and the educational concerns and curricular approaches advocated can be contrasted with those of multicultural education which centralizes the need for schools to celebrate diversity, overcome curricular ethnocentrism and foster mutual understanding and tolerance. The form of political education we have envisaged, on the other hand, attaches high priority to the goal of political autonomy. It sees the role of school as equipping young people with the skills to understand and respond to a range of issues. This entails that young people are encouraged to take a critical stance towards political information; be open minded and show respect for evidence; act in an empathetic manner; extend their appreciation of how power is exercised (and by whom); and explore fundamental questions relating to social justice and equality. Such a programme would invariably necessitate a restructuring of relationships in many schools and classrooms. The aim would be to create a democratic environment in which teachers and learners are 'respected units' (Allport, 1954, p. 511) and where the pedagogical style stresses collaboration and cooperation. We have argued that this is conducive to the development of empathy, humanitarianism, informed scepticism and political autonomy. An authoritarian environment, where teacher exposition prevails and where hierarchy, competition and individualism are revered, would appear to be markedly at variance with these principles and goals.

Partisanship and Objectivity

It is our contention that this educational ideology is congruent with research informed by critical theory. For example, as the work of Lather (1986), amongst others, has indicated, research within this paradigm is essentially 'transformative' in nature: researchers seek not only to highlight forms of inequality and injustice, but view the research act itself as constituting a deliberate challenge to the *status quo*. From this standpoint, the ultimate purpose of research is to contribute to a body of empirically-grounded 'emancipatory knowledge'. This knowledge, by interrogating commonsense conceptions of the world (as well as more systematic forms of 'distorted communication'), may serve to 'empower the oppressed' by enabling them 'to come to understand and change their own oppressive realities' (*ibid*, pp. 261–2). Lather stresses that such research, as a 'response to the experiences, desires and needs of oppressed people' should aim to achieve maximal reciprocity between researcher and researched. She advocates a democratization of the research process. In her view, research should be seen as a 'dialogic enterprise' in which the traditional division of labour between researcher and researched (and its attendant status differential) is abandoned. Lather claims that if subjects (as active, purposive agents) are to be encouraged to be reflexive and question their own taken-for-granted beliefs and assumptions, then researchers must ensure that the 'researched' play a full part in the 'construction' and 'validation' of 'emancipatory knowledge': that is to say, both parties contribute to the analysis of data and formation of theory. It can be seen, then, that this research paradigm bears a strong resemblance to our conception of an antiracist pedagogy.

Whilst we accept Lather's views about the 'educative' purpose of such collaborative research and respect her unequivocal partisanship, we believe that there are some problems with this position. Above all, it declares a commitment to 'underdogs' which is idealist and could be construed as relativist. Criticisms along these lines formed the thrust of Gouldner's (1975) reflections on the work of Howard Becker. It seems to us, that Gouldner's strictures are also important in facilitating an exploration and resolution to the ethical questions associated with research on 'race' and education.

Briefly, when addressing the question 'Whose side are we on?' Becker had contended that the researcher was compelled to affiliate to the perspectives of either 'subordinates'/'underdogs' or 'superiors'/'overdogs'. The inference drawn from his studies of deviance is a sentimental commitment to the 'underdog': marijuana users, jazz musicians, prostitutes and so on. In recognizing Becker's genuine concern to expose injustices through his research, and the potential conflict that such an enterprise entails, Gouldner, nonetheless, argues that it is possible to reconcile such explicit forms of partisanship with objectivity. Gouldner contends that if (partisan) sociologists are to act in the role of arbiter between interest groups (i.e. 'underdogs' and 'overdogs') there must be some appeal to a body of ethical principles if justice is to be realized. Ultimately, Gouldner (1975) insists that: 'It is to values, not to factions, that sociologists must give their most basic commitment' (p. 68).

We take Gouldner's imperative as the starting point for our appraisal of research on 'race' and education. Specifically, this demands that the researcher's preeminent commitment should not be to black or white youth, teachers or administrators, but to the fundamental principles of social justice, equality and participatory democracy. In short, we are arguing for the establishment of principles which are common both to antiracist pedagogy and research. From this perspective, we can now explore the remaining opening questions which highlight, in our experience, the main ethical dilemmas facing researchers in this area. An appropriate starting point for two white researchers contributing to this area is a consideration of the extent to which the 'race' or ethnicity of researchers has a bearing on the realization of these principles.

The Role of White Researchers

Quite clearly, important strategic, moral and political decisions need to be taken about how best research might expedite the attainment of these principles, and it is around this issue that trenchant criticisms about the involvement and concerns of white researchers in 'race relations' and antiracist research have crystallized. In both the UK and USA, a common criticism of such research has been that white researchers have tended to direct their energies towards the study of black people rather than white racism. In this country, such criticisms were voiced during the 'palace revolution' of the early 1970s when black community activists and others criticized the political orientation and research agenda of the Institute of Race Relations (IRR). At the time, the IRR was, in the words of Mullard (1985), 'a white prestigious body' (p. 1). It was engaged in various activities which, its opponents argued, rested on a pernicious and misleading identification of 'the problem'. For those involved in the struggle for control of the IRR the fundamental issues to be considered differed from those which the Institute's researchers had addressed. Bourne (1980) has noted:

> It was not black people who should be examined, but white society; it was not a question of educating blacks and whites for integration, but of fighting institutional racism; it was not race relations that was the field of study, but racism (p. 339).

Clearly these were not simply differences in interpretation which might be resolved by rational, disinterested discourse. They reflected diametrically opposed political positions regarding the cause and nature of racial inequality in the UK and the political actions which were needed to combat this reality. The critique rested mainly on the presumption that (white) social science scholarship had authenticated a scenario in which black citizens played an active role in the generation and maintenance of racial inequality. It was not an unfamiliar debate; the research of Daniel Moynihan and James Coleman in the USA had prompted similar critiques in the 1960s (see Billingsley, 1970). In this country, the dispute continued into the 1980s and formed the *leitmotif* of *The Empire Strikes Back* (CCCS, 1982). Here, black members of Birmingham University's Centre for Contemporary Cultural Studies (CCCS) attacked the research problematics of various white sociologists. Although one of the authors, Lawrence (1981), suggested in an accompanying article that he did not insist that 'white sociologists cannot study black people' (p. 9), his colleagues were less concessionary in their contributions to the main text.

Essentially, the critique comprises three parts. First, that white researchers cannot elicit meaningful data from black respondents because of status and power differences between them. Thus, the absence of shared socialization and critical life experiences inevitably impairs the nature and value of the data. The problem of symmetry, of course, is not merely confined to this particular research relationship. It also features in discussions about the interview relationship between feminist researchers and female interviewees. Some feminists, such as Finch (1984) and Oakley (1981) tend to concur with the view that symmetry provides the *sine qua non* of valuable and reliable data. Others, such as Davies (1985) are more doubtful. Davies, for instance, indicates the possible advantages of the 'cultural stranger' role. The argument here is that those issues and concerns of girls and women which female researchers might take for granted are more likely to be probed and made problematic by a male researcher. Davies also shares with Cashmore and Troyna (1981) a sceptical view of how one might assess the extent to which a male/white researcher might alter the shape and nature of an interview with girls/blacks. As Davies (1985) says: 'It would be impossible to state with certainty . . . the specific effect of gender on any research relationship; all one can ask for again is that it might be borne in mind in planning and execution' (p. 87).

A second and more signficant criticism is based on the way in which the data elicited from black respondents are generally interpreted by white researchers. Here, Parekh (1986) has argued a forceful point: 'Most researchers in the field are white. They have no experience of what it means to be black, and lack an intuitive understanding of the complex mental processes and social structures of the black communities' (p. 24). Consequently, we find accounts of black communities — written, in the main, by white researchers — which are not only ethnocentric but

Barry Troyna and Bruce Carrington

caricature these communities by centralizing empirically questionable concepts such as 'identity crisis', 'negative self-image', 'intergenerational conflict', 'unrealistic and high aspirations' and 'culture conflict'. (See Lawrence, 1982; Stone, 1981.) Analyses embedded within such frameworks have the potential to generate policy and political responses which do little, if anything, to combat racial inequalities or the structures and ideologies from which they stem. On the contrary, they contribute to the maintenance of 'pathological' conceptions of black communities.

Finally, the third element of this critique questions the white researcher's self-appointed role as 'ombudsman', to use Gouldner's (1975) term (p. 40). It is a criticism which has been directed mainly at John Rex and his colleagues at the former SSRC Research Unit on Ethnic Relations. Rex has consistently maintained that his work on 'race' is underpinned by an explicit commitment to racial equality and justice. In Rex's (1981) words he wants 'to use empirical research on racialism and racism in contemporary British society to help all of those engaged in fighting against that racialism;' (p. 151). However, Bourne (1980), Lawrence (1982) and the CCCS collective are impatient with this view. They have suggested that by bringing into the public eye the life situations and life chances of black people, Rex and his colleagues provide the state with essential data which may be used to maintain racial inequalities. Indeed, they go on to assert that this is almost inevitable in so far as Rex and his colleagues were dependent on funding from the state to pursue *policy-orientated* research. Irrespective of the declared commitment of Rex and his colleagues to social justice, the likelihood of their research being appropriated by the state to sustain and legitimate the *status quo* is enhanced by their relatively powerless position *vis-à-vis* the state.

These are important criticisms of the role of white researchers in 'race relations'. What they identify is the profound difficulty in reconciling a genuine commitment to antiracist values and principles with research which focuses on the black communities. The convergence between the taken-for-granted assumptions and values of white researchers about black communities on the one hand, and the delicate situation they occupy as policy-orientated researchers on the other, suggests almost immovable obstacles to the realization of these goals. This is how Lawrence (1982) sees it:

In a situation where *state racism* has intensified, it is disingenuous for policy-oriented researchers to expect that their racist and patriarchal conceptualizations of black people will not be of interest to the state institutions which oppress black people (p. 134).

This is not to deny the role of white researchers in the antiracist struggle; it is to suggest that the principles they avow are in danger of violation should they focus their research activities on the black communities. This constitutes an important ethical issue in the future formulation of research projects and programmes. Nevertheless, a tantalizing question remains: to what extent do we need to have systematic evidence of racial inequality before strategies can be developed to tackle it?

Ethics and Black Educational Experiences

As Troyna (1984) has argued elsewhere, concern about the apparently poor performance of black students (especially those of Afro-Caribbean origin) at all levels of their school career has figured prominently in the literature on 'race' and education. The last twenty-five years has seen the publication of numerous empirical studies into this issue which range from localized case material of performance within and between schools, to comparisons which are both regional and national in nature. As Troyna (1984) noted: '. . . even the most cursory perusal of the literature in this field would show that the notion of black educational underachievement is widely accepted as an irrefutable fact' (p. 153). Nor was this observation disturbed by the publication of the Swann Committee's report *Education for All* in March 1985 (DES, 1985). On the contrary, the data collected by the Committee on ethnic differences in examination performance at 16+ and 18+ suggested that, in the LEAs studied, young people of Afro-Caribbean origin tended to perform less well than their white South Asian peers. On the whole, then, the data endorsed Taylor's (1981) insistence that '. . . research evidence shows a strong trend to underachievement of pupils of West Indian origin on the main indicators of academic performance' (p. 216).

Unfortunately, what this particular statement fails to acknowledge are the conceptual and methodological weaknesses often characteristic of research into this issue. For instance, although it is widely accepted that parental social class and educational level have an important bearing on the school performance of students (Halsey, Heath and Ridge, 1980), the bulk of research into this specific feature of school achievement has failed to take these factors into account. Thus, despite claims to the contrary, there continues to be some confusion as to whether Afro-Caribbean students *qua* Afro-Caribbean students are relatively low academic attainers. It could be that factors other than what Hochschild terms 'racially relevant variables' (1984) have greater salience. The research

Barry Troyna and Bruce Carrington

of Roberts and his associates (1983) provides evidence which supports this view. They found that the educational credentials of Afro-Caribbean school leavers in six working-class neighbourhoods were at least comparable to, and in the case of girls, better than those of their white counterparts. Driver's (1980) study of attainment levels in five urban secondary schools pointed in this same direction although, here, serious questions have been raised about the lack of methodological rigour in the research.

In contrast to these findings, the research of Maurice and Alma Craft (1983) in an outer London borough indicated that the examination performance of Afro-Caribbean students was depressed in relation to their white peers from similar social backgrounds.

We would like to stress that it is difficult to draw any firm conclusions about the respective effects of 'race', ethnicity and class on educational outcomes because of the inconsistencies in the formulation of research.

Clearly, if researchers are concerned to challenge racial inequality in education, it is important that they demonstrate unequivocally the salience of 'racially relevant variables' in the determination of the educational experiences of black students. The ethical issue which this highlights is that, if a 'problem' is to be researched and, more importantly, obviated, then it is imperative that the work undertaken is rigorous and clear. It is simply insufficient to infer cause from effect; this merely absolves researchers from responsibility of testing empirically the relationship between, say, ideologies and practices on the one hand, and the existence of inequalities on the other (Troyna and Williams, 1986).

However, if we remain unsure about those factors which are casually related to the educational *outcome* of black students we are more confident about the existence of differential *treatment* accorded black and white students in school. The research of Carrington (1983), Green (1982) and Wright (1987) has suggested how teacher expectations about black students' presumed academic deficiencies and concomitant sporting prowess may be reflected in teacher strategies, assessment procedures, and in decisions about setting and option allocation. Green's research is especially important in this context for it provides crucial evidence of how racial attitudes and beliefs not only influence the behaviour of teachers towards black pupils but how they may also have an effect upon the pupils' self-concepts and, possibly, academic achievements. Green's fieldwork was conducted in six schools (junior and middle). His sample comprised seventy teachers (all of whom were white) and their 1814 pupils (of whom 940 were white, 449 of Asian descent and 425 of Afro-Caribbean descent). Using a Flanders' Schedule, Green began by analyzing the characteristics of interaction between teachers and boys and girls from each ethnic group. He then invited his teacher respondents to complete a revised version of the British Ethnocentricism Scale. On the basis of these results, he was able to identify two distinctive groups — 'ethnically highly tolerant teachers' and 'ethnically highly intolerant teachers'. A comparative analysis of the classroom behaviour of these groups revealed that, highly intolerant teachers gave their Afro-Caribbean pupils less individual attention, only minimal praise, more authoritative directions and fewer opportunities to initiate contributions to class discussions. Green also found that the mean self-concept scores of Afro-Caribbean pupils taught by 'highly intolerant teachers' were significantly lower than those of their black peers who were taught by 'highly tolerant teachers'. If, as Green's research suggests, teachers' racial attitudes are translated into classroom action, then this is likely to circumscribe the level of educational attainment of black children. Following on from this, and its relationship to our stated ethical position, the imperative must be for educational researchers to develop interventionist strategies which mitigate these clear-cut forms of unequal treatment and contribute towards equity in the treatment of all students within educational settings. This takes us on to our fourth area of concern: to what extent ought the 'research act' itself *actively* challenge commonsense beliefs and perceptions?

Reinforcing or Challenging Stereotypes?

As we have already indicated, the aim of 'emancipatory knowledge' should be to encourage the researcher to be reflexive and question their own taken-for-granted beliefs and assumptions. In effect, the 'research act' is conceived as educative. A perusal of studies into teachers' racial attitudes in the UK shows clearly that this conception has not been in the forefront of researchers' minds. As we will now show, researchers have limited their interventions to encouraging, reinforcing or even forcing subjects to employ prevailing racial stereotypes. We are not aware of any study which has attempted to challenge or undermine directly teachers' racial beliefs and perceptions.

A clear example of how researchers have encouraged teachers to construe the world in racial terms is Brittan's (1976) Schools Council/NFER Survey undertaken in the early 1970s. A questionnaire, comprising mainly items amenable to Likert-Scaling, was administered to a national sample of teachers drawn from both primary and secondary schools. It sought to gauge their opinions about ethnic differences in pupils' and parents' responses to education. The survey showed that Afro-Caribbean pupils were generally seen in a less favourable light than their white or Asian peers. What is more, they were often stereotyped as having lower academic ability and as creating disciplinary problems. By inviting teachers to indicate the extent to which they agreed or disagreed with statements such as 'Asian pupils are usually better behaved than English pupils'; 'West Indian pupils resent being reprimanded more than English pupils do'; and 'West Indian pupils tend to raise the academic standard of this school' Brittan not only encouraged her respondents to employ racist and ethnicist frames of reference but also may have given spurious legitimacy to the process of differentiation along racial and ethnic lines.

Similar criticisms may be levelled against smaller-scale studies, such as that of Edwards (1978). She presented twenty student teachers with tape-recordings of speakers from different social and ethnic backgrounds: a bi-dialectal British-born girl of Barbadian descent (who spoke both in Creole and with a working-class Reading accent); an English boy with a working-class Reading accent; a professor's son who spoke received pronunciation (RP); and a recently arrived female Creole speaker from Jamaica. The respondents were asked to consider 'the relative academic potential of the speakers' and 'their desirability as members of a class'. Not surprisingly, when invited to employ stereotypes of 'race' and class, they behaved 'in accordance with widely-held social stereotypes'. The middle-class male speaker, for example, was perceived as having the highest academic potential and the Barbadian girl was judged less favourably when speaking Creole than in the local working-class accent.

Headteachers were also encouraged to articulate (but not to question) their taken-for-granted assumptions about 'race' and ethnicity in Tomlinson's research on 'special education' in Birmingham. According to Tomlinson, the thirty heads in the sample were asked to describe 'their perceptions of the problems West Indian and Asian children *in general* presented in school ... The questions were designed to elicit the cultural beliefs of heads about the children.' (Rex and Tomlinson, 1979, pp. 198–9, my emphasis.) When asked to generalize, the headteachers obliged by stereotyping Afro Caribbeans as: 'less keen on education than Asians'; 'slower than Asian children, not as bright', and 'volatile, disruptive and easily stirred'.

Carrington and Wood's case study of ethnic differences in extra-curricular sports participation at 'Hillsview School' exhibits similar flaws (Carrington, 1983; Carrington and Wood, 1983). They atttempted to probe teachers' racial frames of reference by inviting them to indicate whether they varied their approach to suit pupils of different ethnic backgrounds. Their responses indicated that 'there were some teachers at the school who operated with pejorative stereotypes of West Indian pupils and viewed their behaviour, academic activities and parent culture in a negative manner' (Carrington, 1983, p. 50). Although some members of the school's staff were unwilling to condone these stereotypical rationalizations, the research, along with those others we have cited, did little to facilitate dissent from such images and perceptions of black and white pupils. By implication, at least, it provided a context for the expression and reproduction of racist and ethnicist views of pupils and their families.

A more explicit example of how research might reinforce such views can be found in Hartley's (1985) study of a Scottish urban primary school. Referring to his respondents' (teachers) use of the term 'immigrant' to describe British Asians, he noted:

> In addition to this matter of nomenclature, there is an argument which says that by the very act of treating ethnic-minority groups as units of analysis in a research undertaking, the researcher may be culpable of unconscious racism. That is, he (*sic*) may actually create a difference associated with ethnicity that might not have occurred to those whom he is researching. He may make an issue out of something that hitherto had not been perceived as such by the participants in the situation he observes. This is a dilemma which is difficult to overcome. My stance here is to state that it was the teachers themselves who offered the 'immigrant'/white dichotomy ... Our purpose is not to condone the teachers' inaccurate nomenclature, nor their use of the ethnicity of the pupil as a basis for differentiation, rather it is to see what consequences these had for the school experience of children labelled in this way (*ibid*, p. 19).

We appreciate that Hartley felt restrained, as an ethnographer, by the self-imposed methodological imperative of adopting 'a position akin to an observer who was both detached and involved.' Leaving aside what we see as the limitations of this paradigm, our main cause for concern is Hartley's lack of consistency. He defends his refusal to combat teachers' racial differentiation by insisting that he wanted to contribute 'nothing to the day to day proceedings of the school' (p. 51). At the same time, however, he appropriates the racist terminology of some teachers, transmits it to the pupils and therefore may have contributed directly to the way those pupils construed relationships at the school. The following extract shows that although Hartley (1985) is aware of the ideological significance of the term 'immigrant' he nonetheless introduces it to a discussion with pupils. It is our contention that this reinforces and extends its legitimacy within the context of that school:

> *White boy:* The teachers take more time with learning the blacks English than with us. My mum and dad says they spend more time with the blacks than they do with us.
>
> *DH:* Do you think the teachers treat the 'immigrants' any differently?
>
> *Girls (3):* Yes.
>
> *Girl:* They are not as strict.
>
> *Girl:* I think they're petted.
>
> *Girl:* Mrs ... favours 'immigrants' more than whites (p. 170).

The studies of teachers' racial attitudes and typifications discussed above show how researchers have both encouraged and reinforced prevailing stereotypes of 'race' (and class). Figueroa's (1986) recent investigation of student teachers' images of ethnic minorities raises further ethical questions. Figueroa administered three questionnaires to a cohort of PGCE secondary students who had attended a short course on multicultural education. The questionnaires were designed to elicit views on the student teachers' perceptions of and attitudes towards 'West Indians' and 'Asians' together with other race-related issues. In common with other studies in the area Figueroa encouraged respondents to articulate stereotypes by completing open-ended statements such as 'when I think of Asians I think ...'. Semantic differential techniques were also used. Figueroa's previous research had shown that when respondents were asked to rate 'White British pupils', 'West Indian pupils' and 'Asian pupils', many refused and elected to use the 'can't generalize' option. As a result, the sample described in the paper under discussion was *not* provided with this option: they were *forced* into a situation where they could do nothing but stereotype. Despite this constraint, Figueroa (1986) reports that 'several respondents made comments about this question indicating that they didn't want to be forced into producing stereotypes' (p. 15). Although Figueroa is frank in his presentation of the research he conveys the impression, nevertheless, that his primary concern is to ensure that his sample generates racial stereotypes. Surely such an approach with an incoming generation of teachers is hardly conducive to changing the *status quo* in education?

In this section we have focused on research on teachers' and student-teachers' racial attitudes and beliefs. It is our contention that the criticisms of these studies also apply to research on childrens' racial attitudes (for example, Davey, 1983; Milner, 1983; Mould, 1987) and professional responses to the role of the school in a multicultural society (Carrington, *et al* 1986; Giles, 1977; Troyna and Ball, 1985). At best, the research has merely highlighted ways in which teachers, policy-makers and pupils tend to evaluate black people in the UK in a negative or dismissive manner. Another problem with this research is its elitist and undemocratic nature which is especially exemplified by the denial of subjects' capacity to scrutinize and change the mode of the research act and their role within it. Ultimately, we are sceptical of the value of this research because it separates conception from execution, theory from practice. Lather's (1986) epithet, 'the rape model', seems to be appropriate to research such as this which takes rather than gives, describes rather than changes, transmits rather than transforms. Whether or not the ethical principles we have espoused here can be reconciled with the demands of external funding agencies and sponsors is, of course, an open question.

Sponsors: Whose Side are They on?

It may seem a truism to note that at a time of severe contraction, expenditure on educational research is highly susceptible to major cuts, and competition for an increasingly limited supply of external funds has intensified. What is more, as Hargreaves (1986) rightly points out, this same period has seen a concomitant decline in 'government interest in investing in independent questioning and self-criticism . . .' (p. 15).

The implications for researchers genuinely committed to implementing educational research based on the antiracist principles we have outlined here should be clear. Firstly, the potential for external funding for radical antiracist research is limited. This is especially the case when one considers the DES as an important source of research funds. After all, it is significant that a commitment to antiracist educational research (or practice) did not appear in the Secretary of State's oral statement on the Swann Report of 14 March 1985 (DES, 1985) which sets out the government's approach and priorities in this area (see Troyna, 1986 for discussion). Secondly, it is increasingly likely that successful applications for external funds would have been compelled to assume explicitly policy-orientated goals. For some researchers, of course, this would not constitute a problem (Hargreaves, 1986). However, as we noted earlier, this poses particular problems for those researchers who may not wish to assume the so-called role of 'ombudsman'. For many antiracists, committed to the principles of research specified by Lather and others, the imperative is to 'empower' oppressed groups, enabling *them* to take action rather than present the research findings to the 'powerful' (for example, policy-makers and professionals) in the (forlorn) hope that they might shoulder some responsibility. Thirdly, the contraction in external funding enhances the researcher's reliance on patronage from sponsoring agencies. Put another way, it has progressively constrained the autonomy of the researcher, not only to initiate research, but also to retain control over its orientation and dissemination. The consequences of the restructuring of the Social Science Research Council (now Economic and Social Research Council) in 1982 demonstrates this point clearly. The reappraisal of the way the Council allocates its limited funds led to a greater proportion of its money being distributed through its Research Developments fund — where Council identifies research areas to which proposals are invited — and to a lesser amount allocated to its Research Grant Scheme, where applications on any topic within the Council's remit are considered. The current economic and, more importantly, political context strengthen Platt's (1976) conviction that the course of research is affected strongly by external factors, especially those which centre on the relationship between sponsoring bodies and the researcher (pp. 64–5).

Three recent examples of how sponsoring agencies can constrain, even control, the nature and dissemination of research on 'race' and education should be sufficient to illustrate the argument. Although two involved the relationship between researchers and one sponsoring body (the now defunct Schools Council) they are instructive in that one of these examples involved Robert Jeffcoate, a self-declared liberal whose antipathy towards radical antiracist principles has been well publicized (for example, Jeffcoate, 1984). The research revealed extensive racism amongst staff in sample schools. Because of this, the Schools Council chose to delay publication of their commissioned report, *Education for a Multicultural Society* for three years. Moreover, the published version, which appeared in 1981, was a heavily censored document. A similar fate was experienced by Dawn Gill, a geography teacher at Quinton Kynaston School in London, who was commissioned by the Schools Council to 'investigate how (geography) syllabuses and examinations at 16+ can meet the needs of all pupils in a multiracial society'. Her eventual report, however, 'eschewed this defining and confining perspective' to use Troyna and Williams' terms (1986, p. 25). Instead it gave primacy to an antiracist perspective in preference to multicultural considerations and specified the limitations of examination reform in the promotion of racial justice and equality in education. The Schools Council refused point blank to publish this report.

Seen from this perspective, it is hardly surprising that the Swann Committee was not provided with access to John Eggleston's report on the educational and vocational experiences of black 16–18 year olds which the DES had commissioned and had available some months before the Committee provided its final report. In view of the difficulties encountered by these researchers, we can only wonder whether future research based on an overt commitment to antiracism would be likely to attract 'official' sponsorship.

A New Direction for Research on 'Race' and Education

Let us conclude by briefly summarizing our argument and suggesting a possible future direction for research on 'race' and education. As well as criticizing much existing research in the area for its failure to provide evidence on the specific effect of 'racially relevant variables' on educational outcomes, we have also shown that it has also tended to reinforce populist images of Afro-Caribbean and South Asian people and culture and done little to surmount the traditional (asymmetrical) division of labour between the researcher and researched. Because of its essentially elitist and conservative form, the research may be regarded as being at variance with antiracist practice. We have argued that both theory *and* practice in this sphere should be informed by the same principles: that is, a commitment to social justice, equality and participatory democracy.

Our analysis suggests that a collaborative, action-research model such as that employed in the GIST project (for example, Whyte, 1986), or by Chisholm and Holland (1986) in their work on antisexist curricula might also provide the basis for future research on 'race'. This approach, as the latter have noted (*ibid*, pp. 358–9) 'can be seen as fostering change during the course of the research process, which includes monitoring or evaluating the change process or outcomes'. In the case of antiracist education, it could offer various advantages. First, in planning, evaluating and appraising an initiative *with* teachers, researchers would find themselves in a position where they could intervene *directly* to influence attitudes and behaviour. As well as providing a forum for reflecting critically on 'race'-related issues, this approach could help to obviate the misgivings that many teachers appear to have concerning antiracist education and, to a lesser degree, multicultural education (Troyna and

Ball, 1985). Advocates of antiracist education, teachers and researchers alike, may then be better placed to persuade those 'lukewarm' or outwardly hostile towards the initiative of its compatability with a 'good' education: that is, an education predicated upon humanitarian, democratic principles and a commitment to equipping young people to play a full part in community-life as decent, fair-minded, responsible and rational citizens. Furthermore, antiracists might also argue that pedagogical strategies compatible with their ideology, such as collaborative group work, not only serve to enhance young people's social awareness, interpersonal and ethical skills, but do so without any apparent, adverse effect on their level of attainment (Yeomans, 1983). In recent years, antiracist policies have been criticized because of the often ambiguous and generalized nature of their prescriptions (for example, Banks, 1986; Richards, 1986; Taylor, 1986). The form of research that we envisage would seek to overcome these problems by helping schools to devise, implement and evaluate their own antiracist policies. As well as providing invaluable data on, for example, the influence of *situational* constraints (school ethos, phase, type, ethnic composition) on such innovations, it would also serve to remind researchers of the varied *institutional* constraints under which teachers currently work. Collaborative, action research would help ensure that antiracist education is better understood (and thus accepted) by teaching staff and its *effects* more systematically monitored. Antiracist theory and practice cannot be founded upon mere articles of faith: both must be reflexive and subject to rigorous empirical scrutiny if their transformative potential is to be realized. This will only be achieved when the present division between theory and practice is eliminated.

References

ALLPORT, G. (1954) *The Nature of Prejudice*, Reading, Mass., Addison-Wesley.
BANKS, J. (1986) 'Multicultural and its critics: Britain and the United States', in MODGIL, S. *et al* (Eds) *Multicultural Education: the Interminable Debate*, Lewes, Falmer Press.
BELL, C. and ROBERTS, H. (Ed) (1984) *Social Researching: Politics, Problems, Practice*, London, Routledge and Kegan Paul.
BARTON, L. and WALKER, S. (Eds) (1983) *Race, Class and Education*, London, Croom Helm.
BILLINGSLEY, A. (1970) 'Black families and white social science', *Journal of Social Issues*, **26**, 3, pp. 127–42.
BOURNE, J. (1980) 'Cheerleaders and ombudsmen: The sociology of race

relations in Britain', *Race and Class*, **21**, 4, pp. 331–52.

BRITTAN, E. (1976) 'Multiracial education—2. Teacher opinion on aspects of school life. Part 2, pupils and teachers'. *Educational Research*, **18**, 3, pp. 182–91.

BURGESS, R. (Ed) (1985) *Field Methods in the Study of Education*, Lewes, Falmer Press.

CARRINGTON, B. (1983) 'Sport as a side-track: An analysis of West Indian involvement in extra-curricular sport; in BARTON, L. and WALKER, S. (Eds) *Race, Class and Education*, London, Croom Helm.

CARRINGTON, B., MILLWARD, A. and SHORT, G. (1986) 'Schooling in a multiracial society: contrasting perspectives of primary and secondary teachers in training' *Educational Studies*, **12**, 1, pp. 17–35.

CARRINGTON, B. and SHORT, G. (1987) 'Breakthrough to political literacy: political education, antiracist education and the primary school', *Journal of Education Policy*, **2**, 1, pp. 1–13.

CARRINGTON, B. and WOOD, E. (1983) 'Body talk—images of sport in a multiracial school', *Multiracial Education*, **11**, 2, pp. 29–38.

CASHMORE, E. and TROYNA, B. (1981) 'Just for white boys? Elitism, racism and research', *Multiracial Education*, **10**, 1, pp. 43–8.

CENTRE FOR CONTEMPORARY CULTURAL STUDIES (1982) *The Empire Strikes Back*, London, Hutchinson.

CHISHOLM, L. A. and HOLLAND, J. (1986) 'Girls and occupational choice: Antisexism in action in a curriculum development project', *British Journal of Sociology of Education*, **7**, 4, pp. 353–65.

CHIVERS, T. (Ed) (1987) *Race and Culture in Education*, Windsor, NFER/NELSON.

CRAFT, M. and CRAFT, A. (1983) 'The participation of ethnic minority pupils in further and higher education', *Educational Research*, **25**, 1, pp. 10–19.

DAVEY, A. (1983) *Learning to be Prejudiced*, London, Hutchinson.

DAVIES, L. (1985) 'Ethnography and status: Focusing on gender in educational research', in BURGESS, R. (Ed) *Field Methods in the Study of Education*, Lewes, Falmer Press.

DEPARTMENT OF EDUCATION AND SCIENCE (1985) *Education for All* Committee of Inquiry into the Education of Children from Ethnic Minority Groups, (The Swann Report), Cmnd. 9543, London, HMSO.

DRIVER, G. (1980) *Beyond Underachievement*, London, Commission for Racial Equality.

EDWARDS, V. K. (1978) 'Language attitudes and underperformance in West Indian Children', *Educational Review*, **30**, 1, pp. 51–8.

FIGUEROA, P. (1986) 'Student teachers' images of ethnic minorities: A British case study'. Paper presented to *World Congress of Sociology*, New Delhi, 18–22 August.

FINCH, J. (1984) '"It's great to have someone to talk to": The ethics and politics of interviewing women', in BELL, C. and ROBERTS, H. (Eds) *Social Researching: Politics, Problems, Practice*, London, Routledge and Kegan Paul.

GILES, R. (1977) *The West Indian Experience in British Schools*, London, Heinemann.

GOULDNER, A. (1975) *For Sociology: Renewal and Critique in Sociology Today*, Harmondsworth, Pelican.

GREEN, P. A. (1982) *'Teachers' Influence on the self-concept of pupils of different ethnic groups'*. Unpublished PhD thesis, University of Durham.

HALSEY, A. H., HEATH, A. F. and RIDGE, J. M. (1980) *Origins and Destinations*, Oxford, Clarendon Press.

HARGREAVES, A. (1986) 'Research, policy and practice in education: some observations on SSRC-funded education projects', *Journal of Education Policy*, 1, 2, pp. 115–32.

HARTLEY, D. (1985) *Understanding the Primary School*, London, Croom Helm.

HOCHSCHILD, J. L. (1984) *The New American Dilemma: Liberal Democracy and School Desegregation*, New Haven, Yale University Press.

JEFFCOATE, R. (1984) *Ethnic Minorities and Education*, London, Harper and Row.

LATHER, P. (1986) 'Research as praxis', *Harvard Educational Review*, 56, 3, pp. 257–77.

LAWRENCE, E. (1981) 'White sociology, black struggle', *Multiracial Education*, 9, 3, pp. 3–17.

LAWRENCE, E. (1982) 'In the abundance of water the fool is thirsty: Sociology and black "pathology"', in CCCS, *The Empire Strikes Back*, London, Hutchinson.

MILNER, D. (1983) *Children and Race: Ten Years On*, London, Ward Lock.

MODGIL, S. *et al* (Eds) (1985) *Multicultural Education: The Interminable Debate*, Lewes, Falmer Press.

MOULD, W. (1987) 'Multicultural education: An LEA response', in CHIVERS, T. (Ed) *Race and Culture in Education*, Windsor, NFER/Nelson.

MULLARD, C. (1985) *Race, Power and Resistance*, London, Routledge and Kegan Paul.

OAKLEY, A. (1981) 'Interviewing women: A contradiction in terms', in ROBERTS, H. (Ed) *Doing Feminist Research*, London, Routledge and Kegan Paul.

PAREKH, B. (1986) 'Britain's step-citizens', *New Society*, 1 August, pp. 24–5.

PLATT, J. (1976) *Realities of Social Research*, Sussex, University of Sussex Press.

POLLARD, A. (Ed) (1987) *Children and their Primary Schools*, Lewes, Falmer Press.

REX, J. (1981) 'Errol Lawrence and the sociology of race relations: An open letter', *Multiracial Education*, 10, 1, pp. 49–51.

REX, J. and TOMLINSON, S. (1979) *Colonial Immigrants in a British City: A Class Analysis*, London, Routledge and Kegan Paul.

RICHARDS, C. (1986) 'Antiracist initiatives', *Screen*, 27, 5, pp. 74–9.

ROBERTS, H. (Ed) (1981) *Doing Feminist Research*, London, Routledge and Kegan Paul.

ROBERTS, K., NOBLE, M. and DUGGAN, J. (1983) 'Young, black and out of work', in TROYNA, B. and SMITH, D. I. (Eds) *Racism, School and the Labour Market*, Leicester, National Youth Bureau.

SCHOOLS COUNCIL (1981) *Education for a Multicultural Society*, London, Commission for Racial Equality.

SHORT, G. and CARRINGTON, B. (1987) 'Towards an anti-racist initiative in the all-white primary school: A case study', in POLLARD, A. (Ed) *Children and their Primary Schools*, Lewes, Falmer Press.

STONE, M. (1981) *The Education of the Black Child in Britain*, London, Fontana Books.

TAYLOR, M. (1981) *Caught Between: A Review of Research into the Education of Pupils of West Indian Origin*, Windsor, NFER/Nelson.

TAYLOR, B. (1986) 'Antiracist education in non-contact areas: The need for a gentle approach', *New Community*, **13**, 2, pp. 177–84.

TROYNA, B. (1984) 'Fact or artefact? The "educational underachievement" of black pupils', *British Journal of Sociology of Education*, **5**, 2, pp. 153–66.

TROYNA, B. (1986) '"Swann's Song": The origins, ideology and implication of Education for All', *Journal of Education Policy*, **1**, 2, pp. 171–81.

TROYNA, B. (1987) 'Beyond multiculturalism: Towards the enactment of antiracist education in policy, provision and pedagogy', *Oxford Review of Education*, **13**, 3.

TROYNA, B. (Ed) (1987) *Racial Inequality in Education*, London, Tavistock.

TROYNA, B. and BALL, W. (1985) 'View from the chalkface: School responses to an LEA's policy on multicultural education', *Policy Paper 1*, Warwick, Centre for Research in Ethnic Relations.

TROYNA, B. and SMITH, D. I. (Eds) (1983) *Racism, School and the Labour Market*, Leicester, National Youth Bureau.

TROYNA, B. and WILLIAMS, J. (1986) *Racism, Education and The State*, London, Croom Helm.

WHYTE, J. (1986) *Girls into Science and Technology: The Story of a Project*, London, Routledge and Kegan Paul.

WRIGHT, C. (1987) 'Black students — white teachers', in TROYNA, B. (Ed) *Racial Inequality in Education*, London, Tavistock.

YEOMANS, A. (1983) 'Collaborative groupwork in primary and secondary schools: Britain and USA', *Durham and Newcastle Research Review*, **10**, 51, pp. 95–105.

A Guide to Further Reading

As the contributors to this volume have indicated there are relatively few discussions of ethical issues in relation to educational research. As a result this list contains more books of a general kind that it is hoped will assist the reader in reviewing, conducting and evaluating educational research practice.

On Education

ADELMAN, C. (Ed) (1984) *The Politics and Ethics of Evaluation*, London, Croom Helm, provides chapters from a range of educational evaluators in the UK. See the chapters by Elliott, Eraut, Adelman and Simons. They are brief but useful accounts.

INNER LONDON EDUCATION AUTHORITY (1987) *Informing Education. Report of the Committee of Inquiry into Freedom of Information*, London, ILEA, provides a discussion of current policies concerning the confidentiality of information about schools, staff and pupils in the ILEA. The report suggests a policy of access to information, together with a policy for discovering what information was needed, the form of presentation and the encouragement of its use. A short guide to the key issues is provided in TOMLINSON, J., MORTIMORE, P. and SAMMONS, P. (1988) *Freedom and Education: Ways of Increasing Openness and Accountability*, Sheffield Papers in Education Management 76 Sheffield, Sheffield City Polytechnic.

PUNCH, M. (1986) *The Politics and Ethics of Fieldwork*, Beverly Hills, CA, Sage, is a short volume in the qualitative research series. It deals with general ethical issues in fieldwork. However, the last two chapters (that constitute half the book) deal with an educational example when Punch discusses the problems of conducting research in Dartington Hall School in England.

On Ethics in Social Research

BARNES, J. (1979) *Who Should Know What? Social Science, Privacy and Ethics*, Harmondsworth, Penguin, is still the best book to discuss the ethics of social research with key examples.

BOK,S. (1978) *Lying: Moral Choice in Public and Private Life*, London, Quartet, is useful for the questions it raises that can be considered in relation to educational research.

BOK, S. (1982) *Secrets: On the Ethics of Concealment and Revelation*, Oxford, Oxford University Press, provides a major discussion of freedom of information in a variety of social contexts.

BULMER, M. (Ed) (1982) *Social Research Ethics*, London, Macmillan, provides a comprehensive discussion about the merits and demerits of covert participant observation drawing on debates and research in Britain and the USA.

CASSELL, J. and JACOBS, S. E. (1987) *Handbook on Ethical Issues in Anthropology*, Washington, American Anthropological Association, is particularly useful for its discussion of ethical problems with commentaries from a range of researchers. Again the issues, can be considered by readers in relation to education.

DIENER, E. and CRANDELL, R. (1978) *Ethics in Social and Behavioural Research*, Chicago, University of Chicago Press, provides a guide to the treatment of participants and professional issues. It also provides a discussion of ethical guidelines.

FILSTEAD, W. J. (Ed) (1970) *Qualitative Methodology Firsthand Involvement with the Social World*, New York, Markham, provides a summary of ethical issues in America in the 1960s.

NEBRASKA SOCIOLOGICAL FEMINIST COLLECTIVE (1988) *A Feminist Ethic for Social Science Research*, New York, Edwin Mellen Press, provides a discussion of research by, for and about women together with accounts of feminist research.

WISE, S. (1987) 'A framework for discussing ethical issues in feminist research: A review of the literature', in GRIFFITHS, V. *et al*, *Writing Feminist Biography 2 Using Life Histories*, Studies in Sexual Politics, Department of Sociology, University of Manchester, provides a very good review of the ethical literature with an emphasis on its relationship to feminist work.

There are also a number of codes and statements of ethical principles, for a British example—see the BRITISH SOCIOLOGICAL ASSOCIATION *Statement of Ethical Principles*, available from British Sociological Association, 10 Portugal Street, London WC2A 2HU and ELLIOTT, J. (1989) 'Towards a code of practice for funded educational research', *Research Intelligence* 31, pp. 14–18.

Examples

For examples of ethical issues you are recommended to examine a range of empirical studies in education and to consider the ethical issues involved in the design, conduct, publication and use of the research.

Notes on Contributors

John Bibby works in Edinburgh as a freelance statistician, teacher and writer. He is currently preparing a textbook on statistics for the innumerate, which will include sections on ethics, and is particularly interested in open learning methods having spent ten years at the Open University.

David Bridges is a former teacher of history, who went on to study and then teach philosophy of education. He wrote *Education Democracy and Discussion* (1979) and, with Charles Bailey, *Mixed Ability Grouping* (1983). Other philosophical writing has focused on teaching controversial issues and parents' rights. He was first drawn into case study research with the Cambridge Accountability Project and then went on to direct a project on School Centred In-Service Education and the Suffolk LEA local evaluation of records of pupil achievement, both based on a mixture of case study and cross-site analaysis, and, currently the evaluation of the Sainsbury/Suffolk Schools and Industry Project and the evaluation of GRIST in Norfolk. He is currently Deputy Principal of Homerton College, Cambridge, and Director of the Homerton Educational Research and Development Unit.

Ivor Bundell works for SIA (Service in Informatics and Analysis) Ltd. From 1984 to 1988 he was a research fellow at the Centre for Educational Sociology (CES), University of Edinburgh, working on database design and data management for the Scottish Young People's Survey (SYPS). His main areas of interest are in relational data modelling, database query languages and metadata modelling. After a first degree in English Literature from the University of London, he taught English as a Foreign Language overseas for three years. He joined the CES after completing an MSc in Information Processing (computing and psychology) in 1984.

Robert Burgess is Director of CEDAR (Centre for Educational Development, Appraisal and Research) and Professor of Sociology at the University of Warwick. His main teaching and research interests are in social research methodology; especially qualitative methods and the sociology of education, especially the study of schools, classrooms and curricula. He is currently writing an ethnographic restudy of a comprehensive school on which he has already published several papers. His main publications include: *Experiencing Comprehensive Education* (1983), *In the Field: An Introduction to Field Research* (1984), *Education, Schools and Schooling* (1985) and *Sociology, Education and Schools* (1986), together with fourteen edited volumes on qualitative methods and education. He is President of the British Sociological Association.

Bruce Carrington has been a lecturer in education at the University of Newcastle-upon-Tyne since 1979. Before taking up this post, he was a lecturer in sociology at St Mary's College, Twickenham and a primary school teacher in North London. He has a longstanding research interest in 'race' and ethnicity and has published extensively in the area. This interest was stimulated by his experiences in the mid-seventies as a teacher-in-charge of a special unit in Tottenham. He is the author, with Geoffrey Short, of *Race and the Primary School — Theory into Practice* (1989).

Pauline Foster came to the University of Warwick as a mature student to study sociology, having previously been a teacher in further education. She returned to Warwick on an ESRC studentship to conduct research for a PhD in Sociology. During her graduate training she obtained a University of Warwick award to spend one year on her research at the University of Wisconsin-Madison in the USA.

Alison Kelly now works in local government. She was a lecturer in sociology at the University of Manchester, where she taught courses on women and society, sociology of education and research methods. Her main research interest is in women's education, especially girls' education in science. She has published numerous articles on girls and science, and was a director of the action-research project Girls into Science and Technology. More recently she edited *Science for Girls?*, a collection of the most important articles on this topic from the last few years.

Jon Nixon is currently based at the University of Sheffield Division of Education. He is involved in the evaluation of local and national education programmes, and has written and edited widely in this field. His main publications include *A Teachers' Guide to Action Research* (1981), *Drama and the Whole Curriculum* (1982) and, more recently, a series on GCSE *Coursework* (1987), all of which he has edited. He is co-author of *Teaching About Race Relations: Problems and Effects* (1982) and the author of *A Teachers' Guide to Multicultural Education* (1985), and *Teaching Drama* (1987).

David Raffe is Reader in Education and Co-Director (with Andrew McPherson) of the Centre for Educational Sociology (CES) at the University of Edinburgh. He has been a member of the CES since 1975 and has been involved in the design, conduct and analysis of the Scottish School Leavers' Surveys, now the Scottish Young People's Surveys. He is co-author of *Reconstructions of Secondary Education* (1983), editor of *Fourteen to Eighteen* (1984) and *Education and the Youth Labour Market* (1988) and author of numerous articles and chapters on secondary and further education, training and the labour market.

Sheila Riddell taught English for six and a half years, before embarking on research into gender and option choice in rural schools at Bristol University School of Education, where she recently completed her doctoral thesis. She is currently working as a research associate at University of Edinburgh Department of Education on a project which is exploring policy and practice relating to provision for children with special educational needs in Scotland.

Pamela Sammons is a senior research officer at the ILEA's Research and Statistics Branch which she joined in 1981. She was seconded to the Authority's Freedom of Information Inquiry which examined ways of widening public access to information about schools. Previously she was Coordinator of the Junior School Project (a longitudinal study of school effectiveness) for four years. Research interests include school effectiveness — the measurement of pupils' progress, attainment and development; the impact of background factors upon pupils' educational outcomes; and positive discrimination. She has published widely in a variety of educational journals and is the joint author of *School Matters: The Junior Years*.

Helen Simons is Reader in Education and Head of the Centre for Educational Evaluation in the Department of Curriculum Studies at the University of London Institute of Education. She has published numerous articles on evaluation and self-evaluation and is the author of *Getting to Know Schools in a Democracy: the Politics and Process of Evaluation* (1987).

Harry Torrance is a lecturer in Education at the University of Sussex. He was formerly research fellow in the Assessment and Evaluation Unit, Department of Education, University of Southampton, and Senior Research Associate at the Centre for Applied Research in Education, University of East Anglia. He has conducted a number of investigations of teacher involvement in examining and is particularly interested in the inter-relation of assessment, curriculum and pedagogy. His publications include *Mode III Examining: six case studies* and *The Changing Face of Educational Assessment* (with Roger Murphy).

Barry Troyna went to school in Tottenham, college in Nottingham, back to school (as a teacher) in Nottinghamshire and then completed postgraduate research at Leicester University. From 1981–1985 he directed the Education programme at the ESRC's Centre for Research in Ethnic Relations before becoming Reader in education, Sunderland Polytechnic. He is currently a lecturer in education at the University of Warwick. He is a member of the National Antiracist Movement in Education, a founder member of Gateshead Federation to Combat Racism and director of research into racist incidents in primary schools. Amongst his publications are *Racism, Education and the State* (Croom Helm, 1986) which he wrote with Jenny Williams, and *Racial Inequality in Education* (Tavistock, 1987). He is the coeditor of *Children and Controversial Issues: Strategies for the Early and Middle Years of Schooling,* (1988) with Bruce Carrington.

Index

Access 3, 5, 6–7, 60, 110, 178
  at Bishop McGregor School 62–3, 64–7
  case studies 118, 123, 128–9, 131–2, 134
  CES 15, 16, 21, 25, 29
  codes of practice 16, 43, 118
  conditions 54, 199–201
  feminist research 77, 81–3, 86–7, 93, 96
  further education college 189, 192–5, 198
  gatekeepers 5, 17, 82, 192
  informed consent 64–7
  to results 33–4, 35–6, 50
  under Official Secrets Act 147, 148, 155
accuracy 15–17, 22, 24–5, 192, 197
  case study 125, 135, 156
  ISI code 39, 40, 42, 45
  SAFARI guidelines 119
action research 3–4, 6, 100–12
  feminism 80
  GIST 77, 100–12, 219
  informed consent 107–11
  race 219, 220
adult retraining 188–9, 191, 199, 200
Adult Training Strategy 200
Afro-Caribbean/West Indian pupils 40, 211–16, 219
analysis of data 17, 22, 166
  CES 15, 29
  feminist research 3, 77, 78, 90–4
  police case study 144
  race research 207, 210
  statistics 33–4, 39, 41, 46–51, 53–4, 56
anonymity 3, 4, 114, 192, 202
  case studies 117, 129–31, 145, 156
  CES code 15, 22, 28–9
  GIST 110–11
  ISI code 44, 46
  teachers 94–5, 182

Asian pupils 40, 211, 212
  teachers' attitudes 214, 216, 219
assessment 4, 172–86
  changes 173–7
  evaluation 183–6
  qualitative research 173, 117–83
  race 206, 212
Association des Administrateurs de l'INSEE 17
Association of Child Psychiatry 51

bias 23, 41, 45, 92
  feminist 80, 92–3, 94, 96
Bishop McGregor School 61–74, 91
  access 62–3, 64–7
  confidentiality 70–3
  deception 67–70
  dissemination 71–3
  fieldwork 62–74
  informed consent 64–7
British Ethnocentrism Scale 213
British Sociological Association (BSA) 7, 17, 82

Caribbean pupils see Afro-Caribbean
case studies 4, 61, 114–36, 182
  access 118, 123, 128–9, 131–2, 134
  evaluation 115–21
  ground rules 155–7
  guidelines 117–20, 122–4, 126–7, 132, 134–5
  internal 128–32
  police training 141–58
Centre for Applied Research in Education (CARE) 142
Centre for Contemporary Cultural Studies (CCCS) 79, 209, 210

231

Printed in the United Kingdom
by Lightning Source UK Ltd.
101838UKS00003B/73-75